THE
SEX-WISE
PARENT

THE
SEX-WISE
PARENT

The Parent's Guide to Protecting Your Child,
Strengthening Your Family, and Talking to Kids
about Sex, Abuse, and Bullying

JANET ROSENZWEIG, MS, PhD, MPA

Skyhorse Publishing

Author's Note: Throughout the book, the author has used gender terms interchangeably. While the support and participation of so many people informed and improved this book tremendously, the author maintains sole and final responsibility for the content. Sex offenders interviewed for this book had been convicted and served time for their offenses. All first names used in personal stories have been changed.

Copyright © 2012 by Janet Rosenzweig
Illustrations by Janet Hamlin

All Rights Reserved. No part of this book may be reproduced in any manner without the express written consent of the publisher, except in the case of brief excerpts in critical reviews or articles. All inquiries should be addressed to Skyhorse Publishing, 307 West 36th Street, 11th Floor, New York, NY 10018.

Skyhorse Publishing books may be purchased in bulk at special discounts for sales promotion, corporate gifts, fund-raising, or educational purposes. Special editions can also be created to specifications. For details, contact the Special Sales Department, Skyhorse Publishing, 307 West 36th Street, 11th Floor, New York, NY 10018 or info@skyhorsepublishing.com.

Skyhorse® and Skyhorse Publishing® are registered trademarks of Skyhorse Publishing, Inc.®, a Delaware corporation.

Visit our website at www.skyhorsepublishing.com.

10 9 8 7 6 5 4 3 2 1
ISBN: 978-1-61608-509-4
Library of Congress Cataloging-in-Publication Data

Rosenzweig, Janet.
 The sex-wise parent : the parent's guide to protecting your child, strengthening your family, and talking to kids about sex, abuse, and bullying / Janet Rosenzweig.
 p. cm.
 Includes bibliographical references and index.
 ISBN 978-1-61608-509-4 (hardcover : alk. paper)
 1. Parenting. 2. Sex instruction for youth. 3. Sex instruction for children. I. Title.
 HQ755.8.R6724 2012
 949'.65—dc23
 2011046576

Printed in the United States of America

To David

The Rockies may crumble, Gibraltar may tumble . . . .

Acknowledgments

With deep and enduring gratitude to the following people:

To everyone who helped bring this book to life by sharing their stories in focus groups and interviews, and for tolerating me when I interrupted a conversation to exclaim, "That's a great example. Can I use it for my book?"

To Beth, Bill, Brad, Christine, Curtis, The Dames of the Oblong Table, John, David, Dennis, Diane, Donna, Elizabeth, Evelyn, Janet, Jeannie, Jerry, Joanna, Julianne, Kathryn, Keith, Gay, Hannah, Herb, Ken, Keith, Lamis, Larry, Mark, Marsha, Maryanne, Maura, Melissa, Michelle, Miriam, Nancy, Phoenix, Ray, Rosanna, Sarah, Shirley, Sonya, Sue, Suzanne, and Zach.

To the very first victims I served in East Tennessee, now grown—you never left my heart or mind; and to the man who built the program that allowed me to serve them, the late Charles E. Gentry, whose vision of service knew no bounds.

To my colleagues who reviewed portions of the content and improved it with their insights: Evelyn Gill, Dr. Jean Levitan, Jim Hmurovich, Dr. Pat Barthalow Koch, Regina Podhorin, Ken Singer, and Dr. Elaine Wilson Young.

To the editors who helped breathe life into my words: David Marcus, Herb Schaffner, and Julie Matysik.

To my family: David, Zach, Shirley, and Irving, who make anything possible and everything better.

Contents

PART 4
What to Do if Problems Arise

Rosenzweig's Rules for Parents to Raise Sexually Safe and Healthy Children

1. Never forget that sexual arousal is an autonomic, reflexive response. Healthy human beings cannot control their reflexive arousal in response to a sight, sound, smell, or memory but they certainly can and must be responsible for what they do with it.
2. Learn Pavlov's lesson; the good doctor and his dogs have a valuable message for us. When Dr. Pavlov's canine experimental subjects completed a task correctly, a bell rang and they were rewarded with food. Soon, they began salivating at the sound of a bell with no food in sight. The sound of a bell became *contiguous*, or "stuck together," with eating. Pavlov taught us that feelings and responses can become stuck together in ways that have no real meaning. Your reaction to your child can cause feelings that become contiguous with sexuality. Be thoughtful and careful to avoid instilling fear, guilt, or shame associated with an autonomic response (see Rule #1).
3. Remember that a parent's job is to provide the tools to alleviate fear and obliterate ignorance, not to add to them. Everyone has fears and questions about his or her sexuality at some point. Your pediatrician, other professionals, and books like this are great tools, so use them!

4. Sometimes really good people do really stupid things, and bad things can happen in any family. Know your community's resources in case this happens to you or someone you love.

5. Never forget that young children are developmentally incapable of protecting themselves from a skilled pedophile. Even the best classroom-based prevention programs in the world are useless unless adults in the community recognize the dynamics of sexual abuse of children in general and pedophiles in particular.

6. Children will rise—or sink—to your level of expectations, even if you don't articulate them.

7. Understand that a criminal background check on someone seeking to work with children is necessary but not at all sufficient to ensure that the prospective person is a safe caretaker for your children.

8. Keep the lines of communication wide open, including ensuring that your child is comfortable using understandable language about every part of his or her body. Kids without sexual language are much more attractive to pedophiles, who traffic in shame and secrecy.

9. Modern American communities have many more resources in place to respond to a victim than to help prevent victimization. Let's hope you never need the former and after reading this book can take a stand and change the latter.

10. Bear in mind that adolescence is, by definition, a time of contradictions. Sociologists tell us adolescence is now lasting longer than ever before, but it will eventually end. Your goal as a parent is to ensure that when it does, the result of your efforts is a healthy, productive adult who will eventually produce grandchildren who will become adolescents and pay your children back for the way they behaved. That can't happen without sex.

For more information, please visit Dr. Rosenzweig's website at www.sexwiseparent.com.

"Sex lies at the root of life, and we can never learn to reverence life until we know how to understand sex."

—**Havelock Ellis**

PART 1

Wake Up and Smell the Pheromones

A Call to Action for Parents

CHAPTER 1

Beyond the Bogeyman

The Dangers We Don't Talk About

Sex is part of life. That's not news. Institutions in our country are doing a lousy job teaching kids about sex, and I mean all institutions—family, schools, church and religious groups, and others. But that's not really news, either. What is news, however, is the lack of accurate information about sex provided by loving, trusted adults to children of all ages, and this is a danger to the health and safety of our kids. You may not realize it, but as parents you have an obligation to do something about it, and this book is written for those of you who are willing to find the courage to take the steps necessary to raise a sexually safe and healthy child. It's never too early, or too late, to start.

As a parent you must possess a broad lens in order to understand sexual health, sexual abuse, and sexual safety, and to understand how vital it is to treat sexual issues as a component of healthy family life. You need the tools to help communicate with your kids and to recognize the multifaceted ways sexuality infuses family life. You can and must learn to weave your own values and beliefs with accurate and age-appropriate information and present it all as a gift to your children.

America's Kids after Megan's Law

The tragic rape and murder of Megan Kanka in 1994 mobilized the nation to be on the lookout for child molesters. Megan's killer was the classic horror-story villain luring an innocent child with stories of a puppy dog to a terrible death. The nation's outrage spurred legislators to act in all fifty states and Megan's Law now makes it possible for parents to find the addresses of convicted sex offenders in their neighborhood. Sex offender registries and Internet searches *may* help prevent further crimes by paroled sex offenders by leveraging public attention to keep violators from acting out. But these potentially dangerous and harmful compulsions are not cured by public scrutiny, and sex-offender registries capture only a small minority of offenders who are reported, caught, tried, and convicted. A realistic look at these limitations makes it clear that Megan's Law is not enough to keep your children safe—not by a long shot.

Policing the Internet is also not the cure we as parents assume it to be. During the late 1990s, public discussion of sexual abuse moved to cyber-crime, notoriously publicized a few years later when a prime-time TV news magazine baited, caught, and televised the shame of men seeking sex with minors via the Web. Parents began to worry about the dangers lurking in cyberspace, dangers streamed directly into our kids' bedrooms through the Internet. In the 1990s, sex-abuse prevention morphed to become about Internet safety—as if monitoring what our kids do online and teaching them chat-room safety rules were sufficient. But even this is not enough.

In addition, government agencies publish statistical reports informing us of how many thousands of children are sexually abused each year, expressing optimism when the numbers decrease and seeking solutions when the numbers go up. Advocates grab onto these numbers as if they are gospel and plan to do something about the rise or take credit for a decline in sexual abuse reports. But statistics fail to capture the individual child being convinced by a teen-aged babysitter to get naked to earn extra TV time, or the school coach whose hugs are just a little too tight.

Too many kids encounter "creepy" teenagers and adults whose behaviors confuse and frighten them, but children often lack the ability, through language or gestures, to tell anyone. Too many adolescents find themselves in sexually-charged situations they barely understand but think everyone else does and are self-shamed into silence.

Most times, we as adults lack the perspective to take notice of such situa-tions and apprehensions in children. Studies show that the overwhelming majority of childhood sexual abuse is perpetrated by someone the child knew, someone who did not have to work very hard to gain his trust. For many parents, the horror of their child's victimization is compounded by the betrayal of the molester they befriended, trusted, and invited into their home or family.

The allegations in 2011 that a serial pedophile operated for years under the cover of Penn State University's highly respected collegiate athletic program may horrify you in terms of the possibility that a trusted, respected adult in your life—and from a revered institution—could sexually abuse your child.

Too many kids are quietly violated by adults in their lives and are stunned into silence and shame that can sometimes last for decades by their body's normal, involuntary response to physical stimulation. Too many kids experience their first sexual arousal in a context riddled with confusion, guilt, shame, or fear. It's time to inoculate our kids from shame by lovingly giving them the adequate knowledge and language about sex and educate ourselves about the multiple ways that abusers can creep into their life.

A child who has knowledge and words about his body is far less likely to ever become a victim. And if he tells you about an adult's attempt to touch him inappropriately, he might just help prevent other children from becoming victims too.

Unfortunately, there is nothing new about adults sexually abusing children. Long before I ever heard the term "child sexual abuse," I was a teenaged camp counselor who didn't know what to do about the little girl who came to camp with bruises on her thighs and blood in her underwear. A decade later, I was working on one of the first federally funded child sexual abuse projects in the United States and a reporter began to cry during our interview as she remembered her own abuse. Months later, a male colleague described being "seduced" as a teen by an adult female neighbor and wanted to know if that counted as abuse. Then there was a woman who had spent more than forty years feeling "sullied" and who spoke for the first time of being fondled at age eight by a man dating her mother.

It was during this time in my career that I began to grasp the scope and depth of this all-too-common tragedy. I began to realize the terrible consequences of sexual abuse on a child and saw that our best efforts were not even close to relieving the problem or the affected families' trauma. Along with the hundreds of families seeking help from the program I managed, relatives, friends, strangers, and colleagues came forward to share their secret shame, profound anger, their sadness, and their continued confusion.

It is a sad fact that almost everyone knows someone whose life has been touched by sexual victimization. Look at the published numbers—different studies suggest 70,000 kids each year; others suggest 90,000 kids each year; some say one out of four kids; others, one out of six. Regardless of the source, the number of affected children is enormous and these findings have become the rallying cries of advocates and many professionals who remind us that these reports are only the tip of the iceberg.

Frankly, I cannot stand the statistics about child sexual abuse. Besides the obvious differences in definitions and counting methods that make statisticians cringe, statistics dehumanize the unbearable pain caused to children who are victims and those who love them. More meaningful than any statistic is the heartbreaking truth that almost everybody knows someone who was sexually abused—a sad friend remembered from childhood, a college friend who confided why they have lousy relationships, someone you dated, a friend of your child's. Startling statistics pose another problem. They can leave us feeling paralyzed and overwhelmed—and rarely inspire any specific action to take place.

Far from the statistics we find stories like Sugar Ray Leonard, who was sexually abused by a boxing coach, or child actor Todd Bridges, molested as an adolescent actor by publicist.[1] On top of that, there are thousands of unreported victims, known personally by many who will read this book. Many of you will shudder as you recognize and remember the touchy-feely coach, the "over-affectionate" stepparent, aunt, or uncle, or the seductive babysitter.

As if we need another reason to look beyond the numbers, ask yourself this question: When you hear the name Monica Lewinsky, do you think *victim*? She was never counted in any database even though she was sexually involved with a teacher for years. If we believe the adage that "children learn what they live," imagine what Monica may have learned from her high school drama teacher—how to trade sex for status, and how to lie about it. An American president faced impeachment and a young woman's life was reduced to a

---

1   Bridges, Todd with Sarah Tomlinson. *Killing Willis*. New York: Simon and Schuster, 2010.

punch line perhaps because a teacher thought his own sexual gratification was more important than the developing spirit of a young woman. As a parent you must look closely at the sexual climate of the institutions serving your child, and this book will help you understand how to do so.

What about Mackenzie Philips? Raised to accept her "special" status in a "special" family, she was never counted as a statistic even though her life was marred in unimaginable ways by becoming her famous father's "lover" while still a child. And speaking of sitcom stars, there's Todd Bridges, whose heart-breaking description (in his biography, *Killing Willis*)[2] of his profound confusion from climaxing while being molested by his publicist is a more compelling argument for educating children about their bodies than any author could ever compose. Bridges's honesty on national television inspired Sugar Ray Leonard to describe his experience of being molested by an Olympic boxing coach in his biography. Hearing Tyler Perry tearfully tell Oprah Winfrey that his body "betrayed" him with an erection during oral sex forced on him by an adult provided another national call to action to educate our kids in this topic. We as parents and protectors of our society's youth cannot continue to let molesters convince victims that they were complicit in forced sexual acts because their body displayed a physiologically uncontrollable, autonomic reflex.

In my early work for a child sexual abuse project three decades ago, I traveled the country lecturing and training professionals on the importance of understanding human sexuality when working with victims, perpetrators, and family members involved with the sexual abuse of a child. I was hired to work on a sex-abuse helpline by a man who believed my degree in health education and certification as a sex educator would make a great match with a social worker experienced in child abuse cases; we would team up, learn from each other, and handle calls that came in. Each month we fielded hundreds of calls from adults and kids of both genders; some just with questions but many simply finding the words to describe their victimization.

Within a year, I found that my unique perspective on the subject was in high demand and national training tours were scheduled. Social workers, law enforcement staff, counselors, youth workers, and educators were among the people I reached out to with good, clinical information on the anatomy, phys-

---

2   Ibid pp. 67–70.

iology, and psychosexual development of children. Lecture halls and seminars rooms always filled and the value of the material was never brought into question. It was, in fact, simply common sense that people needed to understand human sexuality to be able to successfully work in child sexual abuse investigation, treatment, and prevention. It was considered common sense that kids needed language about sexuality to communicate with the adults in their lives about abuse. There was never any controversy over these facts, and I offered this training in churches, law enforcement training centers, university classrooms, and community centers. The positive responses of the professionals who recognized how this information would make them better at their work in child sexual abuse was among the most rewarding aspects of my professional life.

I left the lecture circuit when I became a mother and my career expanded into other areas of public human services in the late 1980s. When I returned to the field of child abuse prevention in 2001, I was shocked to see not only a lack of progress from when I broadened my focus to other areas of public human services but downright degeneration on the point of providing thorough sexuality information—both to professionals charged with preventing and intervening in child sexual abuse cases, and to kids as part of prevention strategies. Sometime during the abstinence-only, anti-sex-education binge of the 1990s, people forgot how important good sexuality education was in promoting overall sexual health, sustaining strong marriages and families, supporting overall personal mental health, preventing child sexual abuse, and intervening if a child is victimized. The politics of fear stopped even qualified and well-meaning adults from talking to kids about sex, and the sexuality component disappeared from many professional training curricula for child sexual abuse. While advocates continue to battle for public education on sexuality and adding the sexuality component back to sex abuse prevention, you as a parent must rise to the challenge of ensuring that your child is not endangered by ignorance.

The Neutered Nineties

While the majority of public school districts mandate sexuality education, researchers found a shrinking of the scope of sexual health curricula from the 1980s to the 1990s as school districts responded to the 1996 boost in federal funding for abstinence-only sexuality education.[3] Cash-strapped school districts and community-based organizations eagerly took advantage of the hundreds of millions of federal dollars allocated in those decades to promote that narrow teaching point. Accepting these funds required teaching abstinence as the only sure method of avoiding sexually transmitted diseases and infections and pregnancy prevention, and it restricted other topics and methods that could be covered. According to the firm contracted by Congress to evaluate this initiative, "Programs receiving these abstinence education funds may not endorse or promote contraceptive use,"[4] which makes little sense in light of the fact that the majority of teens were sexually active by graduation. Objective, federally funded evaluators found early on that " . . . abstinence funds are changing the local landscape of approaches to teenage pregnancy prevention and youth risk avoidance."[5] The amount of accurate information available to kids shrunk in classrooms and youth-serving community-based organizations throughout the United States, leaving kids vulnerable to myths, misinformation, and sexual predators.

Accepting these funds requires schools or youth serving agencies to offer sex education that meets the following criteria:

- Have as its exclusive purpose teaching the social, psychological, and health gains to be realized by abstaining from sexual activity;
- Teach abstinence from sexual activity outside marriage as the expected standard for all school-age children;
- Teach that abstinence from sexual activity is the only certain way to avoid out-of wedlock pregnancy, sexually transmitted diseases, and other associated health problems;

---

3   Dailard, Cynthia. "Sex Education: Politicians, Parents, Teachers and Teens." The Guttmacher Report on Public Policy, February 2001. Accessed at http://www.guttmacher. org/pubs/tgr/04/1/gr040109.html.

4   Devaney, Barbara, Amy Johnson, Rebecca Maynard, and Chris Trenholm. "The Evaluation of Abstinence Education Programs Funded Under Title V Section 510 Interim Report." *Evaluation Interim Report*. Princeton, NJ: Mathematica Policy Research, Inc., 2002.

5   Ibid.

- Teach that a mutually faithful, monogamous relationship in the context of marriage is the expected standard of sexual activity;
- Teach that sexual activity outside the context of marriage is likely to have harmful psychological and physical effects;
- Teach that bearing children out of wedlock is likely to have harmful consequences for the child, the child's parents, and society;
- Teach young people how to reject sexual advances and how alcohol and drug use increases vulnerability to sexual advances; and
- Teach the importance of attaining self-sufficiency before engaging in sexual activity.[6]

This restrictive funding continued to promote the narrow perspectives of sexuality health information even as the researchers found that "programs had no statistically significant impact on eventual behavior."[7] During this same period, "research also suggests that there [was] a large gap between what teachers believe[d] should be taught regarding sexuality education and what [was] actually taught in the classroom."[8] The same source reports that even if a district allowed teaching of contraception and other sensitive topics, a significant number of teachers avoided them because they "feared adverse community reaction." Even if teachers were allowed to teach sex education in a variety of ways, many felt unprepared. (This researcher reports that the United States Centers for Disease Control and Prevention conducted a study around this time that found that many teachers responsible for teaching sexual heath wanted more training in the subject before presenting information to students.)[9]

There were other troubling signs of the restriction on honest discussion about sexuality at this time. In fact, the 1990s were so restrictive that in 1994 Dr. M. Jocelyn Elders, the highly qualified U.S. Surgeon General, was forced to resign after replying to a specific question at a World AIDS Day conference.

6   Catalog of Federal Domestic Assistance Program Number 93.010.
7   Trenholm, Christopher, Barbara Devaney, Ken Fortson, Lisa Quay, Justin Wheeler, and Melissa Clark. "Impacts of Four Title V Section 510 Abstinence Only Education Programs, Final Report." *Evaluation.* Princeton, NJ: Mathmatica Policy Rresearch, 2007.
8   Dailard, Cynthia. "Sex Education: Politicians, Parents, Teachers and Teens."
9   Ibid.

When asked if she "thought that masturbation could serve as a useful tool to help discourage school children from becoming sexually active too early" she stated, "With regard to masturbation, I think that is something that is part of human sexuality and a part of something that perhaps should be taught."[10] Foes of Elders' superior, President Bill Clinton, repeated this one sentence out of context, seeking to paint this dedicated public health official as a pervert who wanted curricula on how to masturbate taught in grade schools. No wonder there were no longer conversations about kids and sexuality in the public sector—such talk could ruin even distinguished careers!

Kids raised in this environment are now young adults, and many are about to become parents and teachers responsible for educating children, and many are less likely to have the benefit of medically accurate, age appropriate sexuality education than their parents!

It's time to get back to basics. The current generation of parents, such as yourself, needs the tools to be the primary sexuality educators of your children, to be the eyes and ears assessing the sexual climate in the community and the institutions serving your children, and to be astutely aware of the signs that something is making your child uncomfortable. You need to know how to respond if you sense trouble, and how to raise kids who share in that knowledge and awareness of sexual predation.

The neutered '90s saw the unfortunate coincidence of sex abuse "prevention" focusing on sex offender registries at the same time as sex education was squelched and public health officials were bullied into silence about sex. And what was the result? *Adults stopped talking about sex to kids!* The politics of fear successfully interfered with health education and common sense. Federally driven abstinence-only policies for sex education and politics frightened too many professionals, and parents, into silence. The sex education component of sex abuse prevention programs disappeared, replaced by stranger-danger coloring books, criminal background checks, and the ratings of nanny cams. Some of these products and programs have value, and Congress rescinded funding for most abstinence-only sex education in 2010 providing more detailed programs to some students, but we must get back to the basics of parent–child communication and the sharing of accurate and age-appropriate information.

---

10 Accessed on December 6, 2011, at http://www.notablebiographies.com/Du-Fi/Elders-Joycelyn.html.

Parents may feel powerless to help the 90,000 sex abuse victims cited in the statistics each year, or the 740,000 adolescent girls who are impregnated out of wedlock each year[11] and the hundreds of thousands of adolescent boys who participate in procreation, but you can help your child, and many more, by examining your own sexual history, your thoughts and feelings, and by developing skills to consciously choose what you transmit to your children about sexuality and abuse prevention.

If you are a parent, especially a parent who completed school when access to comprehensive sexuality education was limited, it is quite likely that you feel woefully unprepared for this challenge. This challenge becomes greater for the many parents who fall into the huge category of uncounted victims; the task of actively working to raise a sexually safe and healthy child can seem even more formidable. But as a parent you must be able to talk to your kids about sex, and you will find the tools you need in the following chapters.

Anyone can feel overwhelmed by a problem of enormous proportions involving a topic so sensitive—maybe even overwhelmed to the point of inaction. But we can't accept that status quo. There are things that every adult can do and they are spelled out here for parents, grandparents, legal guardians, teachers, caregivers, mental health professionals, and public servants. The information herein is provided in a simple, practical, and straightforward manner. An awareness of and open communication about sexual health and safety can make children happier, families stronger, and communities safer.

So Why Don't We Talk?

Throughout the years, in my various professional positions, I have heard parents give many reasons for for their decision not to discuss the topics of sex and abuse with their children. Frequently, parents tell me that they just wouldn't know where to start if they wanted to have a conversation about sex abuse prevention. If they've never had a conversation about sex, they don't want their first one to be about the dangers of molesters. Many divorced parents assume the other parent has covered this topic if they are the same sex

---

11 Ventura, Stephanie J., T. J. Mathews, Brady E. Hamilton, Paul D. Sutton, and Joyce C. Abma. "Adolescent Pregnancy and Childbirth—United States, 1991–2008." *Morbidity and Mortality Weekly*, January 14, 2011: 1–3.

as the child or have custody of the child. And some parents just don't want to think of sex and their child at the same time in any way at all.

You can fool yourself into thinking everything will be fine and that your children will somehow learn all they need to know. Some of you will wait until your kids get to school and hope your district provides a good child safety program. Maybe the scouts will have a special program, or the topic will be discussed in Sunday school. But programs provided by strangers discussing concepts that may be completely foreign to your child can't possibly have the same effect as a loving dialogue; there is no substitute for a permanently open line of communication between you and your child. It's easy to delay opening up that line when you are scared that you won't be able to handle the questions that are put to you by your child regarding sex in any form; your kids may have questions on topics ranging from reproduction to molestation.

Some of you are even unconsciously playing the odds knowing it is better than a fifty-fifty chance your kid will escape abuse (which, when you think about it, is truly terrifying). It's true that odds are strong that your child will avoid a molester, but it's equally important to consider the overwhelming odds that they will have better information about sexuality if it comes from you. The goal of this book is to help you raise a sexually safe and healthy child, and that goes well beyond avoiding abuse. This book provides the strategies and tactics to help you reach your child—and every parent can do that successfully.

I become completely flummoxed when parents state that their parents didn't tell them anything about sex and they turned out "OK." If you insist on dragging out that old chestnut, then I ask you is "OK" good enough for your child? Remember your own confusion, fear, and embarrassment when learning about the topic. Wouldn't you want to spare your child that discomfort? You absolutely can! And your kids will love you for it. Actually, so will their friends when your child shares her new information with less well-informed peers.

Being sexually safe and healthy certainly means a great deal more than avoiding sexual victimization. Avoiding unintended pregnancy and sexually transmitted infections (STIs) are very important issues. There are some pretty good books on the market for those of you who want information specific to these topics and a good librarian can help you find them. Our approach with this book is to focus on the importance of open communication, accurate information, and parental awareness of the sexual climate in the places children spend their time. While my goal is to broaden the definition of sex abuse prevention, developing these habits can have an effect on the overall sexual health and safety of your child as they move into adolescence informed, supported, and prepared.

A Call to Action

In 1962, Rachel Carson published *Silent Spring*, the call to action that sparked the environmental movement in the United States. As a biologist, she could not stand by and watch widespread and casual use of pesticides; she knew there would be dire long-term consequences on all manner of living creatures. Arguing for the curb on chemical use, she wrote:

> We stand now where two roads diverge. But unlike the roads in Robert Frost's familiar poem, they are not equally fair. The road we have long been traveling is deceptively easy; a smooth superhighway on which we progress with great speed, but at its end lays disaster. The other fork of the road—the one less traveled by—offers our last, our only chance to reach a destination that assures the preservation of the earth.

As a sex educator who has witnessed the devastation caused by ignorance of simple facts of physiology, I cannot stand by and watch this silence continue to devastate children, families, and communities. I believe the massive number of children who have been sexually abused, particularly those whose involuntary sexual arousal was used as a tool to gain continued compliance, could be saved from extended grief and pain by accurate information from the adults in their lives who love them. With due respect to Ms. Carson, I offer this call to action to all loving parents:

> We stand now where two roads diverge. But unlike the roads in Robert Frost's familiar poem, they are not equally fair. The road we have long been traveling is deceptively easy; a smooth superhighway on which we progress with great speed, but at its end lays disaster. The other fork of the road—the one less traveled by—offers our last,

our only chance to reach a destination that assures the preservation of *the sexual health and safety of our children.*

Take a stand. Read on. Use what you learn to protect your child and strengthen your family, and be part of a sexually safe and healthy community.

CHAPTER 2

Banishing the Birds, Bees, Storks, and Ostriches

Why Parents *Don't* Talk with Their Kids about Sex

As discussed in the previous chapter, many adults who work with chil-dren have stopped talking to them about sex. But where does that leave you as a parent? Every generation of parents has displayed a wide range of comfort (or discomfort) discussing sexuality, and as much variation in their choice of when and how to teach their children about sexuality. I've heard the fears of a thirty-year-old mother echoing the memories of a seventy-year-old; no generation has cornered the market on having the sex talk correctly or getting it wrong. This generation of parents may be at a disadvantage from growing up in the "neutered nineties," but their great-grandparents didn't fare much better coming of age in the last throes of Victorian repression.

Most adults find the words "birds and bees" easier to say than "penis and vagina." The dreaded conversation about sex has been fodder for many a TV show or comedy skit. But now it's time to be honest about the subconscious reasons these topics are avoided or made into a joke. We as parents don't want to think of our kids as sexual beings. We don't want to embarrass our kids. We don't want to embarrass ourselves. We don't know what to say. We may even be afraid that our kids know more about some things that we do.

If you are a parent whose idea of sex information is to let your kid believe that babies come from a stork, and if you are a parent who deals with sexuality education by emulating an ostrich with his head in the sand hoping that things will come out all right, it's time to wake up. Kids know about sex, and it's silly at best and dangerous at worst to pretend they don't. The real question you should be asking is *what* do they know? If the *information* didn't come from a trusted and prepared adult, it's probably incorrect. If the *values* didn't come from you as the parent, there's a good chance that your children's values around sexuality are a closer reflection to those seen in the media than yours.

Even if it is difficult for us as parents to articulate our fears of speaking with our children about sex, most of us do want effective strategies and tactics to reach and teach our children, so let's look at the most common reasons parents give for not talking with their children about sex.

So Why Don't We Talk?

1. Is it our fear that we don't know what we're talking about?

"She probably already knows more than I do," moaned the father of a twelve-year-old when I asked if he'd talked to his daughter about sex yet. "I'll feel like an idiot if I say something and she tells me I'm wrong!" Adolescents can take great pride in making their parents feel and appear stupid, so the best strategy is to not *be* stupid! The materials presented in chapter 4 are more than enough to put you on a level playing field with your child when it comes to talking about sex.

This father is not alone in his belief that his child already knows more about sex than he. But here's the rub—even if by some chance your child has been lucky enough to have a world-class sex educator in school who did a magnificent job teaching every aspect of reproductive biology, maybe even the physiology of human sexual response, your child still does not know what's important to you in terms of their sexual awareness. Your child needs to know *your* values on the relationship between sex and love, your thoughts on contraceptives, *your* wishes for your son's or daughter's sexual health and safety, and that *you* want to be there for them in this regard. If your child asks you a question that you don't know how to answer, you can feel comfortable replying, "Let me find out more about that and we'll talk again tomorrow." Children recognize, at a certain point, that you cannot know the answers to everything and they will respect you for being honest and showing an interest in finding out an answer to their difficult questions about sex.

2. Is it (small p) political?

Some of you may feel that sex, like driving, is a privilege to be earned and that your child has not yet earned the right to participate. Repressive political regimes seek to control "out-groups" by denying access to education; other societies have denied woman equal access to education to promote domesticity, but revolutions have proven this strategy useless. The truth is that knowledge is power. We send our kids to a good school and save money to get them through college so they can be sent out into the world fortified with a broad range of information. This, in turn, will hopefully allow them to successfully compete in adult society. We cannot deny our children the knowledge of a critical health issue simply because of the mistaken belief that they have not earned the right to know this "grown–up" stuff until a certain age.

3. Is it (capitol P) Political?

Conservative political action groups often use the responsibility of public schools to provide comprehensive sexuality education as an example of government interfering with a family's values. The damage, however, from excluding certain bodily systems and functions from comprehensive health education is aggravated when parents or other institutions aren't adequately prepared to fill in these knowledge gaps in our society's youth.

You can become a partner with your child's school and find a way to participate in making choices about the sexual education curriculum. Do you want your child to take part in an abstinence-only program? Do you want your child to learn about contraception? Do you want your child to know reproductive anatomy? Call your local school district and drill down to find where the decision is made about sex education curricula. Is the content medically accurate? How do the values taught in the curriculum fit with your personal values? Will both genders be taught the same thing about sex? Will the classes be co-ed? If you sense that the values being taught are different than yours, consider this an opportunity to have a frank discussion with your child about your family's values, and why you hold them, and how much you hope that your child will adopt the same ones despite what they may hear in sex-ed classes at school.

In some communities, learning how to influence the content of sexuality education curricula has become a cause celeb among groups with one specific point of view, which may counter your own. This background noise of political confrontation drowns out the important message; young people need age-appropriate, medically accurate information about sexuality. Check out the curriculum, and if it doesn't match what you want your child to know, take the opportunity to ensure that your child knows what you believe and why.

The political conservatives who oppose sex education (who ran Joycelyn Elders out of office), and who want to deny poor women subsidized reproductive health care, claim that sex is a private matter and not the subject of a public discussion. I obviously disagree or this book wouldn't be here for you to read, but I do agree that sexuality education *is* a family matter—the conservatives and I disagree on the issue of sex education being *solely* a family matter. I applaud and support my colleagues who have devoted uncounted political and professional resources to support comprehensive sexuality education in schools. But I lament the lost ground of the last decade and wholeheartedly believe that you as parents have the right and responsibility to ensure that your kids learn what you think is important, including your values. Sadly, it seems to me that the current generation of parents—thanks to the policies of the neutered 90s—is among the least prepared to do so.

Sex education in schools is an important public policy issue; so is public funding for various reproductive health services and maintaining sex offender registries. But reading about them, or even advocating for your particular point of view, does *not* discharge your duties as a parent. When these topics appear in the news, they make great dinner-table conversation and provide an opportunity to voice your values and attitudes to your children and to engage in an important discussion.

You must send your child out into the world (including school) filled to the brim with the values and morals you wish to instill. And if your child happens to be in a school district where the health education curriculum doesn't skip from the belly to the knees, that child will be able to integrate what he learns in class with what he's learned at home.

The sex-education-in-schools debate is important and multi-faceted. While I firmly believe that a well-trained and credentialed sexuality educator is a wonderful resource for a community, this particular debate is too politically charged and changes the subject. The critical common ground is the belief that you as a parent have a crucial role to play in raising a sexually safe and healthy child. Wherever you stand on the polarizing public policy issues, the point of view of this book is that good sexuality education *has* to start at home.

4. Is it just too confusing to untangle your feelings on the subject of sex?

Sex hits on just about every possible emotion, particularly when we add our kids into the mix. Love, lust, fear, anger, excitement, insecurity, and joy are among the feelings we typically associate with sex. Sorting through them can be difficult, and many parents think they need to do this before broaching the subject with their children. It's probably impossible to untangle every thought and feeling about sexuality, but discussing some of these issues with your partner or peers is a good place to start.

Pairing thoughts of kids and anything sexual can be jarring and uncomfortable. While interviewing a pediatrician specializing in child abuse, she lamented that "most pediatricians never spread the labia majora after the child is out of diapers to check for genital abnormalities like labial adhesion or imperforate hymen."[12] Even in my desensitized state of having worked with child sexual abuse for decades, my immediate reaction to "spreading labia" on an infant was momentary shock. But of course this pediatrician is right and I regained my perspective as she explained. "Besides the immediate information on health status, a genital exam has the added benefits of normalizing the genitalia by treating them just like any other body part, providing the doctor with a baseline for comparison if a problem occurs later, and ultimately can make that first visit to a gynecologist as a teenager less traumatic." These are clearly important medical reasons for a thorough examination. I offer my reaction as an example of the many ways that our adult feelings about kids and sexuality can become conflicted and occasionally require clarification. We as

---

12 McColgan, Maria, MD, Director, Child Protection Program St. Christopher's Hospital for Children, Philadelphia, PA. Personal communication in June 2011.

parents and caregivers of children need to have enough self-awareness to evaluate an initial response and let logic, not our discomfort, guide our decision as to how to speak with children about sex.

It's difficult for any generation to think of another generation as sexual, particularly when they share a house. Many families experience the nasty coincidence of adolescents coming into their own sexuality at the same time that parents' hormones start to crash in ways that diminishes their own sexual feelings. The confusing changes that hit at midlife are as profound and comprehensive as those of puberty, and having both life changes occur simultaneously in one home can be a volatile mix.

Perhaps our child's budding sexuality is a reminder of our own mortality—"if my child is sexually mature, then I must be sexually *old*." Multiple generations can be sexually mature at the same time without being sexually attracted to each other. Denying your child's sexuality may seem like a way to reduce the risk of autonomic arousal, but in the long run, it does no good for either you or your child.

As kids become adolescents and they and their friends think they are the first people to discover sexuality, this sense that sex belongs only to them builds a wall in the potential for communication between you and your children. This is one of many arguments for parent-child communication about sexuality starting *before* the child becomes an adolescent. These issues are more real when your child enters puberty and begins to feel these stirrings of their own sexuality—then *your* sexuality may get on their nerves.

Remember, there's nothing wrong with admitting that it's just as difficult for adults to think of kids as sexual as it is for teenage children to think of their parents as sexual beings. It can be pretty unnerving for a vibrant, healthy, sexual, forty-something to look around and wonder how in the world they got old enough to be the parent of a teenager.

5. Are we afraid that anyone who talks to a kid about sex these days will be branded a pervert?

In 1975, a book for parents was translated from Swedish to English entitled *Show Me! A Picture Book of Sex for Children and Parents.* [13] The book was met

---

13   Fleischhauer-Hardt, Helga and Will McBride. *Show Me! A Picture Book of Sex for Children and Parents.* New York: St. Martin's Press, 1975.

with mixed reviews from sex educators and experts in child development, and in 1977, as a graduate student in health education earning my certification as a sex educator, I bought a copy for a graduate course. The pictures of nude children in the book were the basis for obscenity charges brought against sellers in four states, and in all four states the complainants lost in court. Eventually, the publisher chose to stop selling the book in the United States to spare merchants the trouble and expense of responding to continued complaints by vocal opponents.

I still have my copy of the book, along with dozens of other books acquired throughout my career on the topic of human sexuality and education. As strongly as I felt about the right of parents to choose to share this particular information with their kids, as I write this I realize that even I chose not to share this book with my son. Examining the reasons why, I clearly see now that the fear of the opinions of, and even possible sanctions by, others impacted what should have been a very personal, private family decision. My son came of age in the post-Megan's Law era, and I was a public official in the very community where Megan Kanka was murdered. My college-level sexuality text books were on shelves and my now-grown son has confirmed that these books were a resource to him and his friends—yet *Show Me* stayed packed away with old college notebooks. Was I afraid that one of his friends might see *Show Me* and tell their parents they saw naked pictures of children at my house? You don't have to be a public official to be afraid of that happening; any parent could dread an accusatory phone call from another. Even though I was a credentialed sexuality educator, I was sensitive about kids leaving my home with sex information that their parents might find objectionable; any parent might share this feeling. Choosing instead to share materials sanctioned by professional health organizations or religious institutions can alleviate the fear of being labeled inappropriate or worse.

The conversations you as a loving parent have with your child within the privacy of your own home are as personal as can be. They should be based on medical truth and individual family values. "Don't let fear make your decisions" is a philosophy paraphrased in circles from the addiction recovery movement to business motivational speakers. Now I bring it to you, the parent, who is intent on strengthening your family and raising a sexually safe and healthy child. Choose your strategies to reach your child from a position of knowledge, values, and commitment, and not from fear.

If your child chooses to share the books you've bought her with visitors, be ready to answer any disgruntled parents who might call to complain by explaining that your family values include giving accurate information to your children about this topic.

6. Are we harboring a false notion that lack of knowledge about sex preserves some type of innocence?

A poignant and simple response to this question came from a mom of three grown kids. "It's really not so philosophical," she told me. "For me, equating knowledge of sex with loss of innocence was more about not wanting to think about them [her children] feeling their first painful heartbreak. Do you remember how you felt when you saw your child with his first skinned knee? That first wound reminds you of their vulnerability. The thought of a child becoming sexual opens up the possibility of yet another type of pain."

Put in such a way, it's easy to understand why you might fear talking to our children about sex before you think they are "ready" for it. But by failing to do so, we actually leave our children more vulnerable to a harsher and longer-lasting pain as they are left to their own devices in their struggle to reach adulthood sexually safe and healthy. An adult or peer with no concern for your child's well-being will fill in the gaps in ways that might be more treacherous to your child than potential heartbreak. Happily, *this* mom overcame her emotional response and rose to the challenge.

Hopefully, you can find consolation in the knowledge that while your child is no longer a baby, she will always be *your* baby and your open communication about sex information may keep her from *having* a baby.

7. Is it because you don't know the right time or place to have "the talk"?

Ultimately, there is no exact right time and place to speak with you children about sex. However, try doing so in car—you'll at least have a captive audience!

While this answer sounds glib, sitting in a moving vehicle may indeed be a good time and place for you to have a conversation with your child without other distractions; for some of you, the need to keep your eyes on the road gives you the excuse you need to avoid direct eye contact with your child until you become more comfortable with the topic—and that's perfectly OK.

Watching TV with your child also provides ready opportunities—a commercial for an erectile dysfunction medication can provide an opportunity to ask your child if they know what ED is. You then are afforded the opportunity to correct your child's most-likely incorrect answer with an age-appropriate discussion of arousal and erections, and the fact that the way penises behave is different at various ages. I can recall watching TV with my son and ranting against commercials selling products designed to change the scent of female genitals—if the genitals of either sex smell bad, something could be medically wrong. The natural smell of clean, healthy genitals is one to be appreciated and stinky ones of either gender need a good bath or a trip to the doctor. And this is the kind of personal health information that many children lack unless you, as the parent, provide it as a naturally as you would a reminder to wash their hands before a meal.

And that's just the commercials. Lyrics heard on the car radio (or does every single child have earphones inserted in their ears now?), billboards on the highway, or junk e-mail that your SPAM filter misses are all great sex conversation starters. Experiencing the message with your child can be a great opportunity to open the discussion about sexuality. We'll spend a lot more time on what the media is teaching your kids about sex in chapter 10.

8. Do we think that someone else is taking care of this talk?

A highly-educated mom I know was shocked that her twelve-year-old daughter, a straight-A student, didn't know the difference between a vagina and a urethra. When pressed, I learned that the mom never had a mother-daughter anatomy discussion. Many of you may rely on outside sources like teachers or the media to provide this type of basic information to your kids. But the truth is, they can't. Even if you aren't overtly giving your child specific information, your attitudes, non-verbal behaviors, and family norms will stay with your child throughout his life. You must make thoughtful, conscious decisions about what to say and how to say it and not rely on others to provide this information to your son or daughter.

So many parents interviewed for this book assume that their kids will get the information they need in a health education class at school. However, in 2011, only twenty states mandate that sex education be included in the school curriculum. [14] Even if there is a state mandate to include sex education, the actual content of the curriculum may be determined locally and the average parent remains unaware of this content. Once upon a time, youth-serving agencies like Boys Clubs or Girls Clubs or the local community center would offer workshops for kids. That certainly was true when I was the executive director of Girls Clubs of Dallas, Texas, in the 1980s. Now, many public schools and non-profit youth-serving agencies are the recipients of "abstinence education" federal funds, which limit the topics they can cover, as I described earlier. The early twenty-first century is an especially bad time to assume that your child is getting all-inclusive information on sexual health and safety from a credible source outside of the home.

Within a family with little communication about sex, each parent may just assume that the other has spoken to their children. Jim, the dad of two daughters, replied to my inquiry if he'd spoken to his girls about sex by saying, "Their mom will take care of that. She's tough—she'll tell it like it is." He felt like he was off the hook on this one. Sam, the devoted father of two young boys, responded to my question of whether he was planning to discuss sex with his boys by saying, "I don't know."

Studies show that mothers *are* more likely than fathers to provide sex information to both sons and daughters; that means in most families, the odds of mom talking to the kids about sex is greater than the odds of dad doing so. In most families, if mom assumes that dad is talking to the boys, she could be dead wrong. There is no room for assumptions on this important parenting job of determining how and when to speak with your kids about sex, then carrying out your plan. This needs to be a careful and deliberate decision made by you and your partner.

9. Do you think that if ignorance was good enough for you it will be good enough for your child?

If you were raised in radio silence about sex, you can and must do better for your child. Remember your own questions and fears about the topic? Don't you want to spare your child that discomfort? You can. And your kids will love you for it.

---

14   Guttmancher Institute. *State Policies in Brief.* August 2011. Accessed at http://www. guttmacher.org/statecenter/spibs/spib_SE.pdf.

If you are one of the many whose parents skipped talking about sex, you may feel as if you are at a disadvantage, but that's not necessarily true. You can approach the role of parent as sex educator with a clean slate and determine with your partner how to handle issues of sexuality in your home. In some families, one parent may flat-out refuse to have "the talk" with the kids. One focus group mom shared that her husband wouldn't explain anything to their sons because his dad never explained anything to him. So mom prepared herself with good information and stepped up to the task.

Just remember: silence, ignorance, playground misinformation, and Internet sex sites are not good enough for anybody's sex education.

10. Are you afraid that your child will know more (and tell more) than his or her peers?

You may feel like refraining from discussing sex with your kids because you don't want your son or daughter to be the one sharing this type of information on the playground. You may fear receiving a call from an angry parent admonishing your child for using "bad language." But think of it this way: Kids are going to be discussing this stuff anyway, so at least one of the kids (yours, hopefully) should be able to contribute the accurate information to his peers. As part of your preparation to discuss sex with your child, you might role-play with another adult as to how you might react to a call from an angry parent who claims your child has been talking "dirty" to the other kids. As always, stay calm. It may be worth telling your child that other children—especially younger ones—may not be ready for the information he's just learned.

One focus group member shared an especially helpful perspective from his parents. Having enrolled him in the youngest grade in an all-boys school where many older boys could have his ear, they shared the information about sexuality that they believed he needed to know. They ended the conversation by asking him to keep this all to himself because it was a parent's special privilege to tell their children in their own special way. So be that parent who will share sex information with your child in that special way and let pride in your child's knowledge overshadow any fear.

Find the Courage to Be Uncomfortable

It can certainly be uncomfortable to look closely at our own thoughts and feelings about sexuality; it may be uncomfortable to focus on how our own family functions in this regard. When it comes to protecting our children from sexual abuse, it's much easier to focus on the perils of the Internet and take naïve comfort in the thought that the criminal justice system will protect our kids; these thoughts allow us to keep a safe emotional distance from the real problem. These impersonal systems exist far away from the common types of victimization that people face—and that we may have faced and would rather not consider on any level. Every community is home to people who have been scarred through experiences such as unreported assault from an adult, sexually oriented bullying, sexually explicit and violent language, date rape, or worse. Public systems alone cannot protect your children from these risks; your role and responsibility as a parent are paramount despite any natural discomfort.

But you need the courage to be uncomfortable. Keeping your kids sexually safe and healthy requires an extraordinarily brave commitment to healthy family intimacy. We need to pay attention to the real threats in the surrounding world and cyberspace, but not at the expense of looking at and strengthening the most basic institution—the family. Parents must learn and use the tools they need to keep their children safe.

It's hard to open a newspaper and miss a story about a new group that's been started dedicated to the eradication of sexual exploitation of children. It's a great thing that organizations such as the Internet Crimes Against Children's Council, the National Coalition to Prevent the Sexual Exploitation of Children, and other groups are working on policies, procedures, and laws to keep our youth safe from sexual predators. They use legalistic terms such as "demand reduction" in terms of catching the people who sexually exploit children or buy child pornography. But we, as individuals and parents, must address the need for a longer term, more comprehensive demand reduction to be achieved, for example, by helping every parent strive to raise a son (or a daughter) who would find child pornography abhorrent. In this book, we aim to help you as parents to raise a daughter (or a son) whose sexuality is healthy enough so that she avoids the sexualization and objectification that make people vulnerable to exploitation. Healthy sexual attitudes start with the family.

It is unrealistic to assume that a child will not come into contact with someone preaching values about sexuality that don't match yours. If it's not a teacher, it will be someone they hear on the radio or see on TV or online.

Teaching sexual health and safety is a critical aspect of parenting at every stage of childhood and adolescence. Through these strategies you will gain opportunities for your own growth and healing, to open up and identify your own beliefs, messages, and experiences. If you find that these values and beliefs came from bad information or experiences, use the tips herein as you to start the work to make them right. One of the many gifts of parenthood is realizing that you may do something for your child that you neglected doing for yourself.

Furthermore, we must help our children develop understandable language about sex. Pedophiles know that kids who don't have words to describe what was done to them, can't "tell" on them. If you help your child understand how his body works you take away the pedophile's biggest advantage—the knowledge that a child's autonomic, reflexive arousal from stimuli can be used to convince him that his abuse needs to be kept a guilty secret.

Not talking to kids about sex leaves them vulnerable to exploitation. With a little help we can learn to get beyond our own fears or embarrassment and give our children the gift of being sexually safe and healthy. You as a parent and all adults who love and care for children can step up and engage in open, honest, accurate, and age-appropriate discussions with all members of your family about sex in all of its natural beauty with an informed perspective on the very real risks associated with it. Children need their parents and parents need knowledge and support to address these sensitive issues.

You should learn the language, anatomy, and physiology of sexuality and come to understand the stages of psychosexual development. You can learn the meaning of "sexual climate" and determine if the sexual climate in your community, your child's school, and even your house of worship matches your values. You can learn the facts about sex roles, gender identity, and sexual preference, and learn how to support your own children through adolescence with respect for themselves and compassion towards others. You should incorporate this knowledge into daily family life to strengthen your family and protect your children.

A Special Call to Adults Victimized as Children

If you experienced sexual victimization as a child, you may find it even more difficult to broach the subject of sex and the previous talking points with your children. If sex in general or specific sexual acts still carry the pain of your early experiences, consider practicing talking about sex with a professional support person or a trusted confidante before you begin speaking with your child. You want to make sure that you are able to provide your child with the information he or she needs without projecting your pain or sadness onto the conversation.

Keith Smith, author of *The Men in My Town*, describes being abducted by a paroled pedophile, brutally assaulted, and terrorized, and expresses his knowledge that he was lucky to have lived through the experience. Other than the fictional account of the perpetrator's death, Keith reports that the rest of the book is, sadly, true. He further explains that the men in his town stood by him through it all. They showed up at his ball games, they cheered him on, and gave him support in the years following the attack. They may even be the reason that the pedophile never had another victim. But they never spoke of the rape and neither did his family.[15] The publication of his book broke a three-decade silence in that regard. Keith is far from the only adult survivor I've met whose family never spoke of a child's abuse or other sexual issues. These adult survivors knew they had to do better in regard to their own children. One mom of two told me, "My kids know that there is no part of their body that is a secret."

Many victims come from families where sex is never discussed and keeping secrets is the norm. Don't become one of those families. Help your kids enjoy the sexual health and safety that comes from receiving good information from trusted adults and having an open line of communication for their questions or concerns.

A Note for Unmarried Parents

Yes, you have a right to a sex life, and no, it's none of your child's business. Some unmarried parents avoid discussing sex with their kids, hoping that when a partner spends the night, the kids think of it like any other sleepover. This delusion misses the mark on so many levels, though, and must be avoided.

Your choice to have overnights with your partner with your kids in the house is a serious decision. If you are as sure as humanly possible that your partner presents no safety risk to your child, your second question is about

---

15   Smith, Keith, personal conversation, April 2011.

what you are communicating non-verbally to your child about sex when your partner spends the night. Do your kids know you love your partner? Do your kids think you want her there because she makes a mean Sunday breakfast? Kids really learn what they live; if you are not comfortable enough to share your feelings for your partner with your child, consider skipping the sleepover. Even if you think your kids are too young to understand that sleepovers mean sex, their other parent does, and may well add their own unflattering and confusing comments when your child mentions the overnight houseguest.

Communication about sex comes in many forms. For example, if dad has a lady friend sleepover while his daughter is in the house, he is communicating about sex, and the message may be that the way to a man's heart is through sex. When mom tells her kids that her boyfriend is sleeping over so they can get a nice early start to the lake on Saturday, most kids older than ten will see right through that and get the message that we lie to our family members about sex.

Kids who do not get to live with coupled parents may miss an important opportunity to obtain a realistic sense of the real-life ups and downs of human relationships. Most of us want our kids to learn that sex means more than the end to an enjoyable evening, and that real relationships involve commitment. If you are an uncoupled parent, keep in mind that your actions will speak louder than words, especially as your child approaches adolescence.

This list of reasons why parents avoid talking to their kids about sex could probably have hundreds more entries. None of them relieve you of the responsibility of developing the courage to be uncomfortable and acquire the knowledge and skills to reach your child with the information about sexuality that you want him or her to have.

CHAPTER 3

Discussing It for Love

Ten Essential Reasons Why Parents *Must* Talk with Their Kids about Sex

There is sex in your house. You can't pretend there isn't. Actually, you can, but your kids will know that's what you're doing, and that will leave a great big hole in the trust, honesty, and intimacy that characterizes a healthy home.

Your child is sexual. Some adults may cringe at that thought, but we must realize being a sexual being is part of the human condition. As parents, you have an important role to help give your child the tools to prepare him for a safe and healthy adult sex life. And you can make the entire process easier and more effective by discussing all aspects of his body when opportunities arise throughout his childhood.

Silence *can* speak louder than words, even if you are one of the millions who come into adulthood with your own sexual scars. If you have your own healing to do still, take the opportunity *not* to transmit the same unhealthy attitudes to your child.

Even if you are one of the millions who never had any decent sex education—who learned your own information from the playground, magazines, or the Internet—the fact that you are reading this book shows that you want the opportunity to offer your children something more than what you experienced. Families develop their own norms about sexual issues, and most of it happens without much thought. You must find the courage to be uncomfortable and make conscious decisions about what you want your child to know and when.

We live in a sexualized culture and our kids are bombarded with sexual messages. Even the American Psychological Association recommends that parents prepare kids for puberty by age nine or ten so "they will not be caught off guard when the changes occur."[16] If we really want our kids to be sexually safe and healthy, we must not continue to let our children face the developmental task of reaching sexual maturity without our support.

You, as a parent, can prepare for these talks by discussing sex with your partner, other parents, or trusted friends; you can make conscious decisions about the actual information to be shared with your kids and the values you hold regarding sexuality that you wish to be transmitted. When you speak of love and joy while your face communicates fear and embarrassment, you confuse your kids and make the discussion all the more complicated and difficult.

You can rise to this challenge and overcome your fears of speaking with your children about sex and abuse. Here are ten good reasons why you must.

1. When kids have questions, parents are the best source for answers.

Until they leave your home (and perhaps after), your children will have questions about their bodies, your body, their siblings' bodies, about sexual things they've seen or heard, and all matter of related issues. Being in a position to provide answers is a gift—each question is an opportunity to strengthen your relationship with your child, to show mutual trust and respect, and most important of all, to ensure that the answer your child gets is the one you want him to have.

---

16 American Psychological Association. *Developing Adolescents: A Reference for Professionals.* Washington, D.C.: The American Psychological Assocation, 2002. Page 7 accessed in June 2011, at http://www.apa.org/pi/families/resources/develop.pdf.

A member of one of my focus groups recalled her son asking her about the meaning of a word he'd heard at school that day. "Mom, what's a blow job?" he asked. It could just as easily have been, "What's 'cunny-lingus'?"; "Why is sixty-nine a bad number?"; or "Why is pointing the middle finger bad?" These questions, though unsettling at first, are all opportunities to make sure your kids get the information and values you want them to have—imagine the answers a kid might get from other kids!

At almost any age, the oral sex questions could be answered as a matter of fact: "It's a slang term for someone kissing a man's penis/woman's vagina." After the child gets done saying "eeewwww—who would want to do that?" and you reply, "Only grown-ups who really love each other," you may also add, "So where did you see (or hear) that word?" Stay calm and sound matter-of-fact when asking the question; your embarrassment or shock can shut your child down instantly if they sense you are uncomfortable. You really want to know how your child formulated the question. Hopefully, she overheard some older kids talking, but if she was invited to participate in the act, even in jest, you need to find out more and determine if you need to follow up by contacting the person who started the conversation with your child—or his or her parent if the idea came from a child!

Some kids ask questions when they are seeking opinions, as opposed to facts, and these questions are the most important ones for you as a parent. From "When is it OK to have sex?" to "Why is a girl's chest considered a private part but a boy's is not?" being open and available to your kids' questions provides a great opportunity to bring your values to your child and to inform them about sexuality, relationships, and peers.

When you follow up your answer with a gentle probe about why your child asked the question, you may find that someone is being inappropriate with your child, that your child has gotten her hands on adult reading material in your house, or that the song you just let them download has lyrics you really didn't want her to hear. You may be able to confirm your thoughts that your adolescent is sexually active by asking leading questions. A mom was approached by her eighteen-year-old daughter who asked, "How old were you the first time you had sex?" Mom, an experienced social worker, was surprised at how uncomfortable she felt, and chose to probe by responding, "How old were you?" thus opening a long overdue mother–daughter dialogue about sex.

The question about why girls' chests are private but boys aren't could be answered by telling a young child that girls will grow breasts on their chests, and breasts are very special and private. If your child has experienced seeing a mom breastfeed, you could use that as an example of how bodies are shared in special ways with people we love.

Being available to address your children's questions ensures they get the information you want them to have and that you get information about what else they are learning and from whom.

2. It can be very traumatic for a child to hit puberty unprepared.

Kids' bodies can start to show signs of puberty as young as elementary school. Girls will start to develop breasts; both genders will start to grow hair under their arms and in their pubic areas. Girls may experience anything from a little twinge to real pain in the side of their abdomen when ovulation, or releasing of eggs from the ovaries, begins before menstruation. Thoughts such as, "Why is this happening to me?" or "Is it just me?" or worse yet, "What's wrong with me?" can be uncomfortable at best and frightening at worst for children. This fear is one of the few pains of adolescence that parents can actually prevent.

Women who started to menstruate without understanding what it was relate that they thought they had cancer, that they were dying, that they hurt themselves while masturbating or riding a bicycle, and other equally frightening thoughts. Even boys who have been aware of erections their whole lives become anxious over the sudden increase in frequency and intensity of them, and many don't understand ejaculation. We know that boys must deal with social pressures to keep emotions hidden, including their feelings and experiences around their burgeoning sexuality. In countless subtle ways, society tells boys not to cry, to stay in control, and be "strong." All of a sudden, the part of their anatomy that defines them as male—their penis—becomes uncontrollable!

Without the knowledge that this is normal, a boy can be left feeling as if something is terribly wrong with him. Remember in Rosenzweig's Rule #2 we discussed the dangers of sexual arousal becoming associated with fear, guilt, or shame. Ignorance about the normal changes of puberty can lead down this ugly path. And if teasing or misinformation from peers is the only message your son (or daughter) hears about sex, he can stay right on that ugly course for years.

There are also social issues associated with adolescence that are better navigated with loving parental support. One participant in a focus group recalled kissing a girl for the first time around age twelve. Shortly thereafter, he heard a playground rumor that the object of his affection was making fun of him behind his back. He was devastated—and decades later still recalls the shame he felt at believing he did not know how to kiss! What a gift it would have been to hear from a loving parent that adolescent girls can be very fickle and only make fun of the boys they really like. Parental support can help your child navigate these socially, physically, and emotionally turbulent changes. This man's story illustrates another sad fact—silence can leave unnecessary scars on a young person's blossoming sexuality.

3. Kids *need* to learn about sex, *will* learn about sex, and are likely to get bad information if left to their own devices.

Baby-boomers may recall seeing their first nude adults in magazine pictures or as teens in poor-quality X-rated movies. What was considered "mature content" a generation ago can now be viewed on network television. And, of course, the Internet brings remarkably detailed sexual images to anyone who wants them and a lot of people who do not. Among the many dangers from all of this exposure to sexual imagery is that your child will think what he sees and hears is normal, meaning that he or she—who looks nothing like the images they see—may feel like he or she is abnormal.

One focus group member expressed this as she shared her dismay in learning that her eleven-year-old son was visiting online porn sites. "I don't want those images of women to be planted in his head. Those kinds of images are beyond my control," she said. The information her son was getting about sex contained images and messages that came nowhere near conforming to the messages this mom wanted him to have. Her first response was to admonish her son to leave that website immediately, and she still feels regret from not using the opportunity to explain why.

While this passive intrusion into your child's life is bad enough, there are people who will actively seek to plant misinformation about sex into your child's head. From a teen who thinks it's funny to tell a child a lie about sex, to the pedophile who tells your child that all kids do whatever it is he wants your kid to do, to the peer who earnestly passes on incorrect information about sex, your child will be bombarded with incorrect "facts" about a very serious subject. Here are a few "timeless" tales about puberty and sex (do any of these sound familiar from your own childhood?):

- You'll grow hair on your palms from masturbating.
- People look different after they've had sex.
- The other kids can "just tell" that you got your period.
- All the other guys have a foot-long penis, or hair on their testicles.

I thought so. How comforting it can be for a kid to get the truth about puberty and the facts of becoming a sexual being, with love, from a parent and not from a misinformed peer.

It is rare that a parent would not want his or her child to grow up to be happy, but even in the happiest families most adults recall adolescent years as a time of confusion about sex and sexuality. Adolescent angst is developmentally normal, but sex-wise parenting can improve the chance of a successful resolution of these normal developmental conflicts by the time your child reaches young adulthood. Providing accurate anatomical and physiological facts—even if all you can muster up the courage to do is leave a booklet on your son or daughter's bed—is one of the easiest ways for you to promote sexual health and safety.

4. Lacking information, kids fill in the blanks with what they know or can imagine and it usually is wrong.

We can chuckle hearing the story about the junior-high-school-aged girls who thought that "screwing" was another word for deep tongue kissing. If you think about it, you can see their logic—the tongue moves in a "screwing" motion in the partner's mouth—but things became less funny when a teacher intercepted notes the girls were passing in class describing who they planned to screw that weekend. Several frightened parents contacted by the school counselor now had no choice but to discuss sex with their kids. Then there is the story of the boys who thought that because erections were also called "boners" they must have a bone in their penis—and wondered where it went when the penis was not erect. Ignorance can appear cute when we hear the story of the two-year-old girl who points to her new brother's penis during the first diaper change, and asks, "Tail?" But ignorance is far from cute and can be downright dangerous.

These kids filled in gaps in their knowledge with assumptions that made sense to them, but ultimately were wrong. Often leaving an adolescent to their assumptions results in unnecessary pain. Many of us can recall spending what felt like hours in front of the mirror as an adolescent looking at our body wondering if it was normal and desirable by others. Kids subjected to teasing and slang nicknames like "limp dick," "tiny tits," and worse can have reactions more serious than embarrassment and flushed cheeks. Children will take this type of sexual teasing to heart, planting the seeds of a poor body or self-image.

One focus group member, a mom in her thirties, shared a memory she has of a French exchange high-school student who had been sexually active for several years who joined her family for a few weeks back when she was a teen. Being that close to a sexually active peer made this mom feel "as if everyone who was sexually active was in a secret club and looked down on [her] because [she] wasn't—at fourteen!" Providing information and support places you in a position to alleviate much of the pain that results from incorrect adolescent assumptions.

Kids absolutely need the support of you as a loving parent, as an adult who can assure them that their sexual life and their body are both developing in a perfectly normal way. Self-confidence is an important component of sexual health and safety, and knowing that they are growing in a perfectly acceptable, normal, and healthy way helps build that confidence.

Then there's the issue of a child accidently seeing or hearing grown-ups having sex. Kids can experience the sight or sounds of adults making love as anything from a simple hug to an act of violence. Boundaries and privacy are critical in a sexually safe and healthy family, but accidents do happen. Be prepared to explain to your child what sex means to you—perhaps saying that it's a special way grown-ups get as close to each other as possible to show love to each other.

Having gaps in knowledge is absolutely normal for children (and adults as well)—no one is born knowing everything! When your child demonstrates one of these gaps, wouldn't you prefer to be the adult in the position of helping him determine how that gap is filled?

5. Kids with no language about sex lack words to tell if they are being abused.

This one is self-explanatory.

A pediatrician who treats sex abuse victims in a specialized hospital setting shared the story of the little girl who told her teacher that Daddy "hurt my cookie." This child was referring to her genitalia, but the teacher gave the child a snack instead of reporting abuse. Or the example of a little girl who used the phrase "my purse is broke" to tell a teacher that her genitals were bleeding. Both kids were subject to abuse longer than necessary because the adults in their lives who could have helped end the abuse had no idea what the children were talking about.

A pedophile may teach a child that his sexual fondling is "hugging" or "man-touching" or that they play their "special game." A child who lacks any other terms to comprehend what's happening is now trapped! She really may believe this type of touch is part of a special relationship with a grownup who cares about her. That's why you need to probe a little further into their seemingly meaningless banter, to ensure that they have the right words to use when they need to communicate with you about anything, including sex.

6. Kids need to understand the difference between *love* and *lust* in order to be sexually safe and healthy.

Children will experience sexual arousal even before puberty. As they become adolescents, it will happen more often and feel more intense. As your kids develop, you can reinforce the important lesson that genital feelings happen for many different reasons, most of which have little to do with emotions in adolescents. Sights, sounds, smells, memories, movies, pictures, and thoughts are among the stimuli that can lead to sexual arousal. If kids know this and the fact is a routine part of their lives, you may lower the risk of your child making the dangerous mistake of believing lust is love. Knowing the difference is an important milestone on the road to raising a sexually safe and healthy child and young adult.

A sexually safe and healthy person understands that just because his genitals go all warm at the thought or sight of someone, he is not necessarily in love with that individual. Many of us as adults recall feeling our first twinges of arousal while reading a book or watching a movie. Rhett's passion for Scarlett, Catwoman teasing Batman, Kelly Bundy flaunting her stuff, a Sidney Sheldon novel read as a teen, or an explicit magazine stolen from parents—each age has produced its own iconic images that wake up adolescent genitals. Focus group member Jay, a man who has no memories of discussing sex with his parents, recalls being around eight or nine years old when he "realized [his] dick had something to do with girls" but he wasn't quite sure what. Mistaking arousal for affection, as Jay experienced, can lay the foundation for a child's confusion about where sexual feelings fit into their life and relationships.

It is developmentally normal and socially acceptable in the United States for kids to start playing kissing games, like spin the bottle, as early as nine or ten years old. Even in the 1960s, kissing games were the highlights of grade-school graduation parties. Scholarly research (and, most likely, your memory) will confirm examples of early sexual arousal and activity; one study documented "pre-coital" behavior in over one-third of a sample of 1,279 seventh graders.[17] A young person can experience sexual arousal from kissing and may mistake this for affection for their kissing partner. Much social drama could ensue—and usually unnecessarily.

It is equally important for your child to know that he or she alone is responsible for his or her arousal. Ego-centric young people unaware of the autonomic nature of arousal are at risk of believing that the object of their lust actively sought to arouse them. Actually, one teen may actively try to elicit arousal from the other for reasons ranging from curiosity to cruelty. You can keep your child and the people she interacts with sexually safe and healthy by ensuring that she knows no one is responsible for her arousal except herself. It's important that your child know that as thinking, conscious human beings we have the opportunity to *think* about how to deal with our own arousal before we do anything about it.

This issue becomes very important in the teenage years. Adolescent female bodies become flooded with hormones that can make them crave love and nurturing; while adolescent boys bodies are flooded with hormones that

---

17   Markham, et al. *Journal of School Health*, Volume 79, Number 4, April 2009: 193–200.

can make them want orgasms. Both boys and girls are in danger of hearing only what they want to hear from a love or lust object, and many end up with a range of negative experiences from disappointment to outright exploitation. It is dangerous for both teens if the young boy thinks he heard a "yes" because he really wanted to hear "yes," but the girl really meant no. A date-rape accusation can haunt both young people for the rest of their lives. You can read more about adolescent sexual development in chapter 5, but the simple fact is this: it is a milestone of maturity for a child to know the difference between sexual arousal and real emotion. You do not want to raise a son to think that a girl owes him sexual relief because she chose to wear a certain outfit or act in a way that he found arousing. You do not want to raise a daughter who thinks she should have intercourse with a boy because her genitals responded with wet warmth during a make-out session. You want to raise a child who can enjoy the experience of arousal, own these feelings as his own, and make smart choices about sexual partners as he matures into a sexually safe and healthy adult. Even in a loving, committed relationship, lust can overrule all lessons on safe sex, distracting not only from the need to think twice before having intercourse, but the need to find out a partner's sexual health history and to use a condom. These risks—mistaking lust for emotion—are real and you owe it to your children to make them aware of all aspects (and risks) of sexual maturity.

Lust is part of the joy of a healthy sexual relationship; out of context, though, it can fuel stupid decisions. This is a great message for you to be able to share with your son or daughter.

7. Lacking understanding of the reflexive nature of sexual arousal, a child can all too easily be made to feel complicit by their abuser.

Oprah Winfrey used her talk show as a platform to bring sexual abuse of children into the public eye on many occasions. In April 2010, she hosted Todd Bridges, the former child actor known as much for his adult dysfunction as his childhood charm. He was promoting his autobiography, *Killing Willis.*[18] Oprah asked her guest to turn to page 68 of his book and read. At first, Bridges

---

18   Bridges, Todd with Sarah Tomlinson. *Killing Willis*. New York: Simon and Schuster, 2010.

seemed to question her choice of selections, then read this description of being molested as a young teen TV star by his publicist:

"Pull your pants down," he said.

I didn't want to lose everything he had given me. And so I did.

He put his mouth on me. I got hard. I didn't know where to look or how to feel. I squirmed against the back of the seat. He kept on going, getting into it.

I hoped it would be over fast.

Then it happened. I came.

As confused and upset as I was, I liked the feeling.

"No one had ever talked to me about sex before," Bridges writes in his book. "But somehow I knew it was wrong for a man to do that to a boy. I was really confused because having an orgasm had felt good."

None of us wants our child to be molested; the thought of the violation is unspeakable. But if it does happen, we can prevent the lifelong confusion and guilt that can have devastating consequences on our child's psyche just by making sure our kids know that sexual arousal is an autonomic response to a stimulus—that's all. No more, no less. Arousal is not an indication of your feelings about yourself or another person.

Keith Smith, author of the book *The Men in My Town*, was among the 200 men, all victims of child sexual abuse, who made up the audience for Oprah Winfrey's groundbreaking show shedding light on male victims. Over coffee one day, Keith shared with me that when media mogul Tyler Perry, also a victim of childhood sexual abuse, said that his body "betrayed" him with the sexual response, a palpable shock ran through the audience of male victims, and tears of recognition filled the eyes of many. Did anyone teach Tyler, Keith, Todd, and the millions of others that their bodies didn't betray them at all? Loving, responsible parents, such as yourself, can teach young boys that bodies are wired to behave exactly as these young boys' did. Adding self-loathing to violation is awful and one of the effects of victimization that can be prevented with knowledge.

In some ways, girls may be even more vulnerable to the insidious self-blame from unexpected arousal. Girls may think that "everyone knows" that boys will get aroused. But female arousal is a much better kept secret thanks to the more discrete physiological response; vaginal lubrication is much less obvious than a penile erection. A manipulative abuser can make a girl feel special in a way that is ultimately destructive. Healthy kids need to know that regardless of what a calculating molester may say, arousal of either the victim or abuser does not make the relationship with the abuser special. Molesters of little girls have been known to convince the victims that this overpowered, manipulated child is the only person who can arouse or satisfy the man. Female victims of this ruse perpetrated by a father or stepfather recall feeling as if it was their responsibility to keep the family intact, or that it had become their "job" within the family to keep the molester satiated to prevent the breadwinner from leaving or to keep the other kids safe from his advances.

That is a terrible weight for a child to carry. Too many female victims are fooled into thinking they are unique in their ability to arouse their molester. Providing your children with accurate information about sexual arousal can play an important role in helping them find the strength to seek help if ever confronted with this terrible situation.

So many victims blame themselves for all kinds of details of an assault, harboring the illusion that they could have controlled where the lightning struck. If I hadn't been hitchhiking, if I hadn't been wearing those shorts, if I had screamed louder, run faster, been a better step-daughter, not been so nice to the neighbor, or Mom's boyfriends, or Dad's buddy . . . and the like. The guilt is as useless as it is deadly. To add to that the guilt from autonomic sexual response is cruel and unusual punishment.

In 1993, David Kelley's nighttime soap opera *Picket Fences* ran an episode entitled "Unlawful Entries"[19] in which a man filed rape charges after the woman he was on a date with handcuffed him to the bed during a make-out session. She carefully aroused him to erection then had intercourse with him, over his angry protests. The law enforcement characters and judge all needed repeated explanations by the local doctor and medical examiner to actually be convinced of the role of the autonomic nervous system in arousal. Medically accurate information was shared in a pretty responsible way along with some realistic displays of disbelief and embarrassment—and this was decades ago. We don't see many media messages like this in the early twenty-first century. Parents must rise to the challenge of inoculating their kids against fear, guilt, and shame by sharing this simple fact of autonomic arousal, repeatedly.

---

19   Original air date Friday, October 29, 1993.

8. Even if you don't talk, you communicate.

When your kids are very young, they see themselves through the eyes of their beloved caretakers, usually you and your partner. They wonder: Am I lovable? Am I smart? Can I become independent? You are constantly giving your children verbal and non-verbal cues about who they are; the younger the child, the more basic the message is to the child's self image. You are also giving them messages about their body that can form the basis for later body image. Little kids know if they have been labeled "the dirty one," or "the sloppy one," or "the pretty one," and their developing little psyches assume that the label is true. If you ignore your children's genitals all together, then you have absolutely no influence on whether your child thinks genitals are good or bad. Many women recall their fathers making absolutely no comment about menstruation, or sarcastic remarks about more females in the house "on the rag." Very few men can recall getting accurate information about their bodies, and even today, I meet parents who hope and believe their school's health program will take care of all that stuff.

The old adage that actions speak louder than words can certainly apply to teaching children about sex. Several women in my focus groups recalled their dads standing in front of the television set blocking their view when anything sexual showed up on the screen. "Not for you to see," Dad would announce, leaving giggling, confused kids on the family room couch. I certainly recall my mom blushing a vibrant shade of red as she had "the talk" with my sister and me; that blush told me as much as her words! Sex was something to be embarrassed about and to deal with only under duress. My learning to believe otherwise created an unnecessary distance from my mom.

A woman in one of my focus groups, who came from a family with several sisters, shared that if their dad saw even an unused sanitary product in the bathroom, he'd moan some loud complaint such as, "Why do I have to see this stuff?" leaving some of the sisters with ambivalent, if not negative, thoughts about menstruation. And on the topic of menstruation, many kids have memories of seeing what appeared to be bloody objects in the family bathroom, leaving them to wonder who had been hurt. One focus group member laughs now at what was a mortifying experience as a teen—the family dog at a home she was visiting retrieved a used tampon she had wrapped and placed in a wastebasket, and brought it into the living room like a hunting souvenir.

The mom retrieved the tampon and disposed of it but no one in the family explained anything to anyone, leaving only embarrassed silence and confusion. The little kids had been upset by the sight of a bloody object and no one told them what it was. Some parents really think that if they don't talk about sex with their kids, their kids will think that sex is not important enough to talk about. Wake up and smell the pheromones—that's just not going to happen. The feelings children have in their developing bodies and the images and messages all around them tell them that sex *is* important. By not talking to kids about sex, we have absolutely no impact on what they know or think about sex. Is sex good or bad? Fun or evil? Am I normal or not for thinking about sex? Why aren't we talking about this? Silence can teach embarrassment and shame to kids regarding the topic of sex.

Take for example Rob, who was raised by divorced parents in the 1970s before concepts like joint custody and co-parenting were common. Living with his mom meant limited time with his father. One day when he was about twelve, his older sister overheard him talking with his male friends about their (completely made up) sexual exploits. Bossy big sister called their father and said it was time for him to speak with her brother about the birds and bees. Later that night, her brother hung up from a call with his Dad and was completely confused. His dad called and told him a fabricated story that the mother of the girl he had been bragging about "feeling up" called and complained to him about the boy bothering her daughter. This dad thought that it was his job to intimidate his son into leaving girls alone. Dad hit a double here; he gave his son a useless, negative message about sex and a clear indication that he was willing to lie to his son to make a point.

There is a message in no message; and that unspoken message will never meet your child's needs.

9. The parental fear that talking to kids about sex is essentially giving them permission to become sexually active is unfounded.

Here's a true tale of two extremes: One focus group I held while researching this book put me literally between two women with opposite experiences. On my left was a woman whose sex education was so seamless she doesn't ever recall having "the talk"; rather she was one of the lucky people for whom information about sex—from her pediatrician mom—was integrated into any information she received about her body. Occasional nudity in the two-parent family home meant that she knew what male genitals looked like and they held absolutely no mystery or caused any fear. She reported that she was comfortable with sex, and is raising her kids with the same values she got from her parents.

On my right was a woman raised in a strictly conservative, self-described Irish Catholic family where sex was never discussed. Whatever she learned came from books or other kids. As soon as she left for college, she expressed her independence by having sex with any partner that struck her fancy. She learned to like sex, and herself. She is raising her kids in a way that sounds like the woman on my left; she provides age appropriate information, answers any questions, and encourages open communication. Listening to these two women confirmed that parental conversations with kids about sex do not promote sexual activity and that silence from parents does nothing to promote abstinence.

Research also bears this out: "comprehensive education about sexuality does not hasten the onset of sex, increase the frequency of sex, or increase the number of sexual partners teens have."[20]

Open communication is key, especially when you are a single parent or divorcee. Steve is the divorced father of two. Raising his kids in the 1990s, he discussed anything and everything with his kids, often to the chagrin of his extended family. Granted, cultural sexual messages were prevalent, but Steve was no-holds-barred in what he shared with his kids. Both he and his ex-wife dated and kids knew there were occasional sleepover dates. The good news is that as teens, his thirteen-year-old daughter has absolutely no problem sending dad to the store for tampons and his seventeen-year-old son openly discusses his decision to refrain from intercourse with his longtime girlfriend.

Remember, information is a tool to help your child make good decisions, not tacit permission to act in any specific way.

10. My kid shuts me down when I bring up the subject.

Many of you probably remember having excellent conversations looking at young kids reflected in their rear-view mirror while buckled into their car seat. Those days may be gone, but the car is still a great place to talk, as I

---

20 Kirby, Douglas. *Emerging Answers: Research Findings on Programs to Reduce Teen Pregnancy.* Washington, D.C.: National Campaign to Prevent Teen Pregnancy, 2001. Accessed at http://www.sexedlibrary.org/index.cfm?fuseaction=page.viewpage&pageid=877.

mentioned before. You have a captive audience, and even if a sullen teen refuses to answer you, they have no choice but to listen. Use "I-statements" like "I see the changes your friend is going through and I want to make sure you have all the information you need so you're neither confused nor surprised when it happens to you." Recite some facts you want them to know. Remind your son or daughter that you and your partner (or other important adult in your child's life) are there to answer questions. Encourage your child to seek the information that he and his friends want and need. Even if this never progresses beyond a monologue, leave a book on her bed with a note that you love her and want her to be sexually safe and healthy. Remind your child that you're there to answer any questions should they arise.

If you start a conversation about sex with your child where he or she finds a way to avoid you, borrow this line written by a professional writer to be spoken by a father to his son on the TV show *Glee*: "I'm uncomfortable too, but sit down. We'll both be better men for having this conversation."

And, when all else fails, consider a good natured bribe. "Mom, can you drive me to the mall?" Junior asks. "OK, but only if we finish the conversation we started yesterday . . . five minutes is all." And then take it from there.

Make It Easier on Yourself: Collaborate with Formal Sex Education

Ann, the divorced mom of two, lives in a community where the woman who taught human sexuality, marriage, and family life for more than a decade had a PhD in Health Education, specializing in Human Sexuality,[21] and served on the board of every major national sexuality professional organization in the United States. One evening Ann found her daughter, then a high school junior, hard at work studying for an exam. Ann asked which subject she was studying and her daughter replied, "The vagina test, which I had better *ace* because I really did well on the penis test!" Ann's community is an exception; few communities employ credentialed sexuality educators and many communities lack resources for an interested health teacher to get specialized training.

It is not safe to assume that kids will get the sex information they need in a health education class at school; less than half of the states require sex

---

21 http://ncate.widener.edu/CV'S%20FACULTY%20PDF%20FORMAT/CVKon-stance%20McCaffree.pdf

education.[22] As mentioned before, you can become partners with the school and find the way to have input into the curriculum.

None of the parents interviewed for this book reported having input into the health curriculum at his or her child's school. "I received a letter that the school was going to have a sex-ed class . . . that's it. My kid learned about female circumcision in Africa, and I still don't understand why that was included," one parent complained to me during an interview.

Sex education in schools continues to be a politically charged issue, and school is but one of the places where kids will get a good amount of information about sex. However, good curriculum delivered by qualified teachers can balance out all of the inaccurate information from the media and school yard. Rather than argue to keep it out, wouldn't it make more sense for you to review the curriculum and credentials of the people charged with teaching? A good school wants parents as partners.

Considerations for Unmarried Parents

It is entirely possible that a child's two parents can have different values from each other. If you are married, you and your spouse can explore these issues by reviewing the material in chapter 6. Even if you are no longer a couple with your child's other parent, you can communicate about your child's development, questions, and possible fears on a regular basis. Sarah, a focus group member, reports that strongly differing perspectives on how to educate her kids about sex became yet another battleground in a highly contentious divorce. Her kids got entirely different messages from her and her ex-husband and she knows they will have to work to integrate the different messages they've received as they mature. Phyllis, on the other hand, reports that she and her ex were able to keep even that line of communication open—after all, a daughter new to menstruation needs support even when she's at her dad's for the weekend. A boy needs to learn about his penis from someone he loves and trusts—there are pedophiles out there looking for boys with no men to turn to who are all too willing to provide their own form of "education." And remember to practice what you preach; if you are an unmarried parent, you are in a position to role model your values about sexuality in ways that married

---

22   Guttmacher Institute. *State Policies in Brief*. August 2010. Accessed at http://www. guttmacher.org/statecenter/spibs/spib_SE.pdf.

parents cannot. Your kids will be watching and wondering what you're up to, giving you an even more compelling reason to keep the lines of communication open. They may wonder if Mom kisses her boyfriend. Does Dad's girl-friend sleep over when the kids aren't there? Why or why not? These types of questions need to be answered rationally and honesty by you and without any hint of embarrassment or fear.

Even if you think you are being discrete and conducting your sex life only while your kids are away, they will find clues you'd never have thought of—condoms in a drawer, unfamiliar underwear in the laundry, new shampoo in the shower—and know someone else has been in their house. It's hard to preach abstinence until marriage when your kids know you're sexually active, so be prepared for the honest discussions about the meanings of sexual behavior, how you choose partners, and why your knowledge, maturity, and experience have prepared you to do so.

A Special Call to Adults Victimized as Kids

Along with the other reasons discussed in this chapter, failure to discuss sex with your child might cause you to unnecessarily blame yourself if your child tragically becomes one of the tens of thousands who experience abuse each year. This is certainly an emotional experience you neither need nor deserve. Yes, it's acceptable to be motivated by your desire *not* to feel badly. Do whatever it takes to prepare you and your children and open the discussion. The benefits are lifelong.

PART 2

Everything You Should Have Learned in High School and Probably Didn't

What a Parent Needs to Know to Promote Healthy Sexuality

CHAPTER 4

Anatomy and Physiology for Grownups

Why is it imperative for you, as a parent, to know about sexual anatomy and physiology? Here are at least four important reasons:

1. Your child will have questions about his body, and you want him to come to you for answers. The more comfortable you are with sharing age-appropriate information, the more your child will understand about sex and as a bonus, he'll be more willing to come to you with further questions about just about everything.

2. The more you're able to talk with your child about her body before adolescence, the more likely it is that you'll be able to maintain some trust and comfort with her after adolescence, when children naturally turn elsewhere for answers. It's a fundamental right to enter adolescence with a full understanding of the changes puberty is about to bring. I've met women who, as girls, thought their vaginal bleeding meant they had cancer, and men who, as boys, thought their orgasms while sleeping meant they were evil.

3. Knowledge is power. You want to raise sexually safe and healthy children who cannot be misled by the glut of false information waiting for them, in the media, from misinformed but well meaning peers, or from nefar-

ious predators for whom kids' ignorance about sex is an exploitable vulnerability.

4. Finally, you can't teach what you don't know. When it comes to sexuality, many of us don't even know what we don't know! Maybe you were lucky enough to have had a loving, trusted adult who comfortably shared information in small, age-appropriate doses as you grew up. Most of us weren't so lucky, but we want to be that person for our kids.

In this chapter, we're going to look at questions from kids and offer the information you need to answer them, so you are prepared when you child comes to you with a similar question. All of these are based on questions actually posed by kids, to me when teaching, to their parents who shared them with me, or posted on a teen sexual health website. Some questions have been paraphrased and their spelling cleaned up, but the material to follow is exactly what kids want to know about their bodies and about sex.

Remember the fictional dad from *Glee* mentioned in chapter 3? This dad was warned that his son was dangerously clueless about sex. He invited his son into a discussion and the teen balked. I'm repeating the words the writers put into this dad's mouth because I think many parents may want to borrow it: "I'm uncomfortable too, but sit down. We'll both be better men for having this conversation." That TV writer captured the exquisite ambivalence so many parents experience at the thought of speaking with their kids about sex. Knowledge is power, and the knowledge you can get from this chapter can help build your confidence and comfort.

I chose these particular questions to introduce the most important points I want to make about speaking with your children about anatomy, physiology, and sex; there are definitely thousands more; enter "teens and sexual health" into your browser and see what other kids are asking experts.

Let's start with a few core concepts before we move into the questions.

It's important to remember that **anatomy is not the same as physiology**. Anatomy refers to how things are structured, what body part is located where, and what's connected to what. Physiology refers to how these various parts work.

Sex is not synonymous with reproduction. A comprehensive understanding of sexuality goes way beyond an explanation of where babies come from. Sex can be a topic when discussing love, respect, peer pressure, wardrobe, literature, art, music, puberty, brain development, athletics, choice of friends, and almost any other issue that could come up with an adolescent.

There are at least two aspects to our communications with people— **content and affect**. *Content* is *what* we say, and *affect* is the feelings that are expressed while we're saying it. So many adults recall a brave attempt by their parents to have "the talk" with them about sex. Most of us remember our parents' affect as much as we recall what was said. One woman's strongest memory of her "where do babies come from" talk with her mom was how her mother sweated profusely. One man remembers his dad sounding angry during "the talk" and can still only speculate what he was truly angry about. So many of us recall being told we were too young for more information, but were never told why. We communicate volumes to our kids with our emotions when speaking with them and need to pay attention to the unspoken messages as well as the spoken words we are sending them, whether we're having "the talk" or any other conversation about a sexually-related issue.

Life is full of **teachable moments**; those golden opportunities to present your values and ideas to your kids. Waiting until your child reaches a specific landmark birthday and scheduling "the talk" just doesn't cut it. Discussions about issues relating to sexuality can and should be built into conversations on a regular basis. Bath time can be a perfect moment for an anatomy lesson. A pregnant acquaintance is always a great discussion starter for where babies come from. And sitting with your child as he watches TV is a goldmine—one day you may have to explain a Viagra commercial and should be prepared to do so.

Their Questions and Your Answers

"Mommy, why does the baby have a finger growing in his diaper?" —*Three–year-old girl looking at her new baby brother*

Male and female bodies are really much more similar than different. Actually, until about the third month of pregnancy, fetuses of both sexes look pretty much the same. Fetuses all have the same lump of tissue called the "gonadal ridge."

A baby's biologic sex is determined the moment the sperm penetrates the egg; sperm come in male and female varieties and the sperm that hits the

Male	Female
Testes <--------	--------> Ovaries
Penis <-------	-------> Clitoris
Scrotum <-------	-------> Labia Majora
Cowpers Glands <-------	-------> Bartholins Glands

Homologous organs start from the same prenatal tissue called the gonadal ridge in a developing fetus. If the fetus developed from a sperm with a male chromosome, male hormones will be produced starting around the third month of development and the "gonadal ridge" will develop into the male organs. Without the male hormones, the gonadal ridge will develop into female organs.

egg determines the biologic sex. If the sperm carries male genetic material, a male fetus begins to produce male hormones at about nine weeks into the pregnancy. These hormones cause the gonadal ridge to morph into male organs. In the absence of male hormones, the tissue develops into female structures.

The tissue that would have become labia, or outer genitals in a girl, join together and develop into the scrotum. The next time you have the chance to look closely at a scrotum, you can see the seam where the tissue fused called the scrotal raphe. Once joined together, the scrotum forms a very functional pouch to catch the gonadal tissue; the same tissue that would have been ovaries develops into the male gonad called testes.

When exposed to prenatal male hormones, tissue that would have been the clitoris in the females grows around the urethra, the skinny little tube that carries urine out of the body from the bladder, and that tissue develops into the penis.

How you choose to present this type of information to your children says a lot about your values, and you need to choose your affect based on the age

MALE REPRODUCTIVE SYSTEM

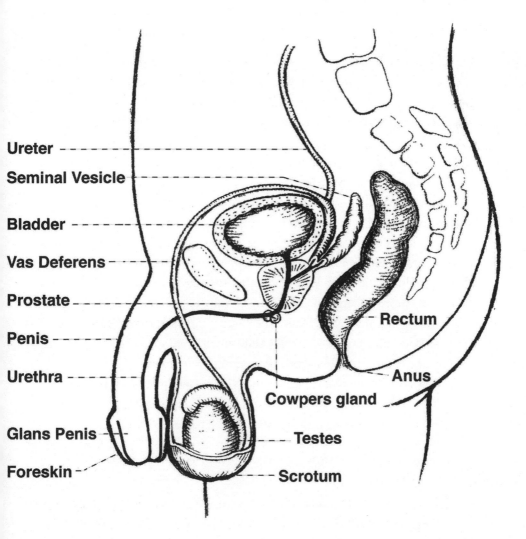

Ureter

Seminal Vesicle

Bladder

Vas Deferens

Prostate

Penis

Urethra

Rectum

Anus

Cowpers gland

Glans Penis

Testes

Foreskin

Scrotum

and state of mind of your child. One explanation that I have offered to young female sex-abuse victims who are frightened of male genitalia is that the male parts are essentially no different than females, just swollen up and turned inside out. This explanation probably wouldn't go over so well with an adolescent boy questioning his own development, but some variation on this theme may be useful in helping young people see that we are more alike than we are different.

"WHY DO BOYS HAVE THOSE BALLS THERE?" —*NINE-YEAR-OLD GIRL*

"Balls" are the most common nickname for the male gonads ("gonad" is the medical term for organs that produce reproductive cells and sex hormones). Male gonads are testicles that produce sperm and testosterone, and female gonads are ovaries that produce eggs, estrogen, and progesterone. You already know that gonads start from the same tissue fairly early in the fetus's development. The gonads are very similar in size and shape, and come in pairs—one on each side of the body.

But gonads differ is some really important ways. One major difference, and the one with the greatest practical implications, is that at birth, the female gonad contains the seeds of every single egg a woman will ever produce and one matures each month during the years a woman menstruates. The male gonad produces the male seed, known as sperm, on-demand throughout a healthy life from puberty on. The internal body temperature of 98.6°F is too warm for sperm, that's why while still a fetus, the male external tissue fuses together and into a pouch, called the scrotum, to hold the testicles and maintain the lower temperature needed for sperm development.

"How cool is that!" you could say in your explanation to your son. Just tell him that Mother Nature is so intent on people reproducing that she gives testicles their own cooling unit and see how he responds.

"WHERE DO MY BALLS GO WHEN I GET REALLY COLD? IS THIS HARMFUL?"
—*COLLEGE-AGED MALE*

Are they "junk" or "family jewels"? Nicknames for the male genitals range from the sublime to the ridiculous. It's also a little misleading to use one name for a complex set of organs. There are three entirely different organs that make up the male external genitals and each has a very different and special job.

We've already covered the testicles; now let's look at the scrotum, a miraculous, multipurpose structure.

The scrotum is the sac that holds the testicles and manages to keep them at approximately 96 degrees, the temperature needed to support developing sperm.

INSIDE THE TESTES

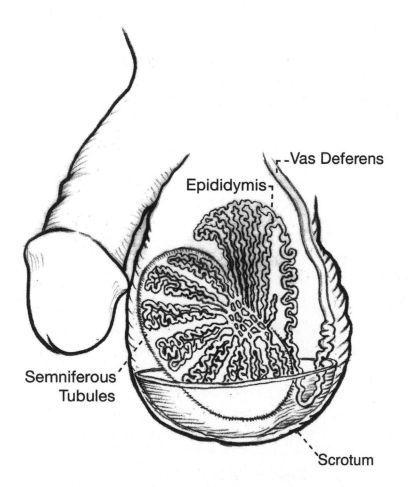

Testicles are suspended within the scrotal sac. Sperm begin developing deep inside the testicle in the seminiferous tubules, and move first through the epididymis then the vas deferens before entering the abdomen to reach the urethra.

Too hot or too cold and the sperm have trouble developing. If a male gets *really* cold, the scrotum will draw the testicles up and inside of the body for warmth, a phenomenon that can scare a boy unless he understands why it's happening. A boy as young as four or five years old may be fascinated with his scrotum in a very warm bath—the scrotum loosens up and his "package" appears bigger. Or, some boys get frightened when their scrotum responds to cold by pulling the testicles closer to the body, sometimes even giving the sense that they have moved inside the body all together. Short, age appropriate explanations are always in order in such a situation. "Your scrotum needs to keep your testicles from getting too warm or too cold" is one explanation that will work for a child lucky enough to have been taught that the testicles are separate organs inside the scrotum.

Men and boys should know the geography of their testes the same way and for the same reasons that woman should know the exact feel of their breasts. The National Cancer Institute reports that "1 in 271 men will be diagnosed with cancer of the testis during their lifetime." [23] As a parent, you should encourage your adolescent boy to know about risk factors, such as an "undescended testicle, previous testicular cancer, or a family member who has had

How to Do a Testicular Self-exam*

The best time to do the self-exam is during or after a bath or shower, when the skin of the scrotum is relaxed. To do a testicular self-exam:

- hold your penis out of the way and check one testicle at a time;
- hold the testicle between your thumbs and fingers of both hands and roll it gently between your fingers; and
- look and feel for any hard lumps or smooth rounded bumps or any change in the size, shape, or consistency of the testes.

NOTE: We didn't forget the girls. The American Cancer Society recommends beginning breast self-exams when a woman is in her twenties.

*All information gathered from The American Cancer Society's website at www.cancer.org/Cancer/TesticularCancer/MoreInformation/DoIHaveTesticular Cancer/do-i-have-testicular-cancer-self-exam]

---

23   http://seer.cancer.gov/statfacts/html/testis.html

this cancer,"[24] and encourage boys with risk factors to gently examine both testicles periodically to get to know what normal feels like; if something abnormal appears, he (and subsequently you) will know immediately and be able to act on it in time to have more treatment options.

Just like the breasts, not all lumps felt through the scrotum are cancer. Any of the internal structures can become inflamed and swell, and skin anywhere can develop a zit-like bump. Look at the drawing of the scrotum and testes on page 59 and you'll see the epididymis. This is the place where the sperm mature and it has been known to become inflamed on occasion. That inflammation has the long and scary name of epididymitis—which means inflamed epididymis. The scrotum also has blood vessels and other perfectly normal structures that can be felt during a self-exam. If anything does change or feel different from your last exam, remember that only a health-care provider can make a proper diagnosis.

"WHY WOULD A GUY EVER HAVE A VASECTOMY AND NOT COME EVER AGAIN?"
—*MALE COLLEGE STUDENT*

When a male reaches sexual climax, one of the many things going on in his body is the release of fluid through his penis. That fluid contains sperm and the other fluids sperm need to survive outside the body. So this question actually needs a three part answer: a male does indeed continue to "come" after a vasectomy; the fluid contains more than just sperm; and an orgasm is a *lot* more than the release of fluid. We'll get to the last point in the section on sexual response; let's start with some anatomy and physiology of seminal fluid.

Seminal fluid is the material released through the penis as one physical sign of sexual climax. The term for the release of fluid is ejaculate, pronounced e-jack-u-*late*. The fluid is called ejaculate, pronounced e-jack-u-*lit*. That fluid is made up of sperm cells and the fluid necessary to keep the cells alive on their journey to meet an egg. Spermatogenesis is the medical word for the process of producing sperm. It happens in several places deep inside the testicle. As the sperm cells mature, they move through a series of little tubes inside the testicle called the seminiferous tubules, and settle in the epididymis,

---

24   http://www.cancer.org/Cancer/TesticularCancer/MoreInformation/DoIHaveTesticular-
     Cancer/do-i-have-testicular-cancer-self-exam

THE STEPS OF A VASECTOMY

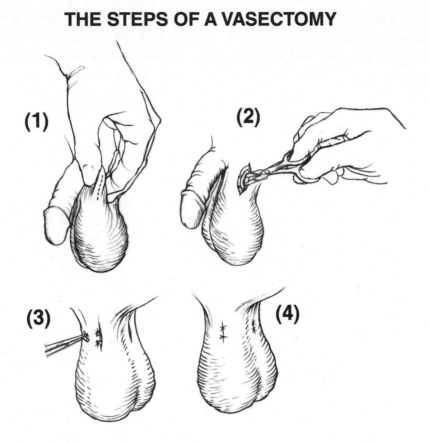

Step 1. The physician numbs the area with local anesthetic and identifies the vas deferens through the scrotal sac.

Step 2. The physician makes a small incision through the sac and locates the vas deferens.

Step 3. The physician severs the vas deferens and closes off each end.

Step 4. The physician repairs the incision on the scrotum. This process is repeated on the other side.

where the developing seeds mature and are stored until ejaculation. When a man becomes sexually aroused, the sperm cells leave the epididymis, travel through the vas deferens (a tube running up the back of the testes within the scrotal sac), and are deposited into the abdomen at the very end of the urethra.

Once in the abdomen, fluid is added by the accessory sex glands and the prostate to protect the delicate sperm cells. Actual sperm cells account for generally less than one-third of the fluids that will be expelled from the penis as ejaculate at the climax of sexual arousal. At least two-thirds of the fluid is from the other organs. A vasectomy blocks off the vas deferens and stops the sperm from mixing with the other fluids. So, men still have both orgasm and ejaculation after a vasectomy. Whew!

"CAN I GET PREGNANT IF HE PULLS OUT BEFORE HE COMES?"
—*HIGH-SCHOOL-AGED GIRL*

Yes! It's important to remember that sperm are really rather delicate living creatures. When they finish their journey through the various parts of the testes, they are stored inside a man's body up until the time when he feels sexual arousal. Then, they start their journey to leave the body through the urethra.

As you will recall, the urethra is also used to carry urine out of the body. Urine is very acidic, and urine makes the urethra a very hostile environment for sperm. Nature has taken care of that dilemma with the Cowpers glands; at the height of sexual arousal, just before orgasm and release of the sperm, this tiny little organ secretes the so-called "pre-ejaculatory fluid" that flows down the urethra and makes it a more comfortable environment for sperm. Every now and then, live sperm hitch a ride in this fluid; the result is that sperm can be released in this fluid *before* sexual climax and ejaculation, so withdrawing the penis from the vagina prior to male orgasm is absolutely not a foolproof method of contraception.

An answer to this question, if your teen brings it up, should also include a reminder that this co-called "withdrawal method" of birth control carries the risk of passing germs as well as sperm. A condom applied as soon as the penis is fully erect is the *best* way to keep unwanted cells—sperm and germs—away from the vagina.

"WHAT'S THAT?" ASKS THE THREE-YEAR-OLD AS HE GRABS HIS FATHER'S PENIS WHILE DAD'S DRESSING FOR WORK.

"It's my penis," says Dad. "Look. There's yours." Dad then points to his son's penis.

A penis, formed from the same fetal tissue as the female clitoris, is the made up of three parallel columns of erectile tissue,[25] one of which carries the urethra.

The cylinder that runs on the underside of the penis contains the urethra, and all of these cylinders fill up with blood when a male becomes sexually aroused. A network of arteries carry blood to the penis, and a network of tiny muscles tighten up and keep the blood in place as it fills up this tissue, making the penis "hard" or "erect."

Many people mistakenly believe that a penis has a bone; it does not. These cylinders of tissue that run the length of the penis do the job of keeping the penis firm. Confusion might come from the slang term "boner" for erection, or because other mammals *do* have bones in their penises, but human penises are, indeed, boneless!

"WILL A BOY GET SICK IF HIS HARD-ON WON'T GO AWAY?" —*THIRTEEN-YEAR-OLD GIRL*

"Have you been drafted into the *Erection Relief Society*?" One mom remembers her high school health teacher asking this question to admonish girls that they are under no moral or scientific duty to relieve boys of their erections. No, they had not been drafted into any society at all. A boy's erection is *his* problem, and a girl is under no obligation to do anything about it, regardless of what a boy might say to the contrary.

As mentioned previously, when a male experiences sexual arousal, his penis, scrotum, and other tissue around his genitals become filled with blood, and a network of internal muscles tighten up to keep it there. The fastest (and the most pleasurable) way to make all of that blood leave the sex-parts is a sexual orgasm, also called climax. But in the absence of a climax, the blood will still slowly seep out of the genitals and no harm will come to the male at all. If an erection lasts more than a few hours, medical attention should be sought but this is highly unlikely and extremely uncommon.

Females also experience a rush of blood to their sexual and reproductive organs when sexually aroused. If arousal is not followed by the release of orgasm, a female may experience discomfort as well. The sensation is gener-

---

25   Strong, Bryan, Christine Devault, Barbara W. Sayad, and William Yarber. *Human Sexuality; Diversity in Contemporary America*. New York, 2005: 111.

INSIDE THE PENIS

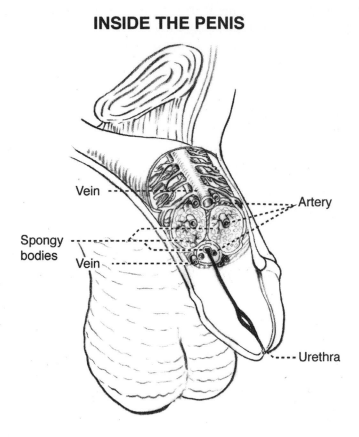

The inside of the penis is made up of three spongy cylinders that fill
with blood when sexually aroused; the urethra runs through the
cylinder on the bottom of the penis.

ally less intense and is spread throughout the abdomen while a male experiences the discomfort very specifically in his external genitals.

"MA! LOOK WHAT MY WINKIE'S DOING!" —*FOUR-YEAR-OLD BOY WITH AN ERECTION*

The human body is capable of experiencing physical arousal from birth on—there are even sonogram photos of babies holding their genitals *before* birth. This is completely normal and healthy. A simple acknowledgment to such an exclamation could be, "Yes. Penises change size sometimes." This may be all of an explanation your child needs, also taking the opportunity to ease your child from your family's term to the anatomical one.

"WHY?" —ASKED BY THE SAME FOUR-YEAR-OLD WHEN TOLD THAT PENISES DO CHANGE SIZES

If confronted with more questions about erections, you may explain, "For the same reason you laugh when I tickle you. Our bodies just do some cool stuff when they get certain feelings." The point here is that no matter how many times the four year old asks "why?" keep your answers very short. A young child may just keep asking why to see how long you'll keep answering; this is not the cue for an entire physiology lesson at this age.

"HOW DID THE BABY GET INSIDE HER?" —TEN-YEAR-OLD GIRL

You always should consider your child's age when answering any question—and in particular this one. A child younger than ten may be satisfied with a simple answer, such as "the dad plants seed in the mom." If your little one asks, "How?" simply answer, "With his penis," or "When moms and dads hug in a very special, loving way."

When detail is requested about female anatomy, kids can understand "moms have a special place near where they pee where dads can plant the seed." If your child asks where the seed goes, an appropriate response would be, "Moms have a place inside where babies can grow." Single sentence answers, given calmly and matter-of-factly, are in order for the youngest kids. Children need time to integrate and process each new piece of information before they can be expected to understand the nuances of reproduction.

Ten-year-olds can, like the one who posed this question, understand most medical facts. Since girls need to understand menstruation by this age, show your daughter a simple drawing like the one on the next page. Here are the basics your child needs to know. Explain that the ovaries produce eggs, and one matures each month. Follow the path of the egg down the Fallopian tube. Show how sperm might enter through the vagina, and when the egg and sperm meet in the Fallopian tube, they join together and begin the process of turning into a baby. Show a diagram of the testicles and penis like the illustration on page 57 (the full page male diagram) and show where sperm are made and how they travel through internal tubes and out of the

FEMALE REPRODUCTIVE SYSTEM

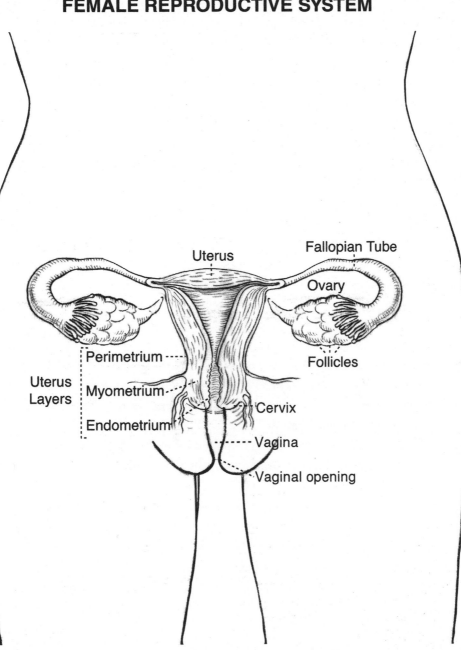

penis. Explain that the joined sperm and egg travels down the rest of the way out the Fallopian tube and plants itself into the wall of the uterus, which has already developed a thick lining full of nutrients to help the fetus grow. If there is no fetus, which is what happens most months, the body disposes of the tissue lining the uterus and it comes out each month through the vagina as a girl has her "period." Periods are also called menstruation.

If a girl wants to know when she might expect to start her period, it makes sense to give a range, such as "most girls start to menstruate sometime before fourteen or fifteen, some as young as eight." Giving a child an average age will make her compare herself to it; better to make her feel "normal" within a range than "different" for not being the exact average.

"How does the baby get out of her?" —*Ten-year-old girl*

Responding that "moms' bodies are specially designed to give birth to the baby" may be enough for a younger child, but a ten-year-old, as stated before, can understand anatomy. Explain that the vagina is surrounded internally by layers and layers of muscle that can stretch a little during intercourse or a lot during childbirth, then bounce back to shape. I've seen health educators demonstrate childbirth to kids using a baby doll and a turtle neck sweater to model the vagina; the turtleneck stretches to let the head go through then goes back to its original shape. For an older child, or one that specifically asks, you might also mention that sometimes a doctor needs to help the baby get out and can perform an operation.

Your affect is important with this question—a preadolescent can find the thought of things coming in and out of her body terrifying if the topic is not presented carefully; specifically, try a variation on the explanation that women's bodies have been designed to let them become mothers when they're ready. Assure your daughter (or son if he asks) that the fact that it all seems weird now is just proof that she is nowhere near ready to be a parent, which is a perfectly normal situation for a kid.

"Do girls pee through the same hole that they have their periods?" —*Eight-year-old girl*

There are actually three seperate openings in the bottom parts of the female body: the vagina, the urethra, and the anus. The *vagina* leads into the reproductive parts of the body and is the outlet for menstrual fluid or a baby, and the entry way for sperm cells. The *urethra* connects to the bladder and provides a pathway for urine to leave the body. The *anus* connects to the digestive system and lets food waste leave the body. You could share a simple line drawing like the one below and point out the different structures. If sharing this drawing leaves you uncomfortable, you could grab a pencil and paper and draw something even simpler, using long lines for the labia, dots for the urethra and vagina, and a larger dot below the labia for the anus. A parent might consider suggesting that an older girl use a hand mirror between her legs and become familiar with her own genitalia, but an eight-year-old like the girl asking this question may not be ready for that.

FEMALE EXTERNAL GENITALIA

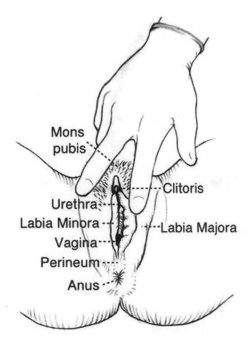

It's important to understand and explain to your child that while all female genitalia have the same structures as shown in this diagram, their actual appearance is as individualized as a face!

"WHAT IS THE SAFE TIME OF THE MONTH TO HAVE SEX WITH A GIRL?"
—*MALE COLLEGE STUDENT*

The female gonads, called ovaries, release eggs, also called ova, through a process called ovulation. Each month—from just before puberty to around the time menstruation stops—one of those eggs developed from cells that have been stored deep inside of the ovary since prenatal time begins to push its way to the surface of the ovary. The egg gets bigger and starts to protrude from the ovary in a little sac that's similar to a little pimple. The inside layer of that pimple, or follicle as it's formally called, produces estrogen. As the follicle gets bigger and bigger, the amount of estrogen produced grows as well. Once the estrogen production reaches its highest level, the pimple pops and out comes the egg, floating down the fallopian tubes, on its course to possibly meet a sperm. The medical term for the release of the egg is "ovulation." The joining of the sperm and egg is called fertilization.

But the follicle is not yet ready to retire; the broken pimple turns yellow (earning the fancy medical name *corpas leuteum*, or "yellow body") and produces the hormone progesterone. Progesterone levels continue to rise until they peak just before menstruation begins.

Let's break down the word "progesterone"; *pro* means in support of, and *gester*, is from the same Latin root as gestation, which is another word for pregnancy. So, we know that progesterone supports gestation. If the egg meets the sperm and fertilization occurs, that broken yellow pimple keeps growing bigger and producing progesterone, which causes the lining of the uterus to thicken in preparation to host a fetus. If there is no fertilization, the *corpas leuteum* shrivels up and stops producing progesterone, and menstruation begins, allowing the now unnecessary tissue that built up in the uterus to exit the body. A few days later, the cycle starts again.

Understanding menstruation is important for both girls and boys, and not just to help predict the "safe" time of the month to have sex. Girls need to be given a good explanation, and luckily, there are many good books available on this topic. As a side note, if you choose to go the book route, make sure you present it as a book about menstruation, or reproduction, and not "sex," since even the best books I've seen for young girls fail to mention sexual arousal.

Girls also need to understand that during menstruation they are not really "bleeding"—blood makes up only a small portion of the menstrual fluid but

HOW AN EGG MATURES

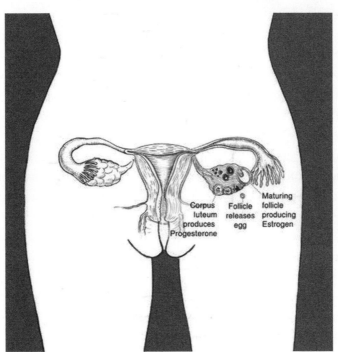

Corpus luteum produces Progesterone   Follicle releases egg   Maturing follicle producing Estrogen

When the maturing egg cell reaches the surface of the ovary, it develops into a follicle that produces estrogen. The egg is released during ovulation and the follicle becomes the "corpas luteum" and produces progesterone.

colors all of it. Boys need to know that menstruation is a sign of maturity, health, and strength. Disrespectful or pejorative terms like "on the rag" or "the curse" should not be tolerated in your home or in your presence. Setting boundaries for this early on should help your son interact more positively with his female peers throughout his life.

A question about the "safe" time for sex presents an important opportunity to remind your teen that there is no safe time to have intercourse without a condom. The lack of an egg in the girl's fallopian tube just before or after menstruation *may* mean a lower probability of making a baby, but safe sex has other aspects to it, including clearly stated mutual consent, sobriety, and prevention of sexually transmitted infections and diseases by consistent and correct use of condoms.

"I JUST WANTED TO KNOW HOW MUCH PUBIC HAIR IS TOO MUCH FOR A GIRL?"
—SIXTEEN-YEAR-OLD GIRL

As a child enters adolescence, the hormones surging through her body cause many changes, and growing hair on the body is second only to developing breasts for girls as being outwardly noticeable. Unless a person suffers from a rare dermatologic disorder, her body cannot produce too much pubic hair. Adolescence has been described as agonizing over the belief that everyone is normal except you and adolescents are exquisitely aware of how their body differs from that of their peers. When adolescent girls only see the shaved or coiffed pubic hair of models in explicit magazines or on websites, they may certainly question their own natural appearance and wonder if they are "normal" or not.

Sex information websites for teens have dozens of questions asked by girls about the best way to remove pubic hair. If your daughter wants to groom her pubic hair for a smooth look in a bathing suit, you may want to give her a lesson in shaving. But a question like the one above implies the judgment that too much pubic hair is bad, which is an opinion your child has most likely learned somewhere and is certainly not a fact. You should be honest and tell your child this and then be ready to answer any additional questions on this topic.

"WHY DO MY PRIVATE PARTS SMELL BAD SOMETIMES?" —FIFTEEN-YEAR-OLD GIRL

The female genitalia are alive supporting a wonderful little ecosystem that must be kept in balance to keep the vagina healthy. In the most basic description, the hormone estrogen supports the presence of glycogen, which is a simple sugar. Glycogen is consumed by so-called good bacteria, lactobacilli, which produce lactic acid and give the vagina a slightly acidic pH of approximately 4.5. [26] Anytime we break that cycle, we risk disturbing the ecosystem and providing a haven for unwanted things to grow, generally yeast cells. And there are *so* many ways to interrupt the cycle. In severe cases of changes in blood sugar, the balance can be affected. Constantly wearing too tight,

---

26 Definition of pH: "A measure of acidity and alkalinity of a solution that is a number on a scale on which a value of 7 represents neutrality and lower numbers indicate increasing acidity and higher numbers increasing alkalinity." Accessed at http://www.merriam-webster.com/dictionary/ph.

synthetic panties can literally suffocate the lacto bacilli or we can kill them off by taking antibiotics for an illness. Many women also unknowingly kill off the healthy growth by using genital grooming products that are not the correct pH.

The Physiology of Vaginal Health

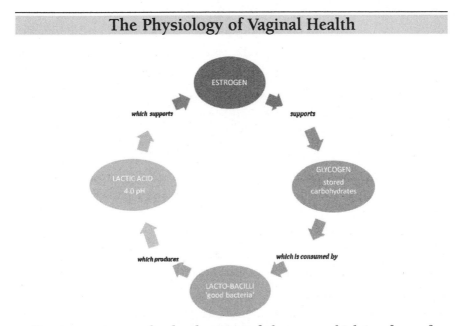

Estrogen supports the development of glycogen, which is a form of stored carbohydrates. Glycogen is consumed by lacto-bacilli, a naturally occurring "good" bacteria. The lacto- bacilli produce lactic acid which maintains a healthy acid/alkaline balance. If this cycle is interrupted vaginitis, or inflammation of the vagina, can occur.

The cycle can be interrupted by changes in the estrogen level from natural changes or using synthetics hormones; from changes in the glycogen level due to changes in health states and, as previously described, from killing off lacto-bacilli with antibiotics, vaginal grooming products, or constant use of tight, synthetic panties that restrict air to the vaginal area.

Infections caused by interruptions in this process are generally not sexually transmitted. In occasional cases, a female who has this type of infection may give it to a partner. But the presence of a so-called yeast infection in a female is not reason enough to assume that she is sexually active. A quick call to a health-care provider will provide instructions for homecare or the advice to come in for an exam. If an over-the-counter remedy has not fixed the problem within a week or two, a girl or woman should see a doctor for a more thorough exam.

Vaginitis is a general term for an inflammation of the vagina, and some types are indeed sexually transmitted. The most tricky to diagnose is Trichomoniasis. A microscopic parasite, Trichomonas vaginalis[27], can live in the male accessary sex glands and produce no symptoms at all. Trichomonads mix with the seminal fluid and are released along with the sperm at ejaculation. If that seminal fluid lands in a vagina, the trichomonads will find the perfect physical environment and they will flourish causing itching and discharge. The discharge usually carries an odor.

Here's how this gets complicated. A woman may start washing a lot, or using some over-the-counter genital perfume to get rid of the odor, which may only serve to make things worse by killing the good bacteria. The odor often gets worse closer to menstruation, so she calls and makes an appointment with her health-care provider. But menstrual fluid typically reduces the number of trichomonads, so an exam right after menstruation may not show signs of the infection. A health-care professional should be consulted and an appointment scheduled as close to the *next* menstrual period as possible. The vaginal secretions will be examined microscopically and treatment prescribed if necessary. The most common prescription for this infection, metronidazole, cannot be taken with alcohol. One reason this infection spreads among adolescents and college campuses is that males aren't usually in a hurry to give up alcohol to treat an infection that rarely shows symptoms in men.

There two types of vaginitis—bacterial and fungal—that can develop without sexual contact. They are referred to by many different names: yeast infection, non-specific vaginitis, candidiasis, bacterial vaginitis. These types of infection are cause for a call or visit to the health-care provider but do not necessarily indicate sexual contact. However, there are many types of genital infections and systemic diseases that are almost exclusively sexually transmitted. One should *never* expect to see trichomoniasis, gonorrhea, syphilis, chlamydia, venereal warts, or human papillomavirus (HPV) in a child. A

---

27   See what the US Centers for Disease Control and Prevention has to say at http://www. cdc.gov/std/trichomonas/

medical diagnosis of any of these infections is almost always an indication of sexual contact. If this is the case, stay calm and read chapter 13 to help you make your plan.

We can't mention HPV without mentioning the vaccine developed in 2006 to prevent contracting this infection. HPV is the most common sexually transmitted infection in the United States, and certain strains of the virus can be a precursor to cancer. The American Academy of Pediatrics joins the U.S. Centers for Disease Control and Prevention in recommending that girls receive their first dose of this three-dose series by age eleven or twelve.[28] HPV can cause cervical cancer, a leading cause of death for women around the world. There are many varieties of the HPV virus, so it is critical for a girl to be immunized before she is exposed to any variety, which means before she becomes sexually active. Physicians are considering immunizing boys as well, and we discuss this in more detail in chapter 11. Have a conversation with your pediatrician around how you both will explain genital health, sexually transmitted infections, and this vaccination to your kids; it will shed light on how your pediatrician handles sensitive issues as your child enters adolescence. You want your child to be comfortable asking his or her health-care provider any question at all.

The Sexual Response Cycle

The entire body, and most of the mind, participates in sexual arousal. In fact, male and female bodies react in a pretty specific and predictable way. It's hard for something to be scary if it's predictable, so sharing an understanding of sexual arousal is an important and helpful gift you can give your children.

Anatomy and Physiology

"WHEN I STARTED RUBBING, MY LEGS GOT STIFF AND STARTED SHAKING. WAS THIS AN ORGASM OR SOMETHING?" —*THIRTEEN-YEAR-OLD BOY*

Dr. William Masters and Virginia Johnson, pioneers of sex research, spent years in the laboratory studying all the wonderful things the body does during sexual arousal and expression and wrote their landmark medical text *Human*

---

28 Accessed on August 23, 2011 at http://www.healthychildren.org and http://www.cdc. gov/vaccines/pubs/vis/downloads/vis-hpv-gardasil.pdf.

Sexual Response[29] in 1966. Their tome is full of anatomical and physiological details written in excruciatingly dry medical terms, but almost half a century later, many of their ideas about the physical aspects of sexual response still rule, particularly the concept of the physical sexual arousal proceeding through a series of phases. They describe the physical phases as excitement, plateau, orgasm, and resolution, the last being the phase in which the body returns to its resting state. Later researchers incorporate the emotional aspects of sexual arousal into the cycle and current thought emphasizes the importance of desire or interest as the first phase. For young people, it can be extremely difficult to separate the physical and emotional aspects of sexual response. Healthy human beings experience all or part of the response cycle very frequently in their adolescent and adult lives. As a parent, your message about sexual response can emphasize that sexual arousal is autonomic, or a reflexive response to stimulation of some kind, but that desire and interest are emotional, and that the entire body is involved when arousal progresses to orgasm.

The young man with this question was experiencing the muscle spasms that are totally normal for many people during an orgasm. Other full-body responses to sexual arousal and orgasm include increased heart rate, rapid breathing, and in some people a full body skin flush.

"WHY DO MY PANTIES GET WET SOMETIMES WHEN IT'S NOT PEE?"
—ELEVEN-YEAR-OLD GIRL

The first phase of sexual arousal is called "desire." Some type of stimuli— a feeling, a touch, a memory, a smell, or seeing passionate kissing on TV—can register with the brain as arousing. The brain sends a signal to a particular region in the spine, and the spinal nerves start sending messages to the genitals. The special spongy tissue in a male's penis begins to fill with blood, and certain little muscles contract to keep it there and the male experiences an erection. For females, the physical response to arousal or excitement that makes panties get wet sometimes are not so obvious.

---

29   Masters, William, and Virginia Johnson. *Human Sexual Response*. New York: Bantam Books, 1966.

When a female is aroused by something, the blood vessels in her vagina engorge with blood and the genitals begins to "sweat," or lubricate, producing a colorless fluid on her external genitals. Boys catch a break here; when their penis gets hard, or erect, there is very little question about what's happening. I have yet to meet an adult woman who recalls being told by a parent or caretaker that vaginal sweating or lubrication is a sign of sexual arousal in a female. Since girls can't see what's going on with their genitals, many never associate the warm feeling "down there" with sexual arousal; in fact it is not uncommon for a girl to see a spot in her panties and think something is wrong. With knowledge and practice, you can prepare yourself to share this important fact of biology with your daughter and help her avoid the confusion that stems from not understanding how her own body works.

"Is it wrong to come when I'm sleeping?" —*Fourteen-year-old boy*

Countless people experience all or part of the sexual response cycle while sleeping. Both males and females have dreams with sexual content, called erotic dreams, and many experience orgasm. If a male goes through all phases of the sexual response cycle, ejaculatory fluid is left as a souvenir. The term "wet dream" refers to this phenomenon. One clue that this might be happening in your house is if an adolescent boy suddenly insists on doing his own laundry. While awake, the response cycle often stops at the arousal stage. Young kids need to know that this is a normal experience and won't hurt them or be seen as wrong, gross, or unnatural. If your son is open enough to ask this question, a simply reply works: "No, son, it's not wrong; it's what healthy bodies do at your age." "Would you like to know more?" is always a good way to end a response to a teen.

"Where's my G-spot? Does everyone have one?" —*Female college student*

A German gynecologist named Grafenberg identified a spot in the internal front of a woman's vagina as being especially sensitive to sexual stimulation. In the 1980s, stories of this so-called G-spot started to appear in the popular media, and women and their partners went in search of it. Many people believe they've found theirs, but there is still debate in the professional literature about the existence of an actual G-spot.

AREAS MOST SENSITIVE TO STIMULATION

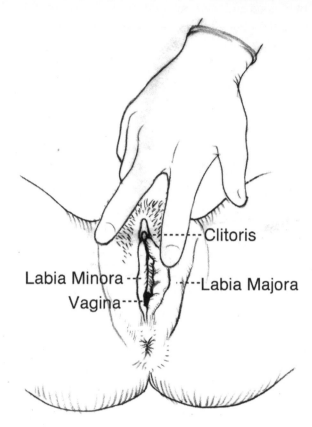

The clitoris, labia minora, and labia majora, in that order, have the highest concentration of nerve endings sensitive to sexual stimulation.

If an adolescent asks this question of a trusted adult, she can be told that human beings are highly individualized in our response to specific stimuli. A sexually healthy person can feel perfectly comfortable determining exactly what type of touch applied to what part of her body brings her pleasure. If a female finds pleasure by stimulating a point a few centimeters into her vagina on the front side below the bladder, then she is welcome to assume that she's found her G-spot. The highest concentration of nerves that respond to sexual pleasure are located in the clitoris followed by the labia minora, or minor lips, which are shown in the illustration on page 78. In fact, the tissue lining the inside of the vagina has very few nerve endings at all.

"HOW MUCH OF THIS DO I HAVE TO KNOW?" —*COLLEGE MALE*

I'm pretty sure the person who asked this question was concerned with the content of my upcoming midterm exam, but it's a very good question for us, as parents, to consider. Knowledge is power and we all need power over our own bodies. This is true for any aspect of health and well-being. Sexual health and safety carry a special challenge because sex is associated with some very strong feelings. As parents, you can help turn those strong feelings into powerful, positive feelings by sharing your knowledge with your children as just one more gift you have to offer them. Any answer lovingly offered is always better than no answer at all. And you can always have another conversation to clear up the details you may have left out or have gotten wrong. Don't be afraid to talk to your child about the anatomy and physiology surrounding sex. And be sure that both your content and affect are in line before you begin these sometimes surprising but important conversations.

CHAPTER 5

Suddenly Sexual

The Journey from Infant to Adolescent

If kids came with an owner's manual, it might read something like "Optimal results cannot be assured if you move on to Step 2 before successfully completing Step 1." Children progress through predictable stages of psychological, social, moral, emotional, intellectual, and psychosexual development. Developmental psychologists may argue about details, but they pretty much agree that children pass through the stages sequentially.

Research shows that all areas of development are *inter*dependent and work together to promote a child's overall health and well-being.[30] Child development is cumulative; completing one stage becomes the foundation for tackling the next.

Advances in nuclear medicine over the last two decades, like the PET scan, have brought a surge in research on how the brain develops, shedding a bright light on the importance of the first months and years of life. As a parent, you play the most critical role as your child develops a strong emotional foundation. In fact, strong give-and-take relationships with a child's primary caretaker(s) are the foundation for emotional development. Being a sexually safe and healthy adult depends in large part on being able to bond with a

---

30 "Zero to Three." *Early Experiences Matter*. 2009: p. 2. Accessed at http://main.zeroto-three.org/site/DocServer/Policy_Guide.pdf?docID=8401.

loved one, show empathy for the feelings of others, and fully understand and appreciate verbal and nonverbal communications.

In order to support our kids through these stages and to ultimately shepherd them toward emotional maturity and health, you need to know what kids can and can't understand at different ages and how your child perceives the world. It takes a truly mature person to understand that people have different perspectives; I'll bet you don't have to think too hard to identify adults who can't do that. Kids, too, see and experience the world differently from adults, and the way they see and experience the world changes as they develop.

A common analogy used to illustrate *perspective* is this: An alien lands in a suburban American community and sees the inhabitants as beings with wheeled shells that they shed when returning to their shelter. This makes perfect sense to an alien and your child arrives in your world equally untrained in our "ways" of living. In fact one mother recalls her three-year-old son sobbing when the only "shell" he had ever known was driven off by the college student who bought it from Mom, excited to be getting a new car.

It can be very difficult to fully understand how differently kids see the world and process information about it. Luckily, child development has been studied diligently for the past century, and brain development research is now being applied to inform child development research, so we have some pretty solid ideas about the stages children pass through, including their perceptions and capabilities at different ages. We can now use the lessons learned from science to help raise sexually safe and healthy children.

You need to understand these developmental phases in order to help your children master each one in sequence, and maintain your patience when your child's developing brain reacts to a situation in a manner completely foreign to you as an adult. Your patience and understanding are key to ensuring that one incomplete developmental task doesn't leave your child unprepared for the rest of them. Completing these developmental tasks gives your child the security that comes from a sense of mastery of his world and makes him feel loved and lovable, all necessary parts of being sexually safe and healthy.

A twenty-first-century call to action among advocates for high quality early childhood programs is to raise little ones who are "healthy and ready to learn."[31] Are you able to raise kids who are also emotionally healthy and ready to love? Understanding where your child is in his development will help you do just that.

You probably already know when your children pass a milestone in a physical developmental stage—they gain weight, they learn to walk, they poop in the right place, they get taller, they grow hair in new places, girls menstruate. These passages are easy to see, and for most parents easy to predict. Knowing that healthy kids will eventually learn to walk makes our back hurt a little less when carrying a thirty-pound child. Similarly, parenting becomes less stressful once you understand where your child is developmentally and what she needs from you in order to move on to a new stage. In fact, no less an authority of children than the American Academy of Pediatrics promotes the practice of "anticipatory guidance," a fancy phrase for preparing you, as a parent, for the next stages of your child's development.[32]

While there are still developmental scientists who debate the "nature vs. nurture" question, current thought on child development focuses on relationships as being the key: "Young children experience their world as an environment of relationships, and these relationships affect virtually all aspects of their development—intellectual, social, emotional, physical, behavioral, and moral."[33]

Whether you believe a child was born with certain personality traits or that they were developed by their environment, those traits will either be encouraged or discouraged through the relationships they have. There is no more important way for a child to learn her place in the world than through her relationships, and there is no more important relationship than with you as her parent, so pay attention! Everything is brand new to a child—when an adult is exposed to a new situation, he can draw from past experiences to adapt; kids have no past experiences, so each new experience they have as a child is a building block for the next. You need to learn to anticipate what's next and normal in your child's development, and respond to your child in a

---

31   See www.ZeroToThree.org.

32   See, for example, http://brightfutures.aap.org/pdfs/Guidelines_PDF/16-Early_Child-hood.pdf.

33   National Scientific Council on the Developing Child. *Young Children Develop in an Environment of Relationships: Working Paper No. 1.* 2004: 1. Accessed at http://www.developingchild.harvard.edu.

way that helps her move from one phase to the next. All through the developmental process, your kids need your unconditional love, your wisdom, and your consistent reaction to their behaviors to teach them about their place in the world.

Major Stages of Development

Infants

What to Expect from an Infant

Babies come into this world physically underdeveloped; in fact, anthropologists tell us that human babies are among the least developed and most helpless of all beings born. Most of us have seen films of newborn animals getting up, testing their shaky legs, and walking on their own just minutes after birth. Not so with human babies.

Infants are barely conscious of the world when they come into it. They can't perceive where their body ends and the rest of the world begins. They *feel*, rather than *know*. Sigmund Freud, a most influential voice in certain aspects of child development, coined the term "psychosexual development." He introduced the words id, ego, and superego in his landmark work and they have made their way into everyday language. Freud described infancy as being dominated by the id, or pleasure principle (*feed me, hold me, keep me warm and dry*). A newborn infant has very little to offer the caretakers in her life until she starts to smile and make real eye contact at around eight to ten weeks. Babies will start to find and use their hands around three months, and use their mouths as a source of comfort, information, and pleasure.

Within months of your infant recognizing you, he may learn to become upset when you leave. This so-called "separation anxiety" is an expected response at this phase—he has finally realized that there is only one of you. He then has to complete the next stage of intellectual development to understand that you will, in fact, return.

What You Should Know

The key developmental task for infants is to learn that the world is safe and that their needs will be met. The key role for you, as the parent of an infant, is to relieve his stress and meet his needs. Babies need to learn to love their bodies, to love touch, to love to be touched. These basic primal needs and feelings set the foundation for a lifetime of feeling safe and secure in the world, and for feeling loved. When an infant needs something—anything—stress hormones are released and the brain enters a state of heightened arousal and awareness. When that need is met, the anxiety dissipates and the brain can go back to a state of comfort where she can interact with the environment and continue on the path to development. If the need is not met, continued heightened anxiety may interfere with important developmental processes.

Dr. Bruce Perry, a pioneer shedding light on the interplay between the environment and brain development in babies, states, "The systems in the human brain that allow us to form and maintain emotional relationships develop during infancy and the first years of life. Experiences during this early vulnerable period of life are critical to shaping the capacity to form intimate and emotionally healthy relationships. Empathy, caring, sharing, inhibition of aggression, capacity to love, and a host of other characteristics of a healthy, happy, and productive person are related to the core attachment capabilities which are formed in infancy and early childhood."[34]

Freud taught that from birth through eighteen months a child seeks pleasure through his mouth; in fact Freud calls this time period "the oral phase." Babies want to suck and put anything they can right into their mouths. They are motivated by feeling good, and learn to "flirt" with the big people who are a source of pleasure and comfort for them. That big, gummy smile you finally see from your infant is actually her way of keeping you coming back.

It's important to remember that every single experience is new for infants and they have no prior knowledge to help them relieve the stress caused by these not-yet-known circumstances—alleviating stress for a newborn is what we have to do as parents in order to make them feel safe, loved, comfortable, and satisfied, and to keep their little brains, bodies, and hearts thriving.

WHAT'S GOING ON IN THE FAMILY?

Just as children pass through predictable developmental sequences, so do families. A most important developmental task for a family when a new baby arrives is to reconnect the sexual relationship between the parents. A strong

---

34   Perry, Bruce. *Bonding and Attachment in Maltreated Children.* The Child Trauma Academy, 2001. Accessed on August 24, 2011, at http://www.ChildTraumaAcademy.org.

adult relationship is the backbone of a family, and it is all too easy to forget this as the family unit moves from a twosome to a threesome (or more). The woman may be in physical discomfort after the birth, and her health-care provider will help determine when sexual intercourse can resume. Kissing, cuddling, and compliments are a great way to stay connected during this time. Reconnecting between partners can be even more challenging if the couple aren't married; patience, understanding, and compassion are critical. A mature, responsible dad can deal with his own sexual needs for a few weeks while Mom's body and mind adjust to her new role, and know that his lover will be back and better than ever soon!

Observing childbirth can also be traumatic for men. Outside of birthing classes, we don't hear much about the physical reality of childbirth—blood, urine, feces, watching strangers with their hands inside their partner's body. All of the stuff of life that accompanies childbirth is not as romantic as we see on TV and can be difficult for the partner to process during and after. Dad needs to think this through and maybe find a confidante to help him deal with the processing of the actual birth. Mom's probably feeling too vulnerable herself to be able to offer this type of support. This stuff is not easy, but it is normal.

One way babies receive oral satisfaction is breastfeeding. As with childbirth, breastfeeding moms learn that it's a lot messier and potentially painful than the romanticists let on. Many a mom recalls the nasty surprise of learning that breastfeeding can hurt. Susan had her first and only child at twenty-nine and found breastfeeding excruciatingly painful for the first few weeks. She shared that only sibling rivalry kept her going beyond the first painful weeks of breastfeeding—her sister was the president of the local La Leche chapter. The rewards of breastfeeding are huge for the mother and baby, and unless there is a strong medical reason not to, breastfeeding is a wonderful way to help a child complete certain developmental tasks of infancy—but it can cause some stress in the first weeks after birth.

When a baby sucks on the nipple of a nursing mom, hormones are released to assist in milk secretion. Once hormones are released into the bloodstream, they can act upon any organ sensitive to their effects. Oxytocin, the same hormone that helps milk release, can also make the uterus contract (great for getting the old body back) and in some women can stimulate auto-nomic arousal. This phenomenon has been known to scare women into believing there is something wrong with them and induce them to stop breast-feeding. If you are feeling this way, please don't! Throughout your child's life, there may be times when a primal part of the brain induces unexpected sexual arousal from a sight, thought, smell, or feeling. Recognize now that this can happen, and file it away under "interesting life experiences." And remember Rosenzweig's Rule #1—the fact that the brain tells the body to be aroused does not by any standard mean that we are responsible for the arousal, *nor do we have to act on it.*

Going from a twosome to a threesome is a tough transition. Making love to a "mother" can be a tough concept for some men. New moms may find their body feels unfamiliar and less than sexy. Some families feel resentment welling up when this tiny intruder robs them of their sleep, and who knows what else. Everybody in the household needs love and affection during this time—a healthy, happy family is the best place to raise a healthy, happy child. I was a single parent and can say without judging lifestyle choices that life with a child is easier if there are two adults in the house. The adjustment to parenting is not easy but worth the effort. Keeping your relationship with your partner intact is very important to raising a sexually safe and healthy child. The early stages of marriage are often referred to as the honeymoon phase. Dirty diapers, sleepless nights, and sexless weekends are a clear sign the honeymoon is over. What lies ahead won't be easy, but teamwork between loving, committed adults can turn your partnership into a robust family filled with joy and gifts for decades to come.

THE BOTTOM LINE: WHY THIS MATTERS FOR SEXUAL HEALTH AND SAFETY

The most primal aspects of human relationships are developed during infancy. For a baby to learn that the world is safe and that she is loved and lovable is a gift that all parents can give to their children. This early emotional and brain development sets the stage for critical aspects of deep relationships, including empathy and attachment. And you and your partner, as new parents, need to find each other again and redefine yourselves within your new family and roles.

Toddlers and Preschoolers

What to Expect from a Toddler and Preschooler

Expect a toddler to exhaust you. They require constant attention for their own safety. They also want your constant attention. From their primitive perspective, they believe that the world revolves around them. A toddler can be strongly attached to his parents in this phase and feel as if you are the center of his world. He takes the first steps in separating from his parents during this stage and learns that it is safe to venture out on his own. An important reason to "childproof" your house with electrical outlet covers, cabinet latches, and similar devices is to enable your toddler to have brief safe adventures into another room, but he is not ready to go far on his own and certainly requires constant adult supervision at this stage. That's one reason why toddlers so exhausting.

Another reason this stage is so exhausting is that toddlers will test you in ways that are cute and also incredibly frustrating. There is just so much of the world that does not make sense to them and some toddlers find this exciting and others find it frustrating. You will get to know your individual child's reaction to external stimulus or boundaries or finding that the world is not being exactly the way she wants, and learn how differently each toddler reacts to stress. One child may find a change in her daily routine exciting while another may hate it.

Expect your toddler-aged child to need you in every way, and to love you unconditionally in the process. Because toddlers experience the universe through their parental love, their loving response to you should not be interpreted as validation of your parenting behavior. Parent your toddler based on the practices and limits you and your spouse have thought and talked about, and be consistent. Gauging your effectiveness by the emotional swings of your toddler will be confusing for you and your child. Her eyes will light up when you walk into a room and you will have moments of sheer parental bliss with a sleeping two-year-old curled up in your arms, waking to gaze up lovingly into your eyes. And within twenty-four hours or twenty-four minutes, this same child may look you in the eye with a lie on her lips and the most stubborn refusal to complete a simple task. You need to be consistent—they can't possibly be.

In this stage, you may find your child telling lies for the first time. While it may break your heart to see what you perceive as a character flaw in your beloved child, take heart from the fact that this is a sign of developing cognition. Your toddler is testing reality—can he really make what he thinks is true be true? At this age, I remember my son announcing one day that my name was now Foo-Foo. Your toddler needs to learn that he can't magically change reality with his wish. This can be the time when a child will stand in front of you with chocolate smeared all over his face and insist he didn't eat the cookie. And a huge mistake that parents make during this stage is to take a toddler's actions or words personally: "How stupid does my daughter think I am?" I've heard young parents moan. This is absolutely the least productive response that you can have. Your child is not thinking about you at all, and that's the point. This is all about the child testing the waters and learning limits. Toddlers have many lessons to learn during these years and will learn the lessons about emotions and feelings best from a consistent, loving parent. Toddlers are curious about everything, and by responding to their curiosity you encourage them to learn.

Curiosity about sex differences is just one part of this need to learn. Curiosity can lead to children wanting to see each other's bodies. This "you show me yours and I'll show you mine" may start toward the end of this phase, so be ready to have simple discussions with your toddler and preschooler about these anatomical differences.

This is also the stage when toilet training takes place; most preschools won't accept a child in diapers beyond age three, so if you are a working parent, you may very well feel the stress to get this done as quickly as possible. However, you should expect a child to learn to use the toilet on her schedule, and not yours. So try to be patient and keep your frustration in check.

What You Should Know

Freud refers to the period of life from eighteen to thirty-six months as "the anal phase," and from thirty-six months to age six as "the phallic phase." Those parts of the body are very important to children during these stages. Many find their genitals and like them. In some ways, touching genitals is a progression from thumb-sucking for comfort during infancy (the oral stage). Children in this age-range may hold their genitals for comfort during naptime.

When choosing a childcare center for your toddler, it makes sense to find out how the staff deals with hands in the pants at naptime. Some childcare centers punish a child who does this, which is not a good idea—others, more appropriately, ignore it. A similar inquiry about reactions to toileting accidents is also a good idea—you never want anyone shaming your child when they are just behaving as any normal growing person.

Many parents choose to toilet train their child during the so-called anal phase and this can be the source of many lifelong messages a child retains about her body. Your child may think, "Am I dirty? Am I unlovable?" A child is learning about control at this age and her body is one of the few things she feels she can control. Can she use it to get negative attention? To avoid giving negative messages to your toddler or preschool-aged child, you could use praise as a reward for proper toileting rather than punishing for mistakes. If first attempts don't work, wait a few weeks and try again.

The id, or pleasure principle of infancy, is joined by the superego, or the conscience, at this stage, which gives a child the sense of right and wrong. Toddlers still want what they want but have started to learn from relationships with their parents, other caretakers, and the environment that certain things they want will not be available to them. This lesson is *very* important. In order for a society to function, people need to be able to learn its rules and live by them, so get ready for the "terrible two's" and hold your ground, knowing that your ability to teach your child right from wrong is another of your gifts to society—and to your child who will have to live in it.

"Young children experience their world as an environment of relationships, and these relationships affect virtually all aspects of their development—intellectual, social, emotional, physical, behavioral, and moral,"[35] reports the National Scientific Council on the Developing Child. Choose your babysitters wisely, especially for your toddlers and preschoolers, and teach your children that they have choices about their bodies. Allow your child to decide who he wants to kiss, and teach him how to say "no thank you" to an over-affectionate relative. There is lots more to say about this topic in chapter 7.

---

35   National Scientific Council on the Developing Child *Young Children Develop in an Environment of Relationships: Working Paper No. 1.* 2004: 1. Accessed at http://www.developingchild.harvard.edu.

What's Going on in the Family?

People who study the lifecycle of marriages often refer to the child-raising years as the "utilitarian" phase. There just are so many things to get done. Many people don't make this transition successfully; in fact, after ten years, one-third of first marriages have disrupted.[36] These early years of parenting place a great deal of stress on parents, and this is the time when a family is likely to add additional kids, so the stress increases even more.

Children at this age are coming into constant contact with new things, and no one is more important to them than their trusted interpreter—you! Kids will be incredibly demanding, and coincidentally you may be hitting the most demanding stages of your career as well during this period. There's a lot to be done here with sharing, scheduling, and coordinating. You and your partner need to support each other in setting and keeping boundaries of all types; it is just too easy to become overwhelmed during these years.

Parenting can be so demanding during this phase that men and women will sorely miss their former, sexier, unencumbered selves. **Pay attention to the marriage!** This is a most critical time to plan date night or, preferably, a weekend away.

The Bottom Line: Why This Matters for Sexual Health and Safety

Kids, by preschool age, will have mastered toileting and learned that their bodies can be a source of great pleasure or pain. They will most likely have found their genitals and identified them as a source of pleasure. Ideally, their genitals have become associated with private contentment and have not become associated with shame. The feelings they developed about their bodies may influence their self-concept and self-confidence, so positive messages about all aspects of their being—including their bodies—are necessary through this stage.

During this time, kids, too, will make remarkable progress in learning about right and wrong and understanding that other people have feelings as well. This is an incredibly important precursor to developing empathy and

---

36   The U.S. Centers for Disease Control and Prevention. *Cohabitation, Marriage, Divorce, and Remarriage in the United States.* June 2002: 17. Accessed at http://www.cdc.gov/nchs/data/series/sr_23/sr23_022.pdf.

integrity, meaning that they are less likely to hurt others and set the foundation to ultimately understand that sex must be consensual.

You and your partner will also be struggling to find yourselves again as the honeymoon phase of your marriage succumbs to the utilitarian phase. Use those "utilitarian" skills for yourselves and keep the relationship going.

School-aged Kids, Age Six through Puberty

WHAT TO EXPECT FROM SCHOOL-AGED KIDS

Called "the latency stage" by Freud (because a child's sexuality is now latent until adolescence), and the golden age of childhood by others, the years between elementary school and entering puberty are wonderful years and a gift that helps prepare children for adolescence. Most of us remember fun-filled events, family outings, and innocent questions during this period of our lives and will enjoy seeing our children grow in the same ways before morphing into defiant, door slamming teenagers. During this time, the family unit is still the most important social influence on your child, presenting a huge advantage for you as a parent. This is the time to fill your child with your values and opinions on everything that's important to you. From manners to hygiene, if you think it's important information, pass it to your child now—because by adolescence, your child's frame of reference will shift to her peer group and you will suddenly seem idiotic in her eyes. Even if your son ignores some of the messages you send him during the preteen years, he won't forget them. But don't waste this opportunity before the hormones start kicking in.

School-aged kids speak, and in some way look, like shorter versions of adults. They're not, though, and this is a fact that can be quite deceiving. They have a lot of internal work to do in terms of integrating their personality. As you will recall from before, the child's id was frustrated by the superego (conscience) developed as a preschooler, and now a child takes a few years to integrate all of these forces into his ego, or balanced sense of self. As the child strives to achieve his own balance, he will have a deep sense of right and wrong (by his standards) and you're sure to hear cries of "that's not fair!" when given boundaries or if he feels he is not allowed to participate in the same areas as his peers. I've even seen school-aged siblings split a candy bar with a ruler to make sure things are equal and democratic!

WHAT YOU SHOULD KNOW

So many *big* developmental tasks have been completed by this stage in your child's life—they can walk and talk, they have developed relationships, they have balanced their id-based desires with a sense of right and wrong, things are integrated and emotionally stable, and it's a great time for your child to learn. Then, just when your child has mastered childhood, it's gone, and now she has to master being a teenager! This time from around age six to puberty is your opportunity to ensure that your child has the best possible information about bodies, puberty, sexual response, reproduction, and sexual health before it starts happening full force. You can help ensure a smooth transition into puberty by ensuring that your child knows in advance what will happen to her body.

Make a clear and conscious decision about the messages you want your child to hear about the sexualization of young children. Girls especially are pressured into appearing sexual at young ages, exposed by the media to baby bikinis and padded bras for eight-year-olds. Boys may need help understanding what is really conveyed by the tough-guy looks. A common problem among latency aged, pre-sexual kids is that they may know that a certain type of look is equated with being attractive without understanding that it has a sexual connotation. When a nine-year-old girl chooses a Halloween costume with a decidedly "hooker-ish" look, a parent needs to supplement their "no" with an explanation about that decision beyond "because I said so." Explaining to kids that certain kinds of clothes carry a certain kind of message (one that is not always appropriate for their age) is a good place to start. Using a uniform as an example ("When you wear shin guards, I know you're getting ready to play soccer") explains to a child that a particular look is seen by some people as a uniform to "kiss" or "flirt" or some other term in that will make a nine-year-old think, "Yuck."

This is an especially important time to monitor all media contact they have. Exposure to explicit sexual acts can be very frightening for this age group—young boys may be exposed to porn-sized penises and young girls frightened by the sight of female bodies invaded by them, and both can be the stuff of nightmares before your child has any knowledge of what loving sexual contact actually is. Media messages as damaging as those explicit images are everywhere—messages about sexual violence, sexual dominance, trading sex for rewards, and others frighten kids even more if they do not have your (their parent's) values as a basis for knowing that these messages do not always reflect the truth.

You can prepare for this stage in your child's development by reviewing the material in chapter 4 and by practicing how to explain anatomy and physiology in your own language with your spouse or a trusted friend. There are many good books that explain the reproductive aspects of sexuality, but I have yet to see one that does a good job explaining arousal; you'll most likely have to do so on your own. If your school district, religious institution, or youth group offers sexuality education, take the time to read the curriculum and then follow up with your child regarding these courses with questions and answers at home.

Half of all prepubescent girls in the United States will be menstruating by age twelve; this means they may be facing a rather grown-up physical issue while still emotionally in the latency phase. The best way to prepare for this is to establish, early on, a good, strong base of information about what her body's doing and why, so she can feel safe about her blossoming sexuality.

WHAT'S GOING ON IN THE FAMILY?

Parents *love* the latency stage and can understand why it's referred to as the golden age of childhood. Kids are now old enough to understand, to have great conversations, and they still like you—their parent! Enjoy it and use this time to infuse all of your values into your children, and to provide accurate knowledge about male and female bodies. Once adolescence hits, you'll have to work much harder get your child's attention on such topics.

With no more toddlers in the house, things seem a *lot* calmer. Now your children can learn responsibilities, such as taking on age-appropriate chores and finding out that privileges must be earned. Lines of communication with you are as strong as they will ever be until your child reaches late adolescence.

For single parents, this may be one of the easier times in the rearing of your child. If a child meets someone you're dating, go easy on the public displays of affection and really reinforce the fact that this person is your friend. If the "friend" part is a lie and you consider this other person just a sex partner, then there really is no reason to introduce them to the kids.

THE BOTTOM LINE FOR SEXUAL HEALTH AND SAFETY

This is a most valuable time for parents. You have your kid's attention and can and must fill your children with your values now. Children should end this phase of their development and enter adolescence with general knowledge about sexual and reproductive anatomy and physiology of both males and females, and a deep respect for the feelings of others. The knowledge will spare them the agony of thinking something is wrong with their bodies as they enter puberty, and the integrity you teach will spare others unnecessary teasing or worse. They should know your rules for adolescent health and safety. In fact, your pediatrician should now begin asking you to leave during the post-exam discussion time during annual checkups to have private time with your child in order to discuss the sensitive topics recommended by the American Academy of Pediatrics: sexuality, mental health, and substance abuse.[37]

Puberty and Adolescence

WHAT TO EXPECT FROM ADOLESCENTS

While developmental psychologists and sociologists do an adequate job describing the sequence of stages a child experiences, there is no map with the exact timeframe for stages in your child's life. In fact, all of the stages overlap, and during transitions, a child will express the characteristics of both the stage they are leaving and the one they are entering. Gail, a divorced mom, tells the story of her twelve-year-old son who decided with complete urgency that he had to absolutely shave one day—not the next day, but right that moment and that he *had* to have a razor immediately. As Gail left for the store her son added, "And don't forget the Mr. Bubble!" This boy needed to shave *and* play with his bath toys. This is just a good example of the overlapping of stages your son or daughter may experience at this and any other transitional time.

By around age twelve, formal and abstract logical processes become available to kids. The bad news is that hormonal and brain changes make them

---

37   Irwin, et al. "Preventive Care for Adolescents: Few Get Visits and Fewer Get Services." *Pediatrics*. April 2009.

want to use this new-found intellectual capacity to get on your nerves as they begin the process of separation and individuation.

Sociologists argue that adolescence is actually a socially-derived phenomenon. Back in the agrarian days when the lifespan was less than fifty years, there was no way-station between childhood and adulthood. As our society became more and more complex, it took longer and longer for a person to acquire all the tools to master it on his own. Throughout the twentieth century, researchers focused on the social and behavioral aspects of adolescence, discussing in great detail the conflicts that arose from having a fully adult body but a dependent social role. As societies become more complex, the length of adolescence—defined as a necessary dependence on adults for survival—increases.

In twenty-first century America, we see some examples of the lengthening period of adolescence. Federal law now allows parents to keep their children on their health insurance until age twenty-seven, and states are maintaining responsibility for foster children to age twenty-one (it had been eighteen years of age for decades previously). So adolescence, one of the toughest times for you as a parent, is now lasting longer than ever. Mary, a mother I interviewed, told me that until she found her twenty-three-year-old son still living at home she never thought she'd be tossing the economy-sized package of condoms in her grocery cart on her weekly shopping excursion.

Even if your family values exclude subsidizing condoms for a young adult, this extended adolescence can have some unexpected consequences. The overwhelming majority of young adults are sexually active and your family must decide together about co-ed sleepovers. Some families are very accepting once their children reach a certain age, such as eighteen or twenty-one; others find it completely out of line at any age. Once again, family communication to clarify your own values is in order.

The twenty-first-century focus on brain development brings important information to the table, particularly around the incomplete development of the parts of the brain responsible for various kinds of judgment found in adolescents. The laundry list of developmental tasks an adolescent must complete is daunting. Ranging from choosing a career path, college, peer groups, and health habits, to determining their sexual values and identity, the list is huge. They have to do all of this with a brain that is not yet operating on all levels, so they need your love and support even though they may look and act as if they do not.

WHAT YOU SHOULD KNOW

This stage is *very* confusing as kids have one foot in childhood and the other in adolescence (and, as some parents may agree, a third in their mouths). Parents have to work a lot harder to find opportunities to get and keep their child's attention.

Brain development is still incomplete, so in some ways adolescents are the most difficult to predict; they have so many traits of both the latency-aged child and the teenager. If you ask a question, you can never be quite sure who's going to answer.

The physical sensations afforded by the bodily changes are very important to a child at this stage. Masturbation, potentially to orgasm, can start early in this stage. "The child who has come to associate sensual stimulation with anxiety . . . is fated to struggle with his emerging sexuality."[38] Remember Rosenzweig's Rule #2, and wonder what feelings your child has learned to associate with sexuality. Parents must let a child know that arousal is normal, healthy, and private.

The same textbooks that point to the sexual arousal and desire to masturbate as a sign of emerging sexual maturity in boys also discuss menstruation as the key sign in girls. Let's broaden this a bit and recognize that in both sexes, bodily changes are occurring that act as a precursor to reproduction. Similarly, in both males and females, bodily changes are occurring that influence sexual arousal and desire, and social changes are occurring that are forerunners to adult coupling.

Girls may hit their growth spurt before boys of the same age. It is possible to see a twelve-year-old girl and boy side by side and think they are five years apart due to their difference in height and variations in their budding signs of adolescence. Because there is such a wide range of "normal" developmental changes in this period, many kids feel like the odd person out; love and positive reinforcement from you and other family members have never been more

---

38 Breger, Louis. *From Instinct to Identity: The Development of Personality.* New Jersey: Prentiss Hall, 1974: 298.

important to your child's ability to feel loved and lovable than they are at this stage of bodily and emotional change.

Although only 13 percent of teens have ever had vaginal sex by age fifteen and the age for young people to engage in sexual intercourse for the first time is about age seventeen,[39] we must be aware that kids are doing a lot of sexual things before then. Kissing and petting start as young as ten or eleven; oral sex can begin as young as twelve. One study of 1,279 seventh graders (average age twelve-and-one-half years) found that "overall, 12% of students had engaged in vaginal sex and 7.9% in oral sex."[40] By their nineteenth birthday, seven in ten teens of both sexes have had intercourse.[41]

The first time someone has sex is a big deal. The typical American boy will have sexual intercourse late in his sixteenth year and the typical American girl midway through her seventeenth. Girls are more likely than boys to have their first experience of intercourse within the context of a relationship. Researchers have found that kids from single parent families or those with stepparents tend to have an earlier onset of intercourse than their peers.[42] Play it safe and assume that your child will be on the early side, and help them prepare with information and a full understanding of your values. The first sexual experiences set certain attitudes and expectations for a young adult that stay for a very long time.

One research study documents that "the odds of having the attitudinal belief that it is OK to have pre-marital sex even if you are not in love is 15 times higher for adolescents who are sexually experienced," [43] meaning that

---

39 Guttmacher Institute. "Facts on American Teens' Sexual and Reproductive Health." January 2011.

40 Christine M. Markham, Melissa Fleschler Peskin, Robert C. Addy, Elizabeth R. Baumler, and Susan R. Tortolero. "Patterns of Vaginal, Oral, and Anal Sexual Intercourse in an Urban Seventh-Grade Population." *Journal of School Health* 79.4, April 2009: 193(8).

41 Guttmacher Institute. "Facts on American Teens' Sexual and Reproductive Health." January 2011.

42 Upchurch, Dawn M., Lene Levy-Storms, Clea A. Sucoff, and Carol S. Aneshensel. "Gender and Ethnic Differences in the Timing of First Sexual Intercourse." *Family Planning Perspectives*, 1998. Accessed at http://www.guttmacher.org/pubs/journals/3012198.html.

43 Tolma, Eleni L., Roy F. Oman, Sara K. Velesy, Cheryl B. Aspy, Sharon Rodine, LaDonna Marshall, and Janene Fluhr. "Adolescent sexuality related beliefs and differences by sexual experience status." *The Health Educator*, Volume 39 Number 1, 2009: 3–9.

once an adolescent is sexually active, he or she tends to remain so even when that initial relationship ends. Conversations about safe sex and sexually transmitted infections (STIs) are important, and it makes a great deal of sense to direct your teen to places where she can get good information. If you absolutely *cannot* bring yourself to have a full-out conversation about this, a good second choice is to find a good book that mirrors your values and has accurate information and leave it on your child's bed with a note, such as: "You're growing up now and this book is full of things adults need to know." Whatever the case, don't forget the note; your teen may think that you felt like you had to buy the book because you thought he was too stupid to know this stuff. You want to make sure your child knows he is loved and cared about and that is why you've provided the reading materials for him.

In his book aptly titled *Why Do They Act That Way?* Dr. David Walsh informs his readers that modern neuroscience provides a window into some of the mysteries of the teen years. I share his strong belief that objective information about a child's developmental changes can help a parent to be more patient, tolerant, and to develop the best strategies to react to his or her child's behavior. Among the important topics he covers are two that are particularly germane to my perspective on sexual health and safety: the development of the ability to accurately assess risk, and the influence of the sudden influx of hormones.

Walsh is among those scientists who remind us of the practical implications of the incompletely developed brain. For example, he writes, "Because the prefrontal cortex's (PFC) wiring is incomplete, the adolescent's PFC can't always distinguish between a good decision and a bad one, no matter how smart a kid is."[44] *What a relief!* I've been wondering for decades why in the world I risked so much to put a tube of toothpaste in my pocket instead of paying for it at thirteen, and why I risked my reputation as the neighborhood's most reliable babysitter by allowing the front lawn of a new babysitting job to turn into a major gathering attracting one hundred kids on a summer Saturday night. I'll bet you can think of similarly bad decisions you made at that age. And it's no different for your adolescent son or daughter.

---

44 Walsh, David with Nat Bennett. *Why Do They Act This Way?* New York: Free Press, 2004.

Couple this undeveloped ability to assess risk and to make good decisions with hormonally-induced physical urges and appetites, and you'll quickly see that adolescents need adult guidance now more than ever—but they want it less, making parenting a challenge, to say the least.

One bad judgment call you can help your children avoid is ensuring that girls and boys both truly understand that any sexual contact must be absolutely consensual; no *always* means *no*. In fact, kids should be advised that they need to hear a "yes" before pursuing any sexual act and that the absence of "no" is *not* enough to assume that a partner is ready and willing to have sex. A colleague who works on a college campus as a counselor shared the story of a young man with an impeccable social and academic record who was shell-shocked when an allegation of date rape against him was upheld by a disciplinary board and referred for prosecution. He really believed that his intoxicated partner had consented to sex, but she claimed that she was unable to do so and thus was raped. Kids should be taught not to rely on their judgment of what they *think* a potential partner means; the story of these two young people remind us that the absence of no does not mean yes—and that mixing alcohol with sexual arousal can send judgment out the window!

It is inevitable that most American teens will experience sex with a partner during adolescence, before the part of the brain responsible for good judgment is completely developed. They will want privacy from their parents, making it a challenge for you to be supportive. You can, however, ensure that they have health care from an experienced provider, and a source of good information about sex. Like all developmental stages adolescence also ends, and with continued effort to parent your child while they demand their independence, you will be rewarded with a functional young adult.

What's Going on in the Family?

While your child enters adolescence, you may begin to feel your own sexuality waning; perimenopause or menopause may be affecting your sexual desire and the male partner may be feeling the effects of blood pressure medications and lowered testosterone production. These experiences may become even more difficult when in close proximity to your adolescent's newly budding sexuality. Resist the urge to try and be one of the gang—you're simply not.

This is one of the more difficult times for a single parent to bring a new adult partner into the family. Your adolescent has so many developmental tasks to complete that she doesn't have a lot of emotional resources to devote to learning to be a stepchild. Of course it's not impossible to blend families that include adolescents, but the degree of difficulty should not be underestimated.

ADOLESCENTS AND PHYSICAL AFFECTION

In some families, it is entirely possible that your child will grow to look very much like your spouse did when you fell in love—a daughter might resemble her mother, or a son his father. As a parent, you may be surprised with an autonomic response of arousal, and here it's important to remember that *the arousal alone does not indicate a problem*. What separates humans from other less developed mammals is that we do not follow our arousal to the nearest source of sexual pleasure. We have the ability to stop and think about what we are feeling and what an appropriate way to deal with it is—in this case, the best thing to do is nothing.

What you should realize is that this potential for arousal is only a response to what our brain associates with memories of sexual attraction, *not* a personal or specific response to your child. And you must not punish your child with any lessening of affection because your central nervous system hiccupped. What you should do is discuss privacy with your adolescent ("You're growing into a young woman now and one way women respect themselves is restricting who sees them undressed"). This is another time when the obvious arousal is a bigger problem for a man—when a man is aroused there's little question about what's happening. For woman, the feeling may be so fleeting and the physical evidence so hard to see that arousal at the site of her son may easily go unnoticed. Many women sadly recall adolescence as the end of physical affection from her dad. Dads may choose to change the type of affection given to their daughters (or sons), but it's awfully painful for a young girl to have this affection disappear altogether without an explanation as to why.

On the other hand, adolescent males can be so hypersensitive that they may become aroused by the touch of a sheet. If a boy is suddenly pushing you (his mom) away, respect his boundary. This may sound like a different standard for male and female teens, but it's not. The common thread is that the child's needs should come first and you are the one who has to learn to cope with these changes.

This should be obvious, but adolescent boys *hate* when their mothers flirt with their friends. Hearing, "Your mom's hot!" may make the day for a forty-something mom, but it will almost certainly ruin the day of any fifteen-year-old son. And some fathers may find themselves the target for adolescent flirting. The last lesson that you want to teach adolescent girls is that their sexuality buys them special treatment of any sort—so if you find yourself in this situation, check your adult ego at the door and tell the young lady to cool it or completely ignore her flirting.

A child wants to develop his own sexuality independently from you (his parents). Keep your sexuality and sex life out of your child's face. If you are married, you can find ways to be creative in finding extremely private times and places to make love, and if a single parent, you should date discretely during this period of your child's development.

One of the most painful developmental tasks an adolescent must endure is determining how to emotionally separate from his or her parent. Devon, a single mom and therapist by profession, recalls her son acting out in hurtful ways toward her at around age eighteen, stranding her at an airport when she flew to his college town for parents' weekend and going weeks with unanswered phone calls. She told me, "I logically knew I didn't want to be the most important person in his life when he was thirty. I guess the separation process had to start by eighteen, and when you're a family of two it can be intense." So, allow your child space to separate and move into the world, but don't let her off the hook when she participates in hurtful acts; a sexually safe and healthy person must understand how her behaviors effect others, especially those who love her.

THE BOTTOM LINE FOR SEXUAL HEALTH AND SAFETY

Watch, listen, ask, and have patience. It may seem like your adolescent's personality, wants, and needs change by the minute but as unpredictable as your teenage may be at times, he still needs you as much as he ever did. He will just make you work really hard to get close enough to help.

Your teen's body and mind are filled with strange new feelings. Your son or daughter can be distracted by sexual arousal, sexual messages, and sexual behaviors. It is inevitable that he will become sexually active during adolescence; and while you may not want to know the details, you do want to be sure that your child knows that you are there to support his sexual health and safety. Teens need to enter adolescence understanding the physiology of contraception and that condoms are the best way to prevent STIs. Your teenager must hear from you how important it is that her first sexual experiences be positive. **It is inevitable that an adolescent will make a few bad judgment calls, and some of those may involve sex.** Be sure you are there to help your adolescent get through these rough times and to move on with a minimal amount of damage to his or her sexual health and safety.

Conclusion

While developmental stages are sequential, expect them to overlap between the current phase and the next. Eventually, the behaviors of one phase will disappear altogether. Since the other side of adolescence is young adulthood, expect to see an occasional glimpse of who your child will become reflected in your frustrating teenager. It's a glorious feeling to see your child act mature, wise, and loving.

By the time your teenager reaches young adulthood, you've hopefully raised a person who is healthy and ready to love in a most positive way.

CHAPTER 6

Articulating Your Family Values about Sexuality

Everyone enters into relationships with expectations. These expecta-
tions are sometimes so ingrained that most of us don't even realize we have
them until they are violated in some way. I can recall a neighbor in my college
dorm freaking out when she saw another resident washing her feet by placing
them one at a time in the sink of the common bathroom. This act is perfectly
normal in some households but apparently unheard of in hers. She evidently
had her own opinions about sinks and feet that she didn't even know about
until it was breached. Another example: Just think about seeing people eating
asparagus with their fingers—a common dining practice in parts of Europe.
Fork-bearing Americans are a bit shocked the first time they see that occur in
a lovely restaurant, but, of course, there is nothing inherently wrong with the
practice. Norms aren't necessarily about what is right or wrong; rather, norms
describe behaviors that are expected or accepted in a group. A family certainly
qualifies as a "group" with norms and each member develops expectations of
their own. Ideally, a family shares similar expectations so no one is caught off-
guard by a family member exhibiting a behavior that seems perfectly normal
to her (washing her feet at the sink?) but is unheard-of to her partner.

When we join a formal group, the norms are usually specified up front.
Groups generally have rules. Formal groups even have bylaws. Even scouts

have a code of conduct. These norms and rules are expected and we know what will happen if one is broken. However, there is no one-size-fits-all set of rules for family life. Each family can and should develop its own norms reflecting its values and beliefs.

Adults come to relationships with expectations or norms about every aspect of sexuality and sexual behavior, and it would be very rare for two people to have exactly the same norms when entering a relationship. Part of building a strong foundation for a relationship includes working to clarify and articulate these expectations, then agreeing on a compromise when differences are discovered. This is particularly important when raising kids; if you and your partner in the household can't agree, your child will be unnecessarily confused as to what your expectations in the household are.

That said, modern media and peer pressure will direct plenty of confusing messages, particularly about sex, to your children without you adding your own. By clarifying your family's norms, living by them, and expressing them to your kids, this confusion can be replaced with knowledge and comfort. And most importantly, your child will know and most likely come to share your values, which is the ideal outcome for most parents.

Many of us experience discomfort when differences in family norms appear. One of the couples I interviewed remembers the confusion their nine-year-old son had at seeing his friend's father move around at home wearing little clothing. It was jarring to him until his parents explained in their own way that families have different expectations. Another parent recalled the shock expressed by grandparents when their child announced that he had to "urinate" in a home where the term "going to the bathroom" was considered explicit enough. And, has anyone ever visited a home where a new mom casually removes a breast to suckle an infant? As normal and natural as that is, it can be shocking at first if going against your family norms.

We generally don't "see" norms until there's a clash between our norms and those of another person. A friend told me of a visiting niece who had a bath ritual that included walking back to the bedroom in a towel, which embarrassed her children who were used to bathrobes. Perhaps your child comes home from a play date upset because the kids have to leave the bathroom door open when using the toilet, a safety rule some parents feel strongly about, while you may place a higher value on privacy. Or maybe your teen comes home and shares that her friend's mother thinks all girls over sixteen should be on the pill, an opinion you certainly don't share. How are you going to manage these conflicts of expectations?

Having a child visit your home, or debriefing your child after a visit, can be like placing a magnifying glass on the differences in family values. This chapter presents value-laden topics related to sexual health and well-being that you should discuss with your partner with the goal of clarifying how you both feel about the issue. You can then be consistent in the values you transmit together to your child. To help you along, I've offered questions to discuss with your spouse or partner. Most of these questions have no absolutely right or wrong answers, but I'm not shy in presenting my opinion in many cases. It is imperative that you and your partner have discussions (based on these questions) and are given the chance to clarify the "rules" you both would like your family to live by. As an added benefit, bringing these issues up can ensure that both of you feel as if your values will be incorporated into how your family functions.

As a side note, you single parents aren't off the hook just because you have no partner to require a compromise on your family norms. Individuals should review their norms and expectations around sex and sexuality periodically; you may be surprised at what you discover about yourself. If you are single, evaluate these questions and consider your own answers, then use them to start discussions with friends or relatives and glean their perspectives. And then, after you've heard and read everyone's opinion, remember this: decisions about your family are entirely up to you. Making decisions and articulating norms of your choice—which may be different than those of your parents, friends, or experts—is a great step in helping your new family solidify its status as a family in its own right.

Here are some of the personal issues that each family must consider and resolve for itself. Address them so that each member understands the values behind your house rules and you'll be well on your way to developing healthy children and a strong family.

Language

Ask yourself this: What terms will you use to teach your kids about all of their (and your) body parts? How and when will you use them?

Think about this: Many parents automatically adopt the terms used in the home where they were raised. Unless the anatomically correct terms were used in the homes of both parents, you and your partner may prefer different terms for these body parts; hence, discussion, and compromise, are in order.

You and your partner should give first priority to establishing recognizable variations of anatomically correct words for genitals and other body parts. This ensures that anyone will understand your child if he or she wants to communicate something to a teacher, babysitter, or other caregiver. Most people know what a little boy means when he refers to his "pee-pee" or a girl refers to her "'gina." Things can be made more difficult than necessary if a little girl tells her nursery school teacher that her "purse" hurts when she actually means her genitalia.

Little girls can learn a generic term for their genitalia, such as "'gina," and learn that they urinate from a little opening right next to it. Little boys can learn that they have a penis and testicles—some parents like cutesy words like to use the word "ballies." The key is to stick with words that can be recognized by someone outside of your family if necessary.

You and your partner may want to begin to have this discussion during pregnancy or soon after the birth of a child. This conversation can be right up there with the discussion of what the child will call each of his grandparents. You may wonder why start so soon, but you and caretakers will babble to your baby during diapering and bath time and will most likely be referencing parts of the baby's body. You may say, "Now I'm going clean your little toes. Ooo, time to see what's behind those precious little ears . . . " and then fail to mention anything while washing your child's genitals. So begins the subtle message of silence about "special" body parts. A child can become conscious of this as early as the first year of life. I'm not suggesting that parents sing a song about genitalia the way we do about toes (this little penis went to market?), but I am suggesting that you be thoughtful and deliberate about the verbal and nonverbal messages you send to your kids. A child will certainly remember his parents referring to washing "the really dirty parts"—a typical negative message that's not a great foundation for sexual health and safety. "But the rectum is dirty," you argue, "or at least germy"; my solution is to use bath time as a teachable moment to inform your kids of their basic anatomy and differentiate among the different parts; call the "really dirty parts" by their real name.

Remember: your goal is to raise kids with an appropriate level of language about each of their body parts, having integrated your values, which can transform as the child develops and the family dynamics change. It's never too late to start this process. If your child is well beyond diapering age, start now. Kids are resilient and will quickly pick up on new language and concepts.

Modesty/Privacy

If either you or your partner grew up in a house where anything is allowed and the other came from a buttoned-down, bathrobe-wearing clan, negotiation is certainly in order on the topic of modesty and privacy. Some people think this is not an issue until a child (or company) arrives. Not so. One partner may be totally comfortable going about his business au natural while another finds it distracting, annoying, unsanitary, or worse. Loving adults want their partner to be comfortable, so decide on this issue together and respect the decision at all times.

Ask yourself this: Will you have a dress code?

Think about this: Being very clear about who sees whom in underwear (or less) becomes a particularly important question in two circumstances—first, when a child approaches puberty and second, when new members are entering the household, such as the blending of families. It's not uncommon for both of these things to happen around the same time, so if you're bringing a new partner into your home and you have an adolescent, this section is especially important for you.

We all have the right to be comfortable in our homes but must remain aware that our appearance may cause discomfort for others. Adolescent boys may be uncomfortable at the sight of braless women of all ages, including mothers and sisters. This is another important time to remember the autonomic rule (see Rosenzweig's rule #1): Sexual response is an autonomic response to stimuli. People in your house who have reached physical sexual maturity may experience involuntary sexual arousal in response to the sight of a scantily clad person. Healthy adolescents and adults are not to blame for becoming aroused, but they certainly have an obligation not to act on their arousal. *Why put sexually mature or maturing members of the household in a position to deal with arousal?* It can add an unnecessary level of discomfort, and possibly create tension in a family unit where the seeds of other problems may have already started to germinate.

Ask yourself this: When will you let your child bathe himself?

Think about this: This question involves child safety, so some concrete facts have to be considered. Just because a child enters the I-can-do-it-myself stage does not necessarily mean he has the skills and judgment to do so safely. A child should be allowed to bathe alone only after he has demonstrated a real understanding of bathtub safety and some personal responsibility, not just because he doesn't want to be seen naked.

If modesty is the issue, bathing should be supervised by the same sex parent or caretaker if at all possible. An opposite-sex parent or caretaker can give the child some privacy with creative use of towels or a shower curtain. It is relatively unusual for a child to hide her nudity from a parent before early adolescence. Any sudden, unexplained change in a child's behavior about nudity in front of you or your spouse should be the cue for a calm, non-judgmental discussion about what has changed and why. Anything from schoolyard anatomical misinformation to being molested in some way may leave your child feeling very uncomfortable about being seen naked, even by you.

Ask yourself this: What rules do you want about having kids in your bed?

Think about this: Experts now agree that safe sleep for an infant means a baby is placed on his or her back in a crib or bassinet within close earshot of parents. By the time your child is several months old, the crib should be moved to a place where you can hear a cry but far enough away so you can sleep through a sniffle.

As mentioned previously, new parents have a huge developmental task to complete after the birth of a child; they have to relearn how to be lovers having taken on the all-consuming role of parents. In almost every definition of "family values," the adult couple is considered the backbone of the nuclear family. A healthy, loving sex life is crucial to maintaining the bond between the couple, and the long-term presence of a child in your and your spouse's bed can get in the way of the intimacy and love that planted the seeds that grew into a family. Once a new mom is medically cleared for intercourse (cuddling and kissing is recommended from day one) plans should be underway for loving private time. Having a child in your bed may be good for contraception, but does not add anything to the marriage. The Consumer Product Safety

Commission reports that there were 180 documented deaths by suffocation from babies under twenty-four months sleeping in an adult bed during a recent two-year study period.[45]

Sleeping arrangements remain an issue long after infancy. Once again, consider the autonomic rule: sexual response is an autonomic response to stimuli. Most healthy people experience all or part of the sexual response cycle while sleeping. People should only share their bed with someone with whom they do not mind sharing their sexual response—this does not include kids!

There are many people who find this reasoning old-fashioned or just too conservative. Many people are strong proponents of "co-sleeping," or a family bed. Molly, a focus group member and mother of three, told me, "Co-sleeping is healthy and normal, at least until age two. It's a warm, intimate family time. Our family did it with all three kids, it never disturbed anyone's sleep, and all three children now sleep remarkably soundly. And no," she continued, "it did not interfere with my relationship with my husband—we just had to get more creative!"

However, autonomic arousal while sleeping is a medical fact. Unless the arousal progresses to an orgasm strong enough to wake us or leaves a physical sign, we just don't know about it. You may think it doesn't happen to you, but if you're healthy, you're wrong; it does. Why chance sharing this with your kid? I felt Molly's earnest passion for sharing this special time with her kids, and respect her opinion, but I just can't share it; I believe that it's best to keep kids out of the adults' bed.

As our children age, sharing sleeping quarters with siblings presents the same challenge. Of course it's not possible for every family to provide each child with his or her own bedroom, but where possible, a separate bed is important for a child approaching puberty. If possible, beds should be placed in a manner that provides some privacy from the sibling or other person sharing the room even if an interior decorator would not approve of the furniture placement.

Have this discussion with a spouse, but reframe the question to "when will we move the baby to their own bed and *keep him or her there*?"

---

45   http://www.cpsc.gov/CPSCPUB/PREREL/prhtml02/02153.html/

Touch

Touch is a fundamental pleasure of human life. We give and receive messages through touch. Harlow and his famous wire monkey studies of the 1960s demonstrated that loving touch or "contact comfort" is a building block to intimacy and trust[46]—the building blocks of human relationships. We touch ourselves thousands of time each day. We long for the touch of someone we love. Humans love touch. Humans need touch. But like anything else so powerful, the potential for abuse is staggering. Thoughtful touch is a vital part of family dynamics and deserves careful thought about how and why it changes as your children age.

Ask yourself this: Will you give your kids a choice about hugging and kissing relatives?

Think about this: Teaching about choice is central to how kids learn that they have rights and responsibilities for their bodies. If both you and your spouse agree that a sign of respect includes kissing relatives, communicate that with your child. You should also give your child permission to have a discussion with you and your spouse if the kissing becomes uncomfortable. If your child has a bona fide reason to refrain from kissing—for example, my child was terrified of an elderly relative after he saw her remove her dentures—she can be taught to offer her hand and aim a glowing smile at the adult while saying, "No, thank you" to a kiss.

If one parent feels very strongly against this—"It would break my grand-mother's heart if our son refuses to kiss her cheek"—involve your child in the discussion and agree on the outcome. When your child expresses discomfort, be present when the disputed kiss might occur; there may be more to your child's discomfort than they can express to you with words.

Ask yourself this: What will you do when your child's curiosity leads him to touch your body?

Think about this: This response is also highly dependent on the age of the child. On one end of the continuum, an infant is welcome to suckle a mom's breast, while an adolescent male is not welcome to even see his moth-er's breasts. The need for thoughtfulness happens in between. A little child

---

46   Breger, Louis. *From Instinct to Identity: The Development of Personality.* New Jersey: Prentiss Hall, 1974: 32.

may be curious and reach out to touch a body part; that said, children as young as two or three can understand when a parent asks for privacy. Any child who can yell, "Mine!" when another child takes her toy can understand when a parent gently says, "Mine" when a child reaches out to touch a private area.

You may find curiosity from a same-sex child easier to handle. You are entitled to your personal discomfort but owe it to your child to be thoughtful when you express it. You must be careful that you own your discomfort; sharing with your child that *you* feel discomfort is a very different message than leaving him with the sense that *he* did something bad. A variation on "it makes me uncomfortable to be touched in one of my private places" does not judge the child, keeps the response on you, and can open a good conversation about private places on the body.

It's much better that a slap on the hand with no explanation.

Ask yourself this: Will your physical signs of affection with your children change over time? How? Why?

Think about this: Many women remember their father's sudden withdrawal of affection as a sad milepost of their entry into young womanhood. On the other hand, many parents can still hear the whiny moan of their adolescent telling them to "stop it" when offering a hug or kiss. With a little forethought and planning, families can navigate these transitions with humor and insight—no one has to get hurt.

In a healthy family, it is far more important for you and your spouse to honor the needs of your child than for your child to honor the needs of you and your spouse. If the mother really "needs" a hug, that's not her fourteen-year-old son's problem—it's hers. If what the mother really needs is to know that her son loves her, it's possible to find a more appropriate way to communicate that. Warning: She may have to wait until he's eighteen to hear it again, though.

A father's refrain from physical affection with adolescent daughters may happen because he fears his own autonomic arousal. If so, the father should respect his need for boundaries and his task becomes letting his daughter know that she is still completely loveable. If you feel a need to limit physical affection, find a replacement—verbal affection, parent-child dinners, or some other means that matches your families' values and circumstances.

Ask yourself this: How will you react when you see our child touching his or her genitalia?

Think about this: The answer to this question will depend on the child's age and the circumstances. A baby with a hand in his diaper is an entirely different situation than a toddler in nursery school or an adolescent hogging the bathroom for forty-five minutes.

Physical sexual arousal is a sign of normal, healthy development. An infant baby boy is as happy to find his penis as he is to find his thumb. Since anatomy hides the source of female arousal, girls may be less likely to find their center of sexual feelings but also feel comfort when they do.

A child's response to his arousal will change as he develops. Remember Rosenzweig's Rule #2 as you decide how to react to a child or adolescent. Ask yourself what feelings you want to become associated with sexual arousal in your child. Is it the poisonous trio of fear, guilt, and shame? No—it is impossible to emphasize this enough. The feelings that become associated with sexual arousal early in life will stay associated with sexual arousal for a long time. Babies will do what they wish. Toddlers can learn the concept of a private behavior. School-aged children are primarily curious, and the line diagrams in chapter 4 can be quite useful for a simple anatomy lesson. Teens combine the characteristics of all three. They'll do what they want and need to be reminded about privacy and boundaries. They will benefit from additional lessons on the anatomy of both genders as well.

There is no single or correct response for every parent that works in every circumstance except to consciously ask yourself what message you want to communicate to your child and proceed from there. Obviously, infants will not understand your words but will sense your emotions. As a child develops the capacity to understand language, your family values about privacy could be shared.

Pleasure

Ask yourself this: How can you support your child's enjoyment of all her senses: the taste of food, the smell of a beloved person, the feel of fabric, the warmth of human touch?

Think about this: In many American communities in the twenty-first century, you as a parent may be tempted to think only about protecting your children from the negative consequences of sexuality such as diseases, pregnancy, and molesters, and ignore the positive aspects of sexuality like pleasure, intimacy, and joy. The topic of pleasure may seem out of place in a conversation about sex and kids, but you need to present the balance.

Remember, your goal is a sexually safe and healthy child, and the ability to feel pleasure is a fundamental part of being sexually healthy. I'm not suggesting you tell your twelve-year-old exactly how good sex feels, but I sincerely hope that you can see how the topic of physical pleasure, or sensuality, belongs in a discussion about parenting a sexually healthy and safe child. Parents can encourage a child to slow down and experience the taste and smell of delicious food, to luxuriate in the feel of a cozy blanket, to enjoy the sense of having their hand held or a protective arm over her shoulder, all of which are age-appropriate ways to learn that the body can be a source of pleasure.

When you see a baby enjoying a meal, a toddler entranced by a beautiful design, or an eight-year-old lost in the delightful cuddle of a favorite aunt, you are witnessing the building blocks of love, trust, and intimacy. Isn't that what we all want for our kids?

Conclusion

Families change over time, and you can prepare for a change by having a family meeting and considering these, and other, questions. The addition of a new baby, a stepparent, and especially the decision to invite a parent's paramour to join the household call for a family meeting where all members agree on new answers to these questions. Even without a major new addition, the answers to these questions will change as your child grows. Pick a date for an annual family and sex values talk—maybe start a new Valentine's Day tradition.

PART 3

The Twenty-four-hour Information Channel for Kids

CHAPTER 7

Earth to Adults

Come Back from Cyberspace and Tune into Your Kids

A Google search for "Internet and child safety" returns over 1 million links. Millions of parents pay $40 or more each for Cybersitter and another filtering software. Even the FBI and the FTC have dedicated educational programs for kids and safety on the Internet. The Internet can be a dangerous place for kids, but focusing on cyber safety does not release you from your responsibility as a parent to focus on personal sexual health and safety—it just adds a new dimension. It is just too easy to focus on and blame the Internet for giving predators access to our children; abusers have been and will continue to use tools both ancient and modern to snare innocent victims.

While parents are worrying about Internet safety, a driver could be fondling their teen as he gets off the school bus, or their daughter may be being ostracized for developing breasts in fifth grade, or their son might be experiencing teasing for his obvious erection when he is called to the blackboard. The current spate of programs promoting cyber safety makes it much too easy to avoid addressing these more personal, sensitive issues that are part of everyday sexual and social life.

In this chapter you'll find advice on everyday issues like safety in bathrooms, hotels, and locker rooms and how to teach your kids to set and keep their personal boundaries. Taking a good hard look at the kinds of people and places that require vigilance is an important step in ensuring your child is sexually healthy and safe.

People Who Can Be Potentially Dangerous for Children

There are several types of people to keep an eye on when considering risks to the sexual health and safety of your child. Let's start with the lighter stuff and work our way into the heavy discussion about child molesters and pedophiles.

Boundary Pushers

Learning to set and hold boundaries is such an important life skill. Adults without boundaries are routinely taken advantage of by others because they lack the skill set it takes to say "no" in various situations. Many don't even realize they have a choice when asked to do something; they become "people pleasers" responding to the needs and requests of others often without considering the cost to themselves. I recall the only girl in my college dorm who had a car had just that problem. She never refused anyone who asked for a ride, no matter how inconvenient it was for her. Eventually, after she and I became pretty close friends, I asked her for a lift and to my surprise she said no, offering the explanation that she could only say no to her friends because they already liked her. This was a young woman who needed to learn to make better decisions about who to keep on which side of her personal boundaries.

Assertiveness training was a popular trend in the 1970s and 1980s for adults both in the workplace and in relationships. Books with titles such as *Your Perfect Right*[47] or *Don't Say Yes When You Want to Say No*[48] became best-sellers, the concepts embraced by millions of readers. Assertiveness training offers strategies to stand up for your rights while respecting the rights of others. You can keep this concept in mind and use it for inspiration as you

---

47   Alberti, Robert E. and Michael L. Emmons. *Your Perfect Right*. California: Impact Publishers, 1978.
48   Fensterheim, Herbert and Jean Baer. *Don't Say Yes When You Want To Say No*. New York: Dell, 1975.

promote assertiveness in young children and teens as a tool for keeping their bodies and psyches healthy and safe.

Talking with your children about setting and keeping boundaries is just another way of describing the act of standing up for one's rights; you need to teach your kids what their rights are and give them the skills, and the permission, to stand up for themselves as protection against boundary-pushers of all types (including, sometimes, their parents!).

A critical part of human development is individuating, which means becoming a discrete individual who is separate and different from others. As infants, your children are attached to the adults who nurture and nourish them—they come into the world with no boundaries at all. As they become toddlers, some boundaries begin to develop, but don't mistake ego-centrism (the belief that the world revolves around them) for boundaries. Just because a child can yell "mine!" when someone wants one of her toys does not mean she has the maturity to set and keep social or bodily boundaries; these are very different skill sets and concepts.

You can start teaching your child bodily boundaries by the age of two or three. Teaching by example is most effective, and one of the best examples is allowing a child to decide with whom they will share physical affection.

Jill, a mother, told me in an interview about finding her four-year-old son standing by the wheelchair of a frail-looking octogenarian relative, who had unintentionally frightened the boy terribly. Her son was repeatedly declaring, "My Mommy says that I don't have to kiss you!" While other relatives who observed the interaction were upset that the child was disrespecting an elder, Jill reports being pleased to see her son setting and holding a boundary. She explained the child's fear to the relative and helped her son understand that he didn't need to announce what he was planning not to do.

Roberta, a focus group member, remembers being about eight years old when she was left with an aunt and uncle while her parents took a vacation. The aunt and uncle insisted on keeping the bathroom door open while she bathed. Roberta, who was just developing breasts at that time, looks back on the situation now and can see that the aunt and uncle were most likely concerned about her safety, but the sense of violation she felt by being forced to reveal her breasts to others than her immediate family stayed with her for decades.

Another focus group member Bernadette shares a memory of being in grade school and spending a night at her grandmother's very small house. She was assigned to sleep in an uncle's bed, and during the night, he rolled over, cuddled up to the little girl, called the child by his wife's name, and fondled her in his sleep. Bernadette was strong enough to tell her parents and while she still believes the uncle really acted unintentionally while sleeping, she refused to ever sleep at her grandparents' house again. This child learned how to set boundaries and thankfully had parents who respected them.

Well-intentioned relatives and friends who agree to watch your kids overnight are a godsend to exhausted parents. However, spend a few minutes with the host and your child to make sure that the sleeping and bathing arrangements won't encroach on a boundary that's important to your child. Have this conversation when you make the arrangement, not when you're on the way to the special event and about to drop your child off.

Remember: If you teach your children to develop and hold their own boundaries, you also have to teach them to respect the boundaries of others.

Bullies

Bullies are boundary pushers, most often crossing social boundaries with verbal abuse but also crossing physical boundaries with violence. Bullying is nothing new and can be terrifying to a child. Make no mistake; no one wants to see a child singled out for terrible treatment by a group of kids with more social or physical power. All adults must be aware of the signs of bullying and intervene to stop it quickly before any child is made to feel unsafe.

The media have been reporting more frequently about bullying in schools or online, but it's important for you, as a parent, to be aware that bullying can also happen within families. In fact, sibling abuse is the most under-reported type of abuse and some researchers believe it may well be the focus of the next great wave of disclosures of bullying. A sibling with more power than the others may exert that power on one or more of the other kids; you need to pay attention to your children and be aware of the differences between good-natured teasing and vicious bullying. How can you tell the difference? One important way is to asses if the target child is mad or terrified. If the answer is terrified, get involved and control the bully, even if it's your son or daughter. There will be a longer, more detailed discussion on siblings in chapter 8.

Bullies generally lack empathy, or the ability to sense the effect their behavior is having on others. Little kids need a constant reminder of the golden rule: "Do unto others as you would have them do unto you." By the time they're adolescents (but still lacking in real empathy), kids will at least have a foundation of the concept of empathy in their minds, if not their gut. Teenagers yet to develop real empathy and who hold power over younger kids, can present a potentially difficult situation and may resort to bullying to meet their own needs, which could be anything from entertainment to sexual relief, all the while lacking any real conception of the pain they are causing their victim.

The only thing worse than having your child bullied is to realize that your child *is* a bully. You should be prepared discuss empathy, role model empathy, and dish out consequences to a child who does not show empathy, particularly if they are resorting to bullying in or out of the home. Promoting empathy is one of the key factors in raising a sexually safe and healthy child. You certainly do not want your child to develop into a person who pushes a sexual encounter after his or her partner says no. You also do not want your child to grow up to be the aggressive half of a couple caught in this epidemic of date rape. To avoid these traps of adolescence, you need to take preemptive measures to speak with your children about empathy and to discourage bullying tendencies. If you are skeptical that your child has the ability to be a bully, the following statistic should wake you up: 25 percent of adolescents report verbal, physical, emotional, or sexual abuse from a dating partner each year.[49]

This is a clear indication of the lack of empathy among young people and is a strong call to action to all parents. Being aware of bullying in your home and teaching your children empathy are important steps any parent can take to slow down and eventually end this epidemic.

When you learn about or observe your child exerting any type of power unfairly over another, ask her this simple question, "How do you think that

---

49   The United States Centers for Disease Control. "Injury Center Fact Sheet." Accessed at
      http://www.nsvrc.org/sites/default/files/IPV%20TDV%20SV%20Fact%20Sheet.pdf.

makes the other child feel?" This is not meant to be a rhetorical question; rather, it should start an important discussion between you and your child.

Empathy is not natural for adolescents; they have too much internal angst going on to spend much energy on anyone else's feelings. Empathy must be learned early on, and you as a parent need to be the teacher. Promoting appropriate treatment of siblings and other younger kids is a great place to start this lesson. You may find yourself repeating again and again, "Stop and think how that makes your sister feel" or, "How would you feel if someone treated you that way?" If done consistently, your message and rules should follow your child from the home into the community.

While a child may be unable to fully grasp the concept of *why* you expect him to be considerate toward others, he can learn to demonstrate the behaviors you expect. Reward the behaviors you're seeking and discipline unacceptable ones; your child will eventually get the point and start to learn the importance of being kind and empathetic.

People You Trust to Care for Your Children

Many parents prefer to have a childcare provider in their home when their children are young instead of enrolling their infant or toddler in a daycare center. There are pros and cons to this decision, but if it's the best one for you and your family, start your search at least six months before you will need childcare services. Many last-minute decisions in this area mean settling for second best, and you and your child deserve better. Make your list of required *and* preferred characteristics, along with a list of things that you do not want, in your childcare provider. When choosing an in-home childcare provider, you should look for an uninterrupted work history in your candidate, unless there is obvious proof for the reason in the lapse of employment. If a candidate tells you she took a year off to care for a dying relative, conduct a quick Google search for the relative's obituary. Really; it may sound neurotic but you are putting your child's health and safety on the line. When you find a candidate who seems to match your list, the real work begins—checking references.

Be sure to speak to both personal *and* professional references for your candidate of choice. It's amazing how many people skip this step and it's a terrible idea. You wouldn't hire an assistant or colleague without checking his or her references, so do the same for your child. Speak to at least six (and no more than ten) people from various points and aspects of the candidate's life—employers, friends, neighbors, clergyperson, and so on. Some nanny applicants have been known to ask friends to pretend to be former employers, so ask lots of questions and trust your gut if the answers don't sound quite right. Whatever you do, do not skimp on questioning references! As much as you want to trust your judgment, even if everyone you know says you've got great antennae for people, for this one situation pretend that you've never heard that before. If there ever was a time to check and double check information, this is it. After all, you're planning to entrust your child to this stranger. And illustrating to a candidate from the start that you are serious about your child's well-being will go a long way in ensuring your child's safety and well-being while in that stranger's care.

Once you are satisfied that you've found someone as close to Mary Poppins as possible, develop a team-like relationship with that person. While you and the caretaker must work together to ensure that you have a happy, healthy child, you are ultimately the captain of the team and must politely, but firmly, make this clear to your counterpart. Young parents can be especially vulnerable to an over-authoritative nanny, and with feelings of inexperience may defer to the "seasoned" nanny's opinion, but remember that your care-taker must be willing to implement *your* values, even if they differ from *theirs*. Make sure your caretaker understands the values you and your partner have established for your child: How long should the baby cry before being picked up? What's the appropriate reaction when the baby finds his penis? Who will be bathing the child? Will she be held and cuddled often?

You want to be sure that your child is getting the same messages about his body from both you and the caretaker. Tell your new employee the terms you expect her to use for the genitalia and how you expect her to react when the baby finds his own. If the caretaker cringes in disgust at this request, then perhaps this is not the person you want changing, dressing, and bathing your baby.

Perhaps the most important tool for you as a parent is to regularly show up unannounced at home or wherever your child is being cared for. Be pleasant about it but consistently walk in to your own home at unexpected times to see how the caretaker is caring for your child. You may want to say that you forgot something, that you're tired and will work from home this afternoon, or that you just missed the baby, but whatever excuse you come up with, this is an important test for both the caretaker and for you. If the baby is in the caretaker's home, pick her up early on random days, or stop to drop off an article of clothing that reflects a change in weather. Take note where your baby is when you arrive and be particularly concerned if there is anyone in the home you didn't expect.

Technology now offers some assistance with checking in on in-home caretakers, but like background checks, these can provide a false sense of security. A daily Skype session or a Nanny-cam may make you feel better and provide some assurance, so if you think that will be a good supplement to unannounced visits, feel free to take that route. Remember, though, that technology cannot provide surveillance of the entire home, and if done without the caregiver's knowledge can cause irreparable trust issues between you and your childcare provider. It's unfortunate, but if a nanny truly wants to slap a child, she'll be smart enough to do it in a bathroom where no one could reasonably place a hidden camera.

If you decided to have live-in help, this also presents an additional set of issues. You and your partner must ensure that the childcare provider has privacy (which also means the family has privacy) and that the new employee is told in advance of all the expectations about dress and conduct. A scantily-clad or flirty young nanny may become an unnecessary distraction, especially if the help is joining the household right after the birth of a child, when you and your spouse are working to readjust your own intimate relationship.

The really tough part of setting rules for your childcare provider is taking action if they are broken. The last thing you want to do as a new parent is to fire a live-in childcare provider just for breaking the dress code, even if she is doing spectacularly well with the child; the thought of going through the whole screening and hiring process is especially overwhelming when you're just getting back to work! But don't hesitate. Failing to act in a situation like this will disrespect the relationship between you, your spouse, and the caregiver. In fact, this is one good reason why you may want to use an agency for the screening and hiring process—if you have to fire a nanny, the agency will be able to find a fully vetted replacement much faster than you can.

Good Coach, Bad Coach

Below is a letter that you'll probably never see printed anywhere else in real life:

Dear Parent:

Welcome to Main Street Sports League! We hope your child has a great experience in our program.

Our policy is to conduct a criminal background check on all of our paid staff and volunteer coaches. This will allow us to identify the approximately 5 percent of child molesters who have been reported to police, caught, charged, and convicted of a sex crime. Protecting your child from the other 95 percent is up to you.

Spectators in our bleachers, vendors in the food stands, maintenance contractors working on the field, and others can potentially be in close proximity to your child. They have not been screened, so we lack even the minimal 5 percent safety net here.

Pedophiles, one type of child molester, are people whose primary sexual attraction is to children. They often develop relationships with children based on friendship and affection that lead to sexual abuse disguised as sex play. Most pedophiles have learned to identify children who really enjoy or even need attention from adults; **they are particularly interested in the children less likely to be supervised by parents or other adults.**

Attending your child's practice and games has many benefits for you and your family, but probably none as important as the added measure of safety it offers your child, our team, and our community.

Sincerely,
Commissioner, Main Street Sports League

Now, of course it's impossible for most busy working parents to attend every single game and practice for each of their children who participate in after-school sports programs. But if a pedophile in the neighborhood (or near your child's school) happens to find that your child matches his attraction, he or she will begin to watch to see how much attention you are paying to your child. So get out of your minivan and talk to your son's coach at pickup or drop off. Arrive a few minutes before practice ends and watch a bit from the bleachers. When you're organizing your schedule for the week, pretend practice ends fifteen minutes before it really does, leave the iPhone on the front seat, and pay attention to your child. Team up with another working parent and take turns doing this—and be sure to cheer on both kids.

You're not just taking my word here; this warning and advice comes straight from the mouths of convicted child molesters I interviewed whose perspectives helped inform this book.

Exhibitionists and Voyeurs

Exhibitionists are people who obtain sexual gratification by showing their genitalia to others, while voyeurs become aroused by covertly watching other people who may be performing private acts, such as undressing or having sex. Some clinicians believe that exhibitionists and voyeurs have previously had experiences that caused sexual arousal to become contiguous or "stuck together with" a negative emotion such as fear, guilt, shame, or, more dangerously, with the fear expressed by another person.

While showing genitals or looking at them will rarely result in physical harm, they are deeply problematic for two reasons: they can terrify a victim and are often an early step on a continuum of sexual acting out by the perpetrator.

Paula joined one of my focus groups conducted for this book and she shared positive memories about her parents handling sexuality issues with her. As she spoke about her parents, Paula was open, animated, and shared many great anecdotes. Her entire affect changed, however, when the discussion turned to memories of being victimized as a child. Terror became visible in her eyes as she described walking up the stairway in her apartment building (generally an open, visible, and safe space) and being followed by a man with his penis exposed yelling at her to come look at it. She ran to a neighbor's apartment, banged on the door, and screamed for help, and the man disappeared. Most likely, the exhibitionist was seeking her screams and terror to enhance his arousal.

On a personal note, I recall as a child learning that there was a peeping Tom looking in the windows of homes in our neighborhood. All the moms seemed upset and I clearly recall the ambivalence among the neighbors about whether or not to call the police once they knew the voyeur was a neighborhood teen and not a stranger.

If you find a voyeur or exhibitionist among your neighbors, avoid the temptation to ignore that reality in order to maintain neighborhood peace. Be sure to document the time and place the voyeur makes appearances, and if you are savvy enough, set up a security camera on your outside premises. Consider keeping vigil by the window where he has been spotted. Of course, you don't want to act on mere suspicion or gossip, but it is important to make sure you and your children are not in harm's way. The safest, most reasonable way to verify any fears or suspicions you have is to keep vigil in a room from which a voyeur has been spotted. Collect solid information and then contact the police.

Exhibitionism and voyeurism may be gateway offenses, which is why it's important for you to be proactive if you hear or see a voyeur or exhibitionist in your community. As the perpetrator requires stronger feelings to obtain sexual arousal, his behaviors may escalate to a dangerous level. You don't have much of a choice if you know what's going on. The consequences of not alerting authorities to these practices could be tragic for adults and children in the neighborhood. No one is totally safe living in proximity to someone who needs to sense the fear of another person to achieve sexual arousal.

Older Kids

Much time was spent reviewing stages of development in chapter 5, and by now you should realize that even when kids reach a point when they sound and look mature, they are still a work in progress. You now know that adolescents do not yet have a fully developed ability to assess risk and to make good judgments. Given this, you need to consider the limits of your teen's judgment when leaving him in charge of younger kids. His curiosity, sexual urges, or heightened sense of power from being left in charge can combine in ways that can lead to sexual acts with younger kids, and I personally believe this is much more common than many of us would like to acknowledge.

In one focus group session, Bernadette recalls a teenage cousin forcing simulated intercourse with her when she was four. She has a powerful memory of her paralyzing fear, but was strong enough to tell her father, who became furious and took her right to the police station to file a charge.

Rayelle, a fifteen-year-old client in a sexual abuse victims' treatment group, came into a session with me one day, terribly upset. Her younger brother had shared her bed recently and he got an erection during the night. She felt the erection as he slept close to her and masturbated him to orgasm. This was a young victim who had learned that erections could hurt her, and she knew how to make one go away. In this case, her own victimization had made her unsafe for her sibling.

A more common scenario is the one shared by Jill, who recalled a teenage male cousin convincing her to show him her developing breasts as a nine year old. She didn't want to, but he was the "most important" of all of the cousins, and she wanted to stay on his good side. Similarly, Neil recalls as a boy, a teenage girl babysitter watched him urinate. He now believes she was taking advantage of the opportunity to see what a penis looked like. These kids were violated in what some may consider minor ways. While there was no need for a criminal investigation, both of these kids could have benefitted from a compassionate conversation with a parent to discuss what had happened and how to process it. As a parent, if your child comes to you with such a scenario, acknowledge how hard it is for someone to know how to act when faced with a behavior she had never considered before, and focus on how your child might react if anything like this happens again.

Parental Partners and Other New Relatives

It is a sad truth that the partner of a parent presents a statistically greater risk for abusing a child than a birth parent, and with divorce and re-coupling so common in our society, it's time to face this fact. One research study concluded that "living with a step-parent has turned out to be the most powerful predictor of severe child abuse yet."[50]

There could be several reasons why this is so. New adults in the home lack the parental bond that increases our tolerance for developmentally normal obnoxious behavior from kids going through certain stages. A new adult may relate to an older child by their physical appearance, which looks a lot like an

---

50   Daley, Martin and Margo Wilson."Violence against stepchildren." *Current Directions in Psychological Science*, Volume 5, Number 3, 1996: 77–81.

adult's, and miss the subtle cues that this really *is* still a child. Further, new partners may resent the intrusion of the child into their love relationship. Most insidious of all, some pedophiles choose partners who have children to whom they are attracted—more detail on pedophiles in the next section.

When you're bringing a new adult into your home, *just take a moment and remind yourself that abuse is possible.* A grandmother was very worried that her divorced son's teenage daughters, who had entered a new phase of dressing provocatively, were getting a new stepfather. The man was from another state and no one in her family knew anything about this man's family or background. The grandmother was close enough to the girls to make it clear that she was always there to talk if they found the adjustment phase difficult in any way. She shared that she considered telling the girls to sleep with their cell phones under their pillow in case he showed up in their bedroom at night, but worried that her former daughter-in-law would take serious offense. Thankfully, this man turned out to be a wonderful stepfather, showing appropriate affection and concern for these young women, but no one knew that when he first entered the extended family.

All of these issues expressed about a new parental partner in the home should be considered when any adult enters the extended family. From grandmother's new partner to brother's new girlfriend, as a parent you need to thoroughly consider safety issues before allowing unsupervised access to your children. Similarly, make sure that you know every adult who will be in the home if your child asks to spend the night with a friend. Speak to the adult in any home where your child will be visiting and ask if anyone else will be there that evening. Mention your child's shyness or extreme modesty—keep the concern focused on your child or family to avoid sounding judgmental or insulting. If you're not comfortable with the answers you receive from the other parent, hold your ground and tell your child you'll pick her up before bedtime. Your kid may scream that you're unfair, but too bad; you can use this as an opportunity to share your concerns about boundary pushers of all types and open the lines of communication about sexual abuse.

Cleavage-baring teenage girls are not the only kids who need attention when a new adult comes onto the scene. There are those who look at eight-year-old boys with thoughts of sex running through their mind. Who are these people, you ask? Pedophiles, that's who.

Pedophiles

When we don't know who to be afraid of, it's our instinct to fear anyone who seems different than we are. When it comes to pedophiles, as with so many other threats, this instinct doesn't help us—but a little knowledge about sex preference does.

Sexual preference refers to the type of partner a person is attracted to in a sexual way—who does that person want to have sex with? We generally define that by the gender of the preferred partner—heterosexual, homosexual, or bisexual—and leave it at that. But if we stop there we miss the entire universe of people who actually represent the real danger to our children.

Beyond the male–female plane, there is a second dimension of sex preference—the *age* of the sexual partner. Pedophiles are people who are attracted to children and their specific body types.

So it's important to consider at least two components of sex preference. It's like describing a body on two dimensions: height (tall or short) and weight (thin or heavy). You need to understand that the preferred *gender* of a sex partner is a separate question than the preferred *age*. When we fail to make that distinction, we wind up fearing the wrong people, and potentially ignoring the dangerous ones.

In some communities or child-serving organizations we find regulations restricting gay people from working with kids. Healthy gay adults have no interest in your kids. In fact no adult—gay or straight—should be sharing their sexual values and opinions with your kid except you. Whether a person is gay or not is not the issue—pushing sexual boundaries with kids is.

It's impossible to provide a description of the stereotypical behaviors of a pedophile besides that he will engage children in inappropriate, dangerous, damaging, and illegal relationships. A graphic description of how a pedophile grooms, then attacks victims, can be found in the Grand Jury finding describing the allegations against Jerry Sandusky, an assistant football coach at Penn State University who founded a charity to serve underprivileged kids.[51] Offering these kids first attention, then companionship, then affection and gifts, this

---

51 Accessed on November 19, 2011 at http://www.attorneygeneral.gov/uploadedFiles/
Press/Sandusky-Grand-Jury-Presentment.pdf.

report describes how he allegedly exploited their trust by progressing from touch to rape and sodomy.

Without question, the most effective practice to keep your child safe is to know everything about every adult in your child's life and keep communication with your child open. Give your child the words and comfort level to ask you questions, and don't be afraid to provide honest answers. Don't pass along prejudices and unnecessary fears to your child; instead, let her know that it's not OK for *anyone* to be sexually attracted to children, and that no one ever has the right to touch her then ask her to keep it a secret.

Pedophiles generally have a specific age range and body type that arouses them, and in therapy, most can trace this back to an early sexual imprinting of some sort. I point this out for two reasons: 1) **your child's early sexual imprinting is crucial to his or her healthy development**; and 2) if you see a child who is sexually acting out, you need to find qualified help for him or her (more on this second point in chapter 12).

Pedophiles have several typical modes of operation. Very few are like the man Keith Smith describes in his book *The Men in My Town* and accost and molest children at random. Some do haunt places such as public restrooms, where they might find a vulnerable child, then hit and run; a discussion about public places will follow in the next section. The overwhelming majority of pedophiles subtly ingratiate themselves into the life of a child, providing something a child wants and needs. This need could be emotional, such as affection and attention from an adult male, or tangible, as Todd Bridges described regarding his abuse by his publicist in *Killing Willis*. By the time sex is introduced, the child may accept sex as the price to be paid for the positive points of the relationship. The Grand Jury report describing how a university football coach funded an organization to help underprivileged boys then allegedly raped several of the young participants provides disturbing and graphic details of this type of predator. [52]

Lawrence, a convicted pedophile I interviewed specifically for this book, spent several years in a federal prison treatment program after his conviction.

---

52   See http://www.attorneygeneral.gov/uploadedFiles/Press/Sandusky-Grand-Jury-Present ment.pdf.

He spoke frankly to me because he wants parents just like you to know how to keep kids safe. He wants to make amends, but unlike the reformed drunk driver lecturing high school kids for MADD, no one is asking a man who molested a child to provide his perspective. He spoke from his experiences as a practicing child molester for decades before getting caught, and from what he learned from and about other inmates in his treatment program. His words frightened even me, and I have been working with child sexual abuse for decades. As Lawrence confided in me, a pedophile will charm his way into the life of a child. A pedophile may woo a single mom with a child to whom he is attracted. A pedophile may single your child out for special attention in a way that seems flattering. Lawrence repeated again and again that parents who are attentive and watch their children generally make their kids unattractive to pedophiles.

It's common knowledge that people have difficulty perceiving things that are out of their realm of experience. If you ever found that a partner had been unfaithful to you, you may have wanted to kick yourself for missing now-obvious clues. You may have considered a thousand possible explanations for the changes in your partner's behavior, but not *that* one—it was just inconceivable. Lawrence shared a story of a young victim whose family he had befriended—a single mom and her son. After a sexual act with Lawrence, the boy told his Mom that his penis hurt, and Lawrence was able to convince the mom that the boy might be irritated because he had changed brands of toilet paper. The thought of Lawrence sexually abusing her son was not even within the realm of possibility to this mom, but in fact, it was quite real. I compare this shock to learning that your spouse has been sleeping with your best friend—totally inconceivable until it actually happens, and it does.

As soon as a kid develops physical signs of puberty, many pedophiles lose interest. But until that time, you must be vigilant and able to consider the inconceivable. Pedophiles are not the only people who prey on youngsters. Once a child develops secondary sex characteristics, he or she may become attractive to other types of predators who prey on children's naiveté.

When I was a very young social worker in my first job for a sexual abuse program, my boss was a divorced father of two teenage boys. He shared with our staff that his boys never spent a night away from home without one of their parents along as a chaperone until they were well past puberty. This sounded extreme to me, until six years later when I had a son and found myself raising him with similar rules. Working with pedophiles may make parents like my mentor and me hyper-vigilant, but all parents need to know what we know: pedophiles are ridiculously skilled at gaining compliance from children. No matter how many workshops your kids have taken or how many books you've given them to read, young kids are developmentally incapable of controlling the interaction with a practiced pedophile they may come to know and trust.

Be vigilant, be visible in your child's activities, and be willing to consider the unthinkable.

Stranger Danger

Even though strangers are the smallest category of offenders, you still need to pay attention to them. In the last section, I stressed parental vigilance when discussing pedophiles, but it is certainly not possible to have all of your children in sight all of the time. You can do your part to choose the safest possible people and places while keeping lines of communication open to reduce the damage if something bad does happens to your son or daughter. But lightning can strike anywhere and you must teach your kids age-appropriate safety skills as a means of prevention.

Little kids should be taught never to wander away from parents while out in public places; this can be compared to not having permission to cross a street alone. You may explain to your child that are a very few people out there who hurt kids and staying with Mom or Dad keeps them away. As kids get older you can share more about the dangers, especially as a child matures enough to hear or read news stories about abductions, or to see posters calling for the return of missing children.

It is highly unlikely that any preschool-aged child is developmentally capable of going anywhere by himself safely, so this should never be considered. You should also make highly individualized decisions about where a school-aged child can walk by herself. Every neighborhood has its own potential hazards, and a parent must be cautious when making this decision. It is possible that your local police department has a community officer who would come out and speak to you and your neighbors about the potentially dangerous places in your neighborhood and how you can keep your children safe. You certainly want to check the online registry of sex offenders in your neighborhood—once again, knowing where to find the convicted molesters is a necessary precaution but avoiding the locations listed on sex-offender registries is not sufficient to ensure your child's safety.

Teach your kids to trust their instincts. If they are about to get in an elevator with just one other person and get the creeps, they should feel free to get off and wait for the next one. Ditto for a public restroom, store fitting room, or any other venue where they could find themselves stuck in an enclosed space with someone they don't know. Teach your children that it is not their fault if someone becomes insulted by this type of behavior; too many victims explain that their offender made their skin crawl in some way and that they wished they'd listened to their instincts. Encourage your child to learn to trust theirs.

And above all else, tell your children that if you ever catch them hitchhiking (or picking up a hitchhiker) they will be grounded for life.

Places that Can Be Potentially Dangerous for Children

Public Restrooms

Public restrooms run the gamut from sparkly clean and well supervised to dirty, dimly lit, and frightening. When you're traveling and nature calls, you don't always have time to be choosy—but there's always time to be careful. You can model safety to your children by getting in the habit of stopping at the entrance of the bathroom and quickly and carefully looking around before entering. If anything looks unusual, leave.

The best option is to use the family restroom now seen in many facilities. A single stall with its own entry provides privacy and security. Some places have such a facility labeled for people with disabilities. Use it if it's your safest alternative. A three-minute trip to a bathroom is not the same as taking a designated parking place.

Stay with a child up to about age ten in a multiple toilet facility, even if your child has hit the "I can do it myself!" stage. Young adolescents should still be supervised in a manner that always keeps them within range of sight and/ or sound.

However, if you are with an opposite-sex child, things can become more complicated.

Boys who are out with their mothers reach an age when they hate being dragged into a ladies' room. Too bad—they'll cope. I learned from my experience as a counselor with sex offenders that pedophiles watch for this behavior when seeking easy targets. *Never* accept an offer from a seemingly nice guy to keep an eye on your son in the public restroom. If you happen to notice a family where the man leaves his wife and takes his son into a bathroom, it may be OK to ask him to keep an eye on your son, but even then, use your best judgment. When a boy absolutely will not come into a ladies' room, let him use a men's room, set a time limit of 300 seconds, and both start counting together. Do not hesitate to walk in, loudly announcing your presence, if you reach 301. Stay totally aware of your child's location at all times; this is not the time to answer your cell phone or to get a soft drink.

Men traveling with girls have a bigger problem as many urinals are in the open in public restrooms; little girls old enough to be out of diapers are also old enough to recognize that men are urinating. If you are a father, you can carry a little girl into a restroom shielding her eyes and head right to a stall with a door. But because of this, girls may be too old to stay with their fathers at a younger age than boys with their mothers. Asking a mom heading into the ladies room with her kids to watch yours is really the best alternative if there is no single stall in the men's restroom. And still play the counting game as women are not immune to pedophilic tendencies.

Adolescents and teens may use a public restroom alone but need to be reminded that unsavory characters can be in restrooms and that they should be aware of their surroundings. I recall being groped by a woman in a restroom as a young teen and walking in on a drug-user shooting up in another, both times in neighborhoods considered safe. Either of those events could easily have turned dangerous, if not tragic. You should scope out restrooms using caution and common sense before letting your children enter alone. If there are a dozen people lined up to use a ladies room, then a teenage girl is most likely safe; "bad guys" (and I use the term generically) typically don't operate well with a crowd around.

As with most safety issues, common sense should always prevail. If you can't stay with your opposite-sex child when nature calls, remember that there is safety in numbers and always know your child's exact location whenever he or she is out of your sight. Kids need to learn that life is not always safe;

discussing public restroom safety before allowing your child to use one on his own is a great opportunity to teach him important safety rules.

Family Travel

It's vacation time and your family arrives at a hotel breathing a sigh of relief that the traveling is over. But don't let your guard down yet—many decisions are still to be made to ensure the safety and comfort of your vacationing crew.

Start at check-in. You have no idea who in the lobby may be observing a member of your family or your possessions with a special interest. Professional desk clerks learn never to announce a room number for safety reasons; they will usually hand a key or key card and point to the room number. This way, no one will know exactly where you're staying unless you decide to tell that person. Speaking of keys, if you give your child a room key, give them one without the number on it—kids lose things and a lost key with the room number on it can be an invitation for trouble.

Many family-themed resorts offer a kids' program. These programs are rarely subjected to the same public standards or regulations as summer camps or childcare centers. Some parental vigilance is required if you decide to place your child in one of these programs. Ask the same kinds of questions you'd ask about any program: Who are the staff? How are they screened? What kind of training do they receive from the hotel? Some hotels contract with licensed local childcare providers for day programs and evening babysitting; you should still ask questions but might be a bit more assured when someone specializing in childcare is in charge.

You must know the whereabouts of your children for the duration of your vacation. Younger ones must be kept within eyesight; adolescents and older kids should be given a time limit to report back to you. Young adolescents can start with a fifteen- to thirty-minute window and earn the right to be gone up to sixty to ninety minutes. These same time limits could apply if you chose to leave an adolescent in charge of his siblings in the room while you enjoy resort life. This can be a risky proposition, though—you deserve privacy and vacation time alone with your spouse, but it's not easy to combine romance and family time. Safety should always come first, and couples' time second—and then only if you have taken every possible precaution to keep the kids safe.

A special thought about beach safety: adolescent girls in bathing suits can often appear to be older than they are. When sunbathing without a chaperone, your daughter may attract attention from men or older boys. A young girl may be extremely flattered by this attention and equally unprepared to respond to it. This topic makes a great pre-vacation conversation and is a wonderful opportunity to share family values and beliefs about topics ranging from respect to puberty to dating safety.

Sleeping space is often limited while traveling, so this is an opportune time to remember some basic physiology: sexual arousal is autonomic and occurs in response to conscious or unconscious stimuli. People do not choose when they become aroused any more than they choose when to blink. Most sexually mature (and maturing) human beings experience all or part of the sexual response cycle while sleeping. As we discussed in chapter 3, sometimes it's only arousal that is gone by the time they wake; other times it goes all the way to climax, which, in males, leaves a calling card. This simple fact of life should be considered when making sleeping arrangements for your family's vacation. If someone in your family is in a developmental stage—like adolescence—where accidental arousal while sleeping is common, it is best not to have that family member share a bed. Put the adolescents on the floor if there are not enough beds to go around.

Don't forget the basics just because you are on vacation—be cautious, use common sense, supervise little ones at all times, and always know the whereabouts of adolescents and teens while you enjoy your time away from your daily routine.

Locker Rooms

If ever there was a time and place where a child feels vulnerable, it's while changing in a locker room. From the type of underwear they choose to the size of their adolescent anatomy, a child can be exposed to taunting from teens who lack judgment, tact, or empathy. And when there is no adult supervision of locker rooms, technology, hormones, and bad judgment can combine to lead to painful if not tragic results.

When I started my research for this section of the book, I thought that bullying, teasing, and subversive cell phone photos were the major locker room risks. Then a search engine search brought this headline up: "Four teens raped another in . . . Middle School locker room."[53] I read the news report of three fourteen-year-old boys and one fifteen-year-old repeatedly assaulting a thirteen-year-old with a broom handle and hockey stick in a locker room. The follow-up to the articles appeared to concentrate on asking where the adult supervision was during this incident. This is certainly a good question; apparently this school district had no policy about adult supervision in locker rooms. The follow-up might also have focused on whether anyone had ever taught these boys the meaning of the word empathy.

When discussing school climate in chapter 9, I'll illustrate how you can make judgments about what kind of sexual climate is present at your child's school; this should help you to avoid schools such as these if possible or work for change in your school district. I emphasize again that adolescence is a time of remarkably bad judgment; the boys accused of the locker room rape mentioned previously are described in very positive ways by members of their community interviewed for the news article. You as a parent need to think that the unthinkable can happen to your child anywhere (even at school) and take precautions, such as promoting adequate supervision in locker rooms and remain sensitive to any inkling that a child is being targeted by bullies.

Three quarters of kids aged twelve to seventeen own cell phones,[54] and schools struggle to regulate their use. It's impossible to stop a teen hell-bent on sneaking a photo of another changing clothes in a locker room. So impress on your child the dire consequences you intend to impose on them if they happen to take an illicit photo, and support the school in their efforts to develop and impose a cell phone policy. Locker rooms will be safer for it, as will your child. Listen to your child if the locker room makes her feel uncomfortable. Pay particular attention if she has been bullied, teased, or made a scapegoat. A vulnerable child is even more so when undressed, physically accessible to bullies, and lacking adult supervision. Empower your child with the knowledge that it's OK to maintain their boundaries in a locker room and that it's important to provide assistance or get help if someone has been singled

---

53   http://www.tampabay.com/news/publicsafety/crime/article999350.ece
54   Hachman, Mark. "More Kids Using Cell Phones, Study Finds." The Pew Research Center's Internet & American Life Project. *PC Magazine*, August 19, 2009. Accessed at http://www.pewinternet.org/Media-Mentions/2009/More-Kids-Using-Cell-Phones-Study-Finds.aspx.

out for bullying in the locker room. Stay open to listening to any problems they encounter in this vulnerable school space.

Childcare Centers

The National Resource Center for Health and Safety in Child Care produced a Parent's Guide to Choosing Safe and Healthy Child Care[55] that includes thirteen important factors to assess health and safely. Sexual issues are not mentioned once in the guide. Along with assessing the education credentials of the staff at a particular center and whether or not they sanitize their hands after diapering, when evaluating a childcare center consider *all* of the issues regarding in-home childcare providers mentioned previously in this chapter—namely, will the staff support your values around sexual issues? What terms do they use for body parts and body functions? Do they punish kids for masturbating during naptime, or leave them alone? Do they teach kids respect for others?

As with any childcare arrangement, be sure to drop in periodically and listen carefully to your child when he discusses his day, his teachers or other staff at the center.

Summer Camps[56]

Summer camps are fun and educational, but you need to make sure the program you enroll your child in is run in a way that ensures your child's wellbeing. Limited adult supervision coupled with the joy of not being in school has been known to lead kids to explore sexuality at summer camp.

In many states, short-term summer camps are not subject to the same stringent licensing requirements as childcare centers, and some faith-based programs may be exempt from public regulation altogether, so it becomes even more important for you to do your homework before entrusting your child to a specific camp environment. To make sure your child will be sexually safe and healthy all day (and night) at camp, start with a typical day and consider all activities that your child will involve your child. If your children will be picked up by a bus or van, will there be someone other than the driver

---

55 http://nrckids.org/RESOURCES/ParentsGuide.pdf

56 Portions of the section on summer camps are based on a publication the author wrote for Prevent Child Abuse–NJ, 2003.

to provide supervision? Excited kids can become unruly and distract a driver. Often, an older child is assigned to lead songs and keep order on a camp-bound bus. This may be sufficient if a staff member is not available, but if the bus is carrying multiple teens, the supervising child may be unable to resist peer pressure and may join the commotion. Moreover, aggressive grabbing or various kinds of showing off can be hidden behind bus seats or crowds of kids, yet another reason to consider bus supervision before sending your child on a bus to and from camp.

If the camp day includes swimming, ask camp administrators if the staff has been prepared to deal with children who get embarrassed changing clothes in front of others, and be sure you're comfortable with the reply. If there is a focus on sports, are all children encouraged to participate? Is competition kept at a healthy level? You also want to know if there is a policy about discipline that is consistent with your values.

You should find out if your child will be supervised as she moves through the camp grounds and facilities. If a child needs to use a rest room, will an adult accompany her? If no, is there a policy in place to carefully monitor the amount of time a child is gone? In addition, if the camp takes your child on field trips, does the camp take adequate measures to ensure the safety of your child? Tight supervision is a must for field trips; whether walking to a neighborhood park or traveling to a local tourist destination, counselors should assign buddies and perform constant head counts to make sure all children are safe and accounted for.

You should always be able to observe your child at camp. The camp should require parents to sign in, and you, in turn, should be respectful and not interfere with camp activities.

The camp should also maintain a list of people allowed to pick up your child. You need to provide the list when the summer session begins and honor the process put in place by the camp by not calling with last-minute changes that the camp can't verify.

Camp administrators should check the background and references for all people who have access to children. This includes maintenance and food services staff as well as the counselors, teachers, or volunteers working directly with the kids. It is common for summer camps to employ students; these young people should participate in pre-service training to learn the rules, values, and standards of the camp, and be assigned an experienced supervisor. Check with the camp director to see if these measures are in place before you entrust your child to their care. Likewise, you can visit the camp or talk to other parents who have sent their child in prior years to get a feel for the workings and safety of the camp environment.

Throughout the summer, you should make it a point to ask your child questions on these topics and be sure that your child feels safe and comfortable at camp. Summer should be a time of relaxed fun for children, and you will be able to relax yourself when you know you have chosen a safe summer program for your children.

Sexual Health and Safety Checklist for Childcare and Summer Camp

- Does the program check the background for all people who have access to children, including maintenance and food services staff as well as the counselors, teachers, or volunteers working directly with the kids?
- Does the program check references and work history for all people who have access to children? Never forget that criminal background checks identify only the small groups of abusers who have been reported, caught, and convicted.
- If the program uses high school or college students as aides, are these young people required to participate in pre-service training to learn the rules, values, and standards of the program? Are they assigned an experienced supervisor? Remember that young people are still developing good judgment and empathy.
- How does the program handle "hands in the pants" at nap time? Ideally, they should let young children sleep peacefully.
- What words do the staff use for genitals when diapering a baby or toddler? Ideally, they should use the anatomically correct terms.
- How does the program handle bullying and intimidation? Many young children have to be taught how to be nice to other children.
- If the program includes swimming, has the staff been prepared to deal with children who get embarrassed changing clothes in front of others?

- If there is a focus on sports, are all children encouraged to participate? Is competition kept to a healthy level? Participation is more important than winning for the development of a young child.
- What is the program's policy about discipline? If it consistent with your values?
- Are children supervised as they move about the building or grounds, for example, to use a restroom?
- Does the program have strong supervision and safety protocols for field trips?
- Can parents observe the day care or camp day? Parents should be required to sign in and be respectful and not interfere with activities.
- If the children will be picked up by a bus or van, will there be someone other than the driver to provide supervision?
- Does the organization maintain tight control over their vehicles, including requiring all trips to be recorded in a mileage logs? I'm aware of a case where a staff member allegedly sexually abused a child in a childcare center's van, and the lack of vehicle logs hindered the investigation!
- If parents drop off the children, do children pass from the parents' supervision directly to a staff member? Is there a safe path to travel when the child leaves the car?
- Does the program maintain a list of people allowed to pick up the child? Parents need to provide the list when they enroll their child and honor the process by not calling with last-minute changes that the program can't verify.
- Does the program have all licenses required by the state and county of municipality? Departments of education or human services may license childcare centers; departments of health may certify centers or camps; and regulations vary by community, so find the expert in your community by contacting the National Association of Child Care Resource and Referral Agencies at www.NACCRRA.org.

Sunday School

Stories about members of the clergy sexually abusing children have been in the headlines since the first high-profile lawsuits were filed in the 1980s. It should be no secret by now that anyone in a position to have access to children should be vetted and watched. Al, a man in his fifties, attended religious school while growing up in the 1970s and recounted that most of the boys knew which guys were the "Father McFeeleys" and did their best to stay away from them. It may be harder to be so blatant now, but abuse still goes on in religious institutions. The addition of child safety seminars by many denominations may be helpful in curbing sex abuse but there is no substitute for parental vigilance.

The many lawsuits settled over the past two decades or two have given us undeniable proof that pedophiles can operate in any kind of setting. We now have proof that when church administrators didn't know what else to do with a pedophile, they frequently moved him to a different church or parish with no warning to the new community (yet another reason not to rely on background checks alone). You now know unequivocally that *any* setting where your children will be without you requires a thorough investigation, unannounced visits, and strong communication with your child about what happens when they are there.

Cyberspace

So much has been written about this topic because so many new dangers are brought right into our homes via the Internet. I stand by my admonition to avoid focusing exclusively on Internet safety; the topics previously discussed are equally important, if not more so. But the threats from cyberspace are among the most insidious, sneaky, and are constantly evolving into new forms to tempt your kids. Could you have even imagined sexting when you were sixteen? Of course not. But unless your profession requires you to be technically proficient, it is entirely possible that your child's online skills far outshine yours—and this can include both computer and smart-phone usage. Level the playing field by keeping up to date with technology. The key is to identify a local expert who understands both kids and technology. Ask your school district technology manager to develop an annual workshop on what parents need to know. Your local library system may also employ experts in online technology who understand parental concerns and child development.

Your Internet service provider may also offer resources for you and your child. Learn about the parental controls and actually use them on your home computer. Do not make your child the system administrator for your computer—keep the highest level password for yourself. Even if your child saves her babysitting money to buy her own PC or smart phone, maintain every possible control of her Internet access. Ensure that you are connected to your child on any social network site and that you have the password to their email accounts. Older adolescents can earn some privacy, but emphasize that online privacy, like driving, is a privilege to be earned, not a right conferred with age.

One particular risk described in some detail by victims of pedophiles is the webcam. Children have been lured into child pornography by online predators who behave exactly as other pedophiles, identifying lonely kids and making friends with them. It used to be easy to just decide there will be no webcams for kids, but most computers and cell phones now come with cameras installed. If possible, disable or password protect the software drivers that run the PC camera. If your child wants to Skype with a friend, let him get your permission then have the call where you can observe it. It is remarkably easy for one teen to convince another to show skin, and pedophiles have an even easier time convincing children to do the same. Along with the pain of actual victimization, these lasting images can be part of a child's life forever. Restricting access to a webcam is an important step to keep your kids safe from being lured into a compromising position online.

Since this is a playing field that is constantly changing, you have to go back to the simplest rules and see how they can apply in this evolving climate. Keep yourself informed, set limits for your children, keep communication open, and know where and with whom your child is hanging out. Monitoring your child's activities in cyberspace is necessary, and we'll go into detail in chapter 10. But potential pitfalls, hazards, and dangers can be found in any unsupervised activity, sloppily managed child-serving program or agency, or any place where your child's undeveloped judgment is put to the test.

CHAPTER 8

If It Takes a Village, What's Up in Yours?

Children and teenagers receive messages on sexuality from many sources, and this chapter's aim is to help you neutralize or moderate the damage from these messages to your children, no matter their age. You'll learn what these messages are communicating to your children and how you can make sure they are getting accurate information and developing sound value systems in terms of sexual health and wellbeing. Media, of course, send messages to your child as well, and this will be covered in chapter 9.

Friends

Life is one big exploration for a child moving through grade school, and there's nothing like a trusted friend to take along on the journey. Grade-school kids are so inquisitive that some conversations with a ten-year-old can feel like being grilled by an investigative reporter. There are just so many things they want to know, and curiosity about sex is often on the list. Many people report learning their first information about sex—for better or worse—from other kids in elementary school. A dominant child in a same-sex group of grade-school kids may establish his status by sharing his wealth of "forbidden" information about sex with his peers—information that is rarely accurate. "The popular girl in our crowd, the one who everyone wanted to be like, provided graphic descriptions of penises and scared everyone to death," one woman shared in a focus group. "For the longest time, I thought that a penis was shaped like an arm and was twice as hairy!"

But peers bring more than information to the table. They reflect a child's self-image, a preview of where a child thinks she will fit into the world, and validates her position among her peers. "Boys will only like you because you have boobs," one woman recalls being told in fourth grade, and as an adult she realizes that this concept stayed with her for decades. "You're too lame to play goalkeeper," a man recalls being told by bigger kids as a child, and he struggled to get beyond that image for years after.

Peers will influence what your child thinks is cool, what he wants to wear, and how he perceives himself. While you can't control what your child hears on the playground or soccer field, you can try to steer your son or daughter towards friends whose values are similar to those of your family. What shows on a family's surface may be nothing like the reality, so making friends with the parents of your children's friends can be one strategy to ensuring your child is hanging with the right crowd. Befriending other parents will make it easier for you to check in with each other routinely to compare notes on what the kids are up to and it can help parents become comfortable imposing shared rules and limits on each other's kids.

Compare that to the experience shared by a mother of a ten-year-old who was told by a misbehaving neighborhood eleven-year-old that his mom said he didn't have to listen to her. In this neighborhood, the highest fence may never make that family into a good neighbor, but a social boundary is a good idea; this mom wants her child to avoid learning anything from an unsupervised, undisciplined child who disrespects adults.

As your children grow older, it is unrealistic to think that you can influence their choice of friends or limit them to spending time with children of simpatico families. But you can allow extended visits or sleepovers only to homes where you know or trust the parents. There really are parents who think it's cool to help a child deceive his own parents—parents who buy the seventeen-year-olds alcohol, or allow coed sleepovers against your regulations, or even cover for a teen to date someone forbidden by her family. If you ever find this to be the case, create a permanent distance from this family; don't allow for a second opportunity to be misled. Integrity is rarely situational.

Spend as much time as possible listening to and observing your children's interactions with their peers. Chaperoning school events, or showing up fifteen minutes early to pick them up from a game or practice can provide a wealth of information to an observant parent. Who is being nice to your kid? Which kids are showing respect to the coaches or teacher? Who insults her parents when they arrive for pick-up? Discuss your observations with your child, using this as another opportunity to promote values of respect and empathy, which are critical components of sexual health and safety.

Kids pick up information and values from friends, so use every opportunity possible to check that the information is correct and the values match your own.

Let's revisit the car ride. So many kids sitting in the backseat come to regard the driver of the vehicle as just another automobile accessory. However, rather than feeling insulted by this, if you're the driver, think about what you can learn from your kids while they pretend you don't exist. Playing chauffer can provide a treasure trove of information of what's going on with your kids and their friends. While you most likely will not be privy to the most private conversations among BFFs, and should refrain from jumping into your kids' conversation unless you hear egregious misinformation, you will have the unique opportunity to use what you've seen and heard to open discussions with your child when you get home.

So What Can You Do?

- Take every possible opportunity to observe your kids with their friends— be the chaperone or driver whenever you can.
- Befriend the parents of your children's friends, speak regularly, and compare notes. Listen closely to conversations among kids and discuss what you've heard with your child later at home. Your child will stop speaking in front of you soon enough, so capitalize on the opportunity while you can.
- Only allow your child to have lengthy or overnight visits at homes where you know and trust all of the adults—the ones who live there, including older siblings, as well as anyone who might be visiting at the time of your child's stay.
- Make sure your child has correct information to counteract misinformation from friends. By adolescence, kids are almost guaranteed to share

information about sex with each other; if you don't want your younger child sharing what you've taught them, borrow this line a focus group participant shared: "My parents told me to keep this new information (about sex) to myself, because it was the special job of parents to get to tell their own kids."

School

In the next chapter, we'll spend a great deal of time learning to understand the sexual climate of your child's school and both the formal and informal messages that flourish in that environment. For our purposes in this chapter, we'll discuss how the treatment by school personnel can play an important role in your child's developing self-image. Karen, a focus group member, told me that when her nine-year-old daughter got her first period at school, the school nurse called her and said, "Something exciting is happening. I want Susan to tell you herself." There was nothing bad, mysterious, or dirty in the message from this school nurse—just the support and acknowledgement of a life event. How different this mindset was than the memory of a woman I spoke to who, in the 1960s, was sent home as "sick" when her period began.

Schools also send messages about sex roles. Are chores and toys for the little ones assigned along traditional sex roles? Do your kids have the opportunity to experience members of both genders demonstrating both nurturing and authoritative behaviors? Preschool children accept things at face value, so finding a school that demonstrates role equality is important. School-aged and older kids can engage in discussions about what can be expected from males and females and the value of options being open to both genders.

And of course we have the issues of sex education in schools. While a school may or may not have a specific sex education class, you still want to know that all body systems are covered in science class by junior high school so your child has accurate information to draw from.

Learn what your child's school is doing to support sexual health and safety among its students. Has the school contracted with a local prevention agency to deliver a proven program? Most comprehensive sex abuse prevention programs in schools have a parent component; be sure to participate when your school brings it in. Does the school have a gay–straight alliance? Even the U.S. Centers for Disease Control and Prevention recommends in-school inclusive organizations to promote a climate of tolerance and safety for all, no matter a person's sexual preference.

I've worked with a great many school administrators over the years, and I know one reason that parental concerns go unheeded is because administrators know that a parent's interest generally extends only as long as their child is enrolled in that particular school. An administrator can repeatedly stall on taking the action you request, waiting until your kids graduate and you and your concern go away. If something is amiss in your child's school, *don't be stonewalled* by this attitude. Feel free to borrow the phrase that I had to use with a summer camp director who invited me to withdraw my son when I found the camp's safety policies lacking: "If it's not safe enough for my kid then it's not safe enough for any kid." Of course it didn't hurt that I was a government official at the time, but the safety improvements sought by myself and other parents were implemented at the camp within weeks. You, your children, and their classmates will benefit much more if a school administrator knows that your concern will not simply go away once your child graduates so be vocal and proactive to make your school a sexually safe and healthy environment for children of all ages and cohorts.

So What Can You Do?

- Contact your local school district if you have not seen information indicating curricula or programs on sexual health or safety by the time your child reaches the fifth grade. Assist the overworked school administrators by finding a reputable sexual abuse prevention program in your community and offer to help arrange to bring them to your school. The information in Appendix 2 can help generate ideas.
- When contacting your child's school about a perceived problem, be very specific about identifying the issue that you find unsatisfactory and suggest a reasonable solution including a timeline for implementation.
- Follow up on your concerns, politely seeking periodic status reports, but don't hesitate to take your concerns higher up the administration if solutions are not forthcoming.

Health-care Professionals

Health-care professionals can be an excellent source of sexual information for your child. Pediatricians should start asking to speak to your pre-adolescent child without you as part of an annual physical exam. These talks are supposed to provide the opportunity for your child to ask any question on his mind, and for the physician to provide "anticipatory guidance" by informing your child of the changes he can expect in the coming year. Some pediatricians develop a sensitive way to ask a child if someone is being abusive in any way. Many states require that pediatricians attend a child abuse identification and prevention seminar as part of their annual continuing education requirement; this may provide the impetus to ask sensitive questions. Children lucky enough to have the same pediatrician year after year may actually feel very comfortable asking or answering questions, but many will not. However, even if your child stares at the floor while alone with the doctor, he will still hear the content of the anticipatory guidance message and just may feel empowered to ask his questions later.

So What Can You Do?

- Choose a pediatrician who follows the American Academy of Pediatrics (AAP) guidelines and provides anticipatory guidance to you *and* your child.
- Speak with your child's pediatrician and express your wish that he or she address sexual health and safety with your child in an age-appropriate way.
- See if your state requires a child abuse identification and prevention seminar as part of pediatricians' continuing education requirements. If not, contact your state legislator—it seems reasonable that advocating for this change in law would be popular with most voters.

Religion

People who choose to send their child for religious education generally want to ensure that their child learns the traditions and values passed down for generations. Mainstream religions practiced in the United States promote tradition, family unity and service, and offer rituals to commemorate life events. Regardless of the specific religious tradition, the concept of spirituality provides a perfect backdrop to teach the values of love, empathy, honesty, and respect, which are all critical components of sexual health and safety.

Religious leaders and institutions are among the most respected in many communities and are in a perfect position to support you as a parent with programs to provide medically accurate information within the context of their specific theology. People look to their religious institutions for advice and guidance, and national surveys show that many people believe that religious institutions can do even more in the area of sexuality awareness and education. One national study found that the majority of teens and adults surveyed believe "religious leaders and groups should be doing more to help prevent teen pregnancy."[57]

But using the bully pulpit is not enough. The program evaluations demonstrating the ineffectiveness of abstinence-only sex education programs have a lesson for religious institutions: They must do more than put an authority figure on the pulpit and preach the evils of non-marital sex. Responsible and responsive religious institutions can partner with health educators, sex educators, or medical personnel in the congregation or community, offer workshops for parents to support them as they develop the comfort and skills to speak with their kids about sex, or invite vetted experts into youth group meetings. At the very least, faith-based institutions can provide pamphlets to parents and remind them of their responsibility to provide sex information to their children. So if you are involved in a religious institution, help to establish a sex-information program for children and parents or become involved in one it may already offer.

Jeff, father of three kids in their twenties, recalls that his wife "had 'the talk' with our oldest daughter, and I bought our second child, my son, a book. By the time our youngest hit adolescence our church had developed the OWL program."An acronym for Our Whole Lives, OWL is a curriculum developed by the Unitarian Universalist (UU) Church and is offered to parents *and* their children. OWL offers specific modules for people from kindergarten to adults

---

57   Albert, B. *With One Voice 2010: America's Adults and Teens Sound Off About Teen Pregnancy.* Washington, D.C.: The National Campaign to Prevent Teen and Unplanned Pregnancy, 2010.

over the age of thirty-five, making it clear that sexuality is a lifelong progression.[58]

The UU initiative may be among the most comprehensive, but faith-based groups representing every major American religion have something to say about the sexual education of children. From Methodists to Muslims, from the LDS to Catholics and Jews, **there is not a single mainstream religion that denies the importance of sex or the responsibility of parents to prepare their children for a sexually healthy adulthood.**

The major religions in the United States promote the sanctity of the family unit and acknowledge that loving sexual relations among adults is a part of family life. Many of their national governing bodies or auxiliary organizations offer resources infusing medically accurate information with the specific religious values, yet religious and faith-based organizations are largely untapped resources for parental support. Unfortunately, it is easier to find material from denominations opining on the evils of comprehensive sex education in public schools than it is to find denominations offering support to families and congregations. Everybody loses when congregations and faith-based organizations abandon their opportunity to help parents be the primary sexuality educator of their children providing values and information.

So What Can You Do?

- Contact your clergyperson and offer to help them bring your denomination's perspective on sexuality to the parents and children in your congregation.
- Do your own online or library research to find materials that match the values of your religious tradition and bring them to the institution's leaders and other parents.
- Encourage your religious institution to use medically accurate, faith-based sexuality education materials and get the discussion going! An easy first step could be to organize a parents' workshop. You can start with something as simple as reviewing pamphlets and information together; see Appendix 2 for some ideas.

---

58   See http://www.uua.org/religiouseducation/curricula/ourwhole/.

- Is there a member of your congregation comfortable with and knowledge-able of sexual issues? A physician, nurse, health teacher—even a pharma-ceutical salesperson working with reproductive health might be able to blend medically accurate information with your faith's perspective and lead the parents' group.

Community

The word "community" means different things to different people. Communities tend to be defined by something shared, so the term may refer to a specific, contained geographic location or a group of similarly minded people within a larger geographic community. People refer to their parish community, the Black community, the GLBTQ community, and so on. Community members communicate messages to your child about behaviors and sexuality, and these messages may go either way in supporting sexual health and safety.

Community values and norms, even the unspoken ones, can have a dramatic impact on the sexual health and safety of children. The tragedy surrounding the 2011 allegations of the long-term, serial rape of children by a respected member of the State College, Pennsylvania community will continue to provide both pundits and scholars the fuel to speculate about how so many people in one community failed to act in the face of so much evidence. The grand jury findings of the initial investigation[59] indicate that some people believed that there may have been a steep price to pay for speaking up on behalf of children, such as potentially losing a job. In this case, we now see that being different from the rest of the community, no matter how difficult, might have meant being a hero and saving many children from victimization.

One focus group mom expressed a common concern about the possibility of being different in some way from the rest of her community in a very different way when she said, "I have a huge concern about how I raise my children, in relation to how the world operates." She shared her surprise that two visiting children had values about modesty so different than hers that they became alarmed when her five-year-old son came downstairs in his bathrobe.

---

59   See http://www.attorneygeneral.gov/uploadedFiles/Press/Sandusky-Grand-Jury-Present ment.pdf.

"There are just too many mixed messages from home and the world," she told me. You have a great opportunity to share your values and beliefs as a parent when you help a child decipher the mixed messages she receives in the community.

Another mom offered the suggestion that "we need to express to our kids what [we] the parents believe," then help them understand the world surrounding them, and ultimately "they must learn to assimilate in that world." Still other parents hold values that disdain assimilation; you should pay attention to the range of values expressed within the various communities you claim to be part of, and openly discuss with your children how and why these values relate to your own.

You can find additional challenges raising kids when they're moved from one community to another. Differences can be subtle or blatant in new environments. A mom who spent the first twelve years of her children's lives in a Scandinavian country before returning to the United States shared the culture shock her adolescent children found when their peers in a well-regarded school in a liberal, affluent suburb were completely unschooled in sexual issues. Her son, who casually mentions his wet dreams at home, was sad that so many of his friends were left to figure out this normal, healthy phenomenon without parental support.

"Communities" can also refer to formal groups that our kids join as teens. Athletic teams, leagues, arts groups, and other clubs can become a community for kids, a place where they find acceptance and the first sense of belonging somewhere outside the home. Clubs, teams, and other groups can have a powerful influence on teens. They establish their own rules, norms, expectations, and social hierarchies. At best, they can provide mutual support and encouragement to help teens become their very best selves. At worst, they can have all of the attributes of a gang. A very closed group can teach your child values like exclusion and marginalization. In chapters 5 and 7, we discussed in detail how and why teens are naturally lacking in empathy and have yet to develop the brain capacity necessary for good judgment. Loyalty to an exclusive "community," whether formal or informal, may hamper an adolescent's ability to develop empathy, compassion, and respect for people unlike themselves. You as the parent must intervene if you see this happening with your child. A critical developmental task of adolescence is to truly understand the impact one's behavior has on another person, but that's just the first step. You want your kids to care if that impact is positive or negative. So-called in-groups can be remarkably cruel; no matter how proud you may be that your son or daughter is accepted by a club, team, or social circle, look and listen to make sure that it is a community with values that match your own.

So What Can You Do?

- When feasible, observe events sponsored by actual clubs or formal groups.
- Listen to how your child describes who gets to be a member of the group he or she is a part of. Is it tolerant or harmfully exclusive?
- Encourage your child to find "community" among groups whose values match your own.

Siblings: The Good, the Bad, and the Ugly

Sibling relationships are among the most significant for impacting a child's developing self-image and personality, yet sibling relationships are the least studied and discussed by social researchers. Many kids spend the first years of their life sharing the most intimate human experiences with their siblings, from sleeping in the same room or bed to sharing baths, fights, made-up words and games, secrets, and drowsy cuddles. It makes perfect sense that siblings have a strong influence on what and how the other kids in the family learn. There's a lot to be gleaned from and about sibling relationships, and we can apply their lessons to keeping our kids sexually safe and healthy.

Bullying Often Begins in the Home

I was raised by a mother who had no siblings, and I can still recall the horror on her face when my siblings and I fought. Our mom had no idea that this was typical, and in fact sociologists now tell us that there may even be some benefits from kids learning to resolve conflicts with people they actually love. Balance in the family is key. Kids who experience love and nurturing from siblings, along with conflict and resolution, have been found to "be more socially skilled and have more positive peer relationships compared with children who lack this experience."[60] So when your kids fight, comfort yourself that they actually may be helping to socialize each other in a very positive and productive way.

But pay close attention to the overall quality of the relationship between your children and the fights among siblings, particularly to whether or not the conflicts really are resolved. An ongoing conflict can mask the fact that one sibling is actually terrifying or bullying another. Siblings lacking empathy, or a real understanding of the impact of their bullying, are a risk to the other kids. We know from sociologic studies that oldest siblings, particularly males, are the most common family bullies; in fact, the presence of an older brother is the best predictor for in-family bullying.[61] Personality characteristics also come into play here; active, outgoing kids are more like to be bullies than quiet, introverted kids.

An older son (or any child) lacking empathy is a red-flag situation for you and your partner. Learning to have empathy for others is a key developmental task, and one that should be completed during your child's adolescence—this allows your child to enjoy healthy relationships later as an adult. If you have a child who is bullying his siblings, you must be sure he receives specific personal attention from you and other significant adults in his life to learn that his behaviors affect people in negative ways. Model appropriate behaviors and reward your child when he shows them.

Older kids may naturally relate with the parental authority figures, having been in the family before the younger ones arrived. Older sisters may be more predisposed to caretaking and nurturing, while older brothers often exert dominance. As soon as you see the first signs of inappropriate or excessive teasing or bullying from the bigger or older kids in the family, remind them that they have not earned the right to exert authority or dominance over the younger siblings.

60　Hetherington, E. M., as cited in Brody, Gene H. "Siblings' Direct and Indirect Contributions to Child Development." *Current Directions in Psychological Science*, 2004: 124–126.

61　Ersilia Menesini, Marina Camodeca, and Annalaura Nocentini. "Bullying among siblings: The role of personality and relational variables." *British Journal of Developmental Psychology*, No. 28, 2010: 921–939.

Kids Learn from Their Siblings in Significant Ways

In happy, healthy families, kids are important early teachers for their younger siblings. By middle school, older siblings have the skills to teach important cognitive and social skills to their younger brothers and sisters. More importantly, older siblings often act as the translator between younger kids and parents, with younger kids turning to trusted older siblings to obtain a sense of what the adults think about a particular topic. "How can we get around Mom on this one?" or "Who's more likely to let me go out with my friends?" or "Mom will kill you if she sees that!" are the kinds of communication common among siblings sharing the inside information of their family norms and expectations with each other.

Once we acknowledge the importance of siblings in teaching and socializing each other, it is not at all surprising to learn that siblings play an important role in how kids learn about sexuality. Focus group members and professionals participating in my training sessions routinely refer to their older siblings as sources of information about sex when they were growing up. Siblings are not just providing the facts; social researchers have found that they are among the most vital sources of messages to young people as they learn family and community norms and expectations about sexuality.

Kids really get the message when both you and their siblings discuss safe sex. Attitudes toward sex "were safer when they also reported more frequent discussions about these issues with both their parents and siblings."[62] This same study also found higher levels of skill for communicating with partners about condom use and for buying and using condoms. [63] In other words, when kids speak both with their siblings and you about sex, they show safer attitudes about sexual behavior out in the world. Some studies even recommend targeting adolescent boys for training on how to share sexual health information with their younger brothers,[64] especially since boys are at a higher risk for unsafe sex practices than girls.

---

62 Kolburn Kowal, Amanda and Lynn Blinn-Pike. "Sibling Influences on Adolescents' Attitudes Toward Safe Sex Practices." *Family Relations*, No. 53, 2004: 381.

63 Ibid.

64 Ibid.

Siblings are a source of lessons on broader aspects of sexual health and safety as well. Jean, a focus group participant in her thirties, reports that she "wanted to date and marry someone who had a sister. Boys with sisters grow up to be more considerate men. I really believe this after dating both men who did not did not have sisters." Nan, another focus group participant, said that her older brother completely changed the way he treated the women he dated when he saw how happy she was at the kind and considerate treatment of a high-school boyfriend. Lessons about relationships don't get any more basic or important than these.

Older siblings can also function as parental substitutes. Cal, a man in his forties, described that having a sister ten years his senior was like having a second mother. Marilyn, another interviewee, described her older son taking on a parental role when his twelve-year-old sister starting her first menstrual period in school while her parents were traveling. This twelve-year-old was excused from her own class, made her way to her brother's classroom in another wing of the building, and called him into the corridor; he escorted her to the nearest drug store to buy tampons.

Not all sibling memories are of warm, supportive, or educational behavior however. Sue, a woman in her fifties, recalled that her older sister—with whom she shared a bedroom—saw her dancing in front of the mirror and screamed, "Ooooo . . . that's disgusting—that dance looks like sex," when of course the younger sister had no idea what sex really was or what it might possibly look like. But Sue recalled, "I never danced like that again." Len, a man in forties, said that he and his sister negotiated a "you show me yours and I'll show you mine" session as grade school kids, but he confounded his sister by hiding his penis between his legs. "She kept staring at my crotch and all she saw were my thighs closed tight," he reported, still pleased with his deception.

Another woman remembered her surprise at finding her copy of the popular menstruation education pamphlet "Growing Up and Liking It" she'd received from her divorced mother hidden under the pillow of her younger brother. "It never occurred to me that he had to learn this stuff somewhere; here he was in a house full of women—who was teaching him about what was going to change in his body? Not our father, I'm sure." That brother had a passive lesson from his sister, but in other families, older siblings take the initiative. Leslie, a health-care professional and mother of three, reported that her eldest child took it upon herself to ensure that her little brothers knew what she thought they needed to know about sex. "She felt responsible for them not going out there unprepared," Leslie proudly announced.

At best, siblings can be helpful, supportive, and responsible. Some siblings want to lovingly help their brothers or sisters make the transition into adulthood. But harmful behavior abounds in family circles, like shaming a younger sibling for an innocent dance or planting frightening images of intercourse worthy of a horror story, complete with blood and screaming, in a young child's mind. And at worst, siblings can be the perpetrators of sexual abuse in their own households.

Siblings and Sex Abuse

Abuse by siblings is probably among the most under-reported forms of sexual victimization. We know that siblings hurt each other; one study estimates that over 29 million children commit an act of violence against a sibling each year.[65] In one widely cited survey of college students, results showed that 13 percent of this population reported sibling incest.[66] Higher and lower estimates can be found, and researchers agree that the real prevalence is still unknown. But case studies and anecdotes are plentiful in professional literature on childhood sex abuse; there is no denying that sexual activity and abuse does occur among siblings.

Most of the cases reported involve an older male sibling abusing his younger sister. Most cases described also seem to involve problems with the family dynamics in general; the older, victimizing child is favored in some way, or the victimized child is shunned or made a scapegoat within the family. We've all seen families like this, where one child clearly is the family superstar, or another seems ignored.

Frankly, the dynamics involved with sibling incest are such that a parent aware and concerned enough to be reading this book has most likely paid enough attention to the relationships among their own kids so there is little to worry about. But watch for these dynamics in the families that are part of your

---

65   Straus, M. and R. Gelles. "How violent are American families: estimates from the national family violence survey and other studies." *Family Abuse and Its Consequences: New Directions in Research.* Edited by G. Hotaling et al., 1998.

66   Finkelhor. "Sex Among Siblings: A survey on prevalence, variety and effects." *Archives of Sexual Behavior* (9), 1980: 171–194.

or your child's life. The obnoxious, entitled teammate of your adolescent son just may think he's entitled to use his little sister to relieve his sexual tension. The cousin whose tickling keeps going on when a younger child cries for her to stop may believe her fun is more important that another child's distress. Many more kids sexually victimize each other than the adults lucky enough to reach adulthood unscathed would like to believe.

So What Can You Do?

- Model respect and love for all family members.
- Teach empathy by emphasizing the Golden Rule: "Do unto others as you would have them do unto you."[67]
- Stop bullying between siblings the minute you see it. What you see is most likely the tip of the iceberg of how they're interacting with each other.
- Pay close attention to complaints from a child about a sibling—while some kids do make up stories to get a sibling in trouble, most have a legitimate concern. Remember that statistically, oldest brothers present the largest risk to younger siblings.
- Do not allow one child to become the family scapegoat or the one child always teased, punished, or treated poorly. If you see this happening in a family you're close to, consider helping the parents see this dynamic and start to take measures to eliminate it.
- Make sure that your adolescents—particularly boys—know that erections from unexpected autonomic sexual arousal is a big part of adolescence and that the erection is his own issue to resolve.
- Pay attention to reports of what happens when the kids are left alone without parental supervision. Ask each child individually how the time was spent and follow up if their answers don't match. Follow the same suggestions offered for monitoring daycare providers, particularly occasionally stopping home unannounced.
- Praise and encourage older siblings for being responsible and loving to their younger siblings.

67   Singer, Ken. *Evicting the Perpetrator: A male survivor's guide to recovery from childhood sexual abuse*. Massachusetts: NEARI Press, 2010. page 83

- Listen carefully if one child claims to be a target for mistreatment; while the injustices of the juvenile community in your home may be invisible to adults, these complaints reflect someone's legitimate feelings and should be given time and attention.

You, the Parents! Parents Underestimate the Power of Their Influence

When I ask adults where they learned about sex and sexuality, almost all mention the messages they received from their parents. Not all messages were direct; indirect messages like blushing bright red when discussing menstruation or standing on front of the television when passionate kissing came on the screen figure prominently in the memories of many adults. With all of their authority, parents tend to underestimate the impact they have on their own children, so be wary of this with your own children. My observations echo a 2010 national survey by The National Campaign to Prevent Teen and Unplanned Pregnancy, who found that:

- "Teens continue to say that parents (46 percent) most influence their decisions about sex.
- By comparison, just 20 percent say friends most influence their decisions.
- Eight in ten teens say that it would be much easier for teens to delay sexual activity and avoid teen pregnancy if they were able to have more open, honest conversations about these topics with their parents.
- Six in ten teens (62 percent) wish they were able to talk more openly about relationships with their parents."[68]

This was a well-constructed national survey with very good statistical validity so pay attention: **Kids report that their parents have more influence on their decisions about sex than their friends!** If nothing else you've read so far empowers you to talk with your kids about sexuality, I hope this does. If you don't believe this, you're not alone; this and other research

---

68 Albert, B. *With One Voice 2010: America's Adults and Teens sound Off About Teen Pregnancy.* Washington, D.C.: The National Campaign to Prevent Teen and Unplanned Pregnancy, 2010.

surveying parents show that they routinely underestimate the importance they played in the sexual socialization of their children.

When your kids communicate with you about sex, they are more likely to develop healthy attitudes about sex. "Adolescents' attitudes toward sex were predicted by discussions with parents," reports another study. [69] Your child's feeling of closeness with you and your partner, parental communication, comfort in discussing sensitive topics, and supervised television viewing all play a role in promoting sexually safe and healthy behaviors like postponing voluntary sexual activity. And these conclusions are based on feedback that comes from teens. Younger children who have not yet developed the natural desire to ignore parents are even more open to hear age-appropriate parental messages about sexuality.

Here's another good reason to keep the communication open, one that I've repeated throughout this book: These same parenting activities known to reduce voluntary sexual activity will help enable your child to seek your support if someone initiates involuntary sexual activity or if they are sexually abused. Clearly, kids believe that you, their parents, play an important role in promoting their sexual health and safety. These same human beings who brush you off and act disinterested actually report to researchers that they really want advice and information, so keep at it even when your child does not seem to be listening.

So What Can You Do?

- Never underestimate the influence you have on the sexual health and safety of your child.
- When you're getting ready to start a conversation with your child, remind yourself of the statistics provided in this section. Repeat to yourself: *Parents routinely underestimate the influence they have on their kids decisions about sex. The majority of kids wish they were able to talk openly to their parents about sex.* Let that be your internal pep talk when gearing up to speak with your kids about sex.
- Remember that your kids want to hear what you have to say about sexual health and safety, even adolescents who act like they don't.

---

69   Kolburn Kowal, Amanda, and Lynn Blinn-Pike. "Sibling Influences on Adolescents' Attitudes Toward Safe Sex Practices." *Family Relations*, No. 53, 2004: 377–384.

What If You Suspect Unstable Dynamics in Another Family or in Your Community?

First, here's the basic rule: Every state in the United States has a law in its books regarding the required reporting of child abuse to the child protection or law enforcement authorities. An explanation of the public systems can be found in chapter 13, and contact information for each state's child abuse reporting hot line is in Appendix 1. If a child is physically injured, or tells you that sexual abuse is going on in their home, school, or other institution, there's nothing to think about—call the authorities immediately. You don't have the proper judgment to know if the child is telling the truth, and you don't want the responsibility of sending a child back into a potentially dangerous situation.

Most of our concerns aren't so cut and dried. Imagine that a child says an uncle gives her the creeps. Your daughter's best friend hates that her newly single parent is having sleepover dates. A young child who visits your home seems to be precociously sexual, at least by your standards. Once again, communication is the key in each of these instances to determine if sexual abuse is at the forefront of the behavior and statements.

Listen carefully to children, being careful not to plant ideas with poorly worded questions; use the information on structuring questions offered in chapter 13 to hold discussions in your home. Make a considered decision to contact the child's parents, and practice sounding *concerned* rather than *judgmental*: "I thought I'd share that Jill expressed discomfort with something, and whether it's real or not, I thought it would be irresponsible of me not to let you know." Work at maintaining a non-judgmental tone—one good hint is to start your sentences with "I" instead of "you"; keep comments about your concerns and not the other person's behavior. The parent of your child's friend may be going through a difficult emotional time, and adults in pain may find it hard to tune into their kids. Offer support without judgment but do follow up to ensure the child is safe at home.

What if you see something disturbing in public? Most of us have considered that question of what to do if we see a parent unloading on a child in a public place, and most people choose to stay away. This is a difficult personal decision, and if you choose to offer assistance, remember the rule to show empathy for the parent and use "I-statements" to express your concern: "I'm upset to see you in such distress—can I help?" is much better than "What are you thinking talking to a child that way!"

What kinds of signs might you see in public that indicate a child is being sexually abused? One of the easiest to see, and the one most overlooked, is an adult in the neighborhood with an extraordinary array of kids visiting his or her home. If there is one home where children seem to congregate, pay greater attention. Pedophiles often engage kids in fun-filled activities and build on the intimacy of these shared activities to initiate sex. Adults seeking sex with adolescents may do likewise. So the nice older man who gives out candy when the kids get off the school bus may have his own needs in mind—needs that are unsafe for your child's sexual wellbeing. Don't be paranoid, but definitely be aware of the adults in your child's life.

So What Can You Do?

- Practice a supporting, empathic, non-judgmental phrase you can use if you see a problem with your child or another.
- Consider learning more about the community prevention programs sponsored by Stop it Now! (www.StopitNow.org) or your states, chapter of Prevent Child Abuse-America (www.PreventChildAbuse.org).
- Don't be afraid to pay an unexpected visit to the neighbor's house where kids like to hang out; maybe you need to borrow a cup of sugar?

CHAPTER 9

Assessing the Sexual Climate in Your Child's School

What Is "Sexual Climate"?

How often do you think about the weather? Most of us pay no attention to the actual climate surrounding us unless something extraordinary happens—a horrible storm or a gloriously sunny day in the middle of winter. Likewise, most people pay no attention to the sexual climate in the places they spend their time each day until something doesn't feel right. Maybe the jokes are just a little bit too risqué or displays of affection don't leave you with a good feeling, or questionable photos are hanging over a colleague's desk; something just feels unsafe and at times downright creepy.

Your child spends most of her waking hours in school, and schools each have their own climate or "social feel." Education experts conduct studies highlighting the relationship between school climate and bullying, school climate and achievement, school climate and discipline, and other similar issues. In the same way, you need to examine your child's school climate and sexual safety and understand how to recognize signs that the climate may be turning dangerous.

According to one authoritative study of school *culture*, this is defined as "the shared beliefs and attitudes that characterize the district-wide organization."[70] In simpler terms, this means that a district might have documents such as a mission statement or policy manuals that define the formal expectations for conduct and behavior. School *climate* describes how it actually feels to be in a building, that intangible attitude that's so vital yet so hard to measure. A healthy school climate supports an environment where people treat each other with dignity and respect not only because the policies dictate those in the school must do so, but the people in the school actually want to. School climate very much depends of the personalities of the administration and staff and how they treat each other and the students.

This concept can be hard to grasp because most of us spend time in very few schools—only the schools we attended as a child and now the one our child attends. This limited experience makes it almost impossible to grasp how widely the climate can vary from building to building. As a parent, you'd like to be able to answer the question, "What affects the way students and faculty feel about being in the same building all day every day?"

If you think about your own school experience, you may remember at least one teacher who gave you the creeps—the history teacher who spoke to young women's breasts or the biology teacher whose risqué jokes made her popular while making some students cringe. In recent years, tainted sexual climates in schools is one reason why locker room discomfort has become so prevalent that many schools no longer ask students to shower after physical education classes.

I'll bet if you ask your friends, you'll find at least one who will say that there was a sexual relationship between a teacher and student that everyone suspected or knew about when she was in school. Throughout my career, I have come in contact with people who work in schools where "everyone knows" that a teacher is sexually involved with a student but take no action, and with people who work in a school where a teacher is subject to maximum sanctions for uttering as much as an inappropriate word while teaching a class. The laws and rules are the same in each place, but the context, or school climate, is behind the differences.

---

70 Tableman, Betty, and Adrienne Herron. "School Climate and Learning." *Best Practice Briefs*, Number 31. University-Community Partnerships at@ Michigan State University, 2004.

Younger Kids

My first job working in child sexual abuse was as a staff member of a twenty-four-hour hotline specifically aimed at reaching victims of sexual abuse. Once I answered a call from a young-sounding girl who asked, "Is this the sex police?" After assuring her I could listen to her concern, I learned that she wanted someone to help her because boys were lifting up her dress on the school playground. It's possible you might be thinking, "Well, boys will be boys," and be absolutely right. But this can move quickly into the "not OK" category when a child continues to ask that a behavior stop and no one gives her support by disciplining the aggressive child. With younger children, sexual climate issues are expressed in ways that may not appear to be sexually explicit—such as bullying, teasing, or disrespect—but you should be cognizant of them anyway and be prepared to speak with your child and the staff at any school or daycare where this is happening.

A parent of a grade school child heard his son refer to another eight-year-old as a "faggot." The dad asked the child what this meant and was told by his son that it meant the other child was weird, and that all of the kids knew that the other boy was a faggot. If you hear this language from your child, pause and consider if a teacher ever heard this in the schoolyard or lunchroom. If so, did he take any steps to intervene? Would he know how? A young child may have no idea that his word for weird has a sexual connotation, but the victim of the taunt *will* remember that word. The danger of this aspect of sexual climate is gaining more attention as the public becomes aware of the damage this does to sexual minority youth, exemplified by a higher-than-average suicide rate. Teaching young children respect for differences of any kind at a young age will most certainly pay off for decades.

Not too long ago, one would have considered risk of sexual exploitation at school to be an issue primarily for girls in middle or high school. Then Mary Kay Letourneau "had a sexual relationship" with a male grade-school student and the world was shocked into reality. Likewise, clergy scandals and other high profile cases remind us that young children can be at risk from faculty, staff, and religious leaders, and there is the ever-present possibility of a pedophile gaining access to children through the school or religious institution. Your child's risk of exposure to a pedophile is dependent on the more formal aspects associated with sexual culture—pre-employment interviewing, background checks, rules limiting out-of-school contact, and the like. But a teacher's willingness to speak up if she sees something wrong is dependent on the sexual climate in the school.

My son was attending a much respected preschool and one day I received a call that all parents dread—one of the male staff had been arrested for sexual contact with a child at the preschool. My mind immediately flashed to memories of this staff member sitting on the front steps of the school with his arm around my four-year-old as I arrived to pick him up after work. By that point I had been working with child sexual abuse cases for a decade and was working on my PhD research in child welfare—how could my child be at such risk with all that I knew? Had other staff noticed anything amiss and kept it to themselves? Had the owner of the school sensed something but was blinded by the popularity of this staff member? Those unanswered questions continue to haunt me decades after this experience.

Pedophiles are generally careful to behave publicly in distinctly nonsexual ways. They often begin a relationship with a child as a trusted friend or mentor. Since pedophiles are attracted to prepubescent bodies, you should be concerned with the classic pedophile issues if you have little kids, as discussed in more detail in chapter 7. These serious issues are very different from the trap of a teacher succumbing to the overt sexuality swirling around adolescents and teens.

The hormonal surges of puberty start younger and younger these days with girls averaging age twelve for their first periods and age eight for beginning breast development. The average age for America's boys to experience the physical changes is approximately thirteen years old. Long before the hormones start to rage, however, kids show important interest in the basic components that influence sexual health, issues such as relationships with others, self-confidence, bodies, bodily functions, and sex roles; an inappropriate sexual climate in a grade school can leave lifelong scars in these areas while a healthy, supportive sexual climate can help you build a foundation for lifelong sexual health and safety.

It is typical for younger children to come home from school using sex words with incorrect meanings, embarrassed about their physical development or lack of it, or with an outlandish rumor about a faculty member and a student. You need to use your communication skills to determine if the staff at your child's school endorses or encourages any problematic behavior you are hearing about or witnessing firsthand. Ideally, faculty and staff have the training, supervision, and skills to intervene appropriately to bring children going through a normal developmental phase back to reality by offering constructive criticism and alternative acceptable behaviors. If you have reason to believe the staff lacks these skills, express your concerns to the person in charge and suggest they invite a local expert in child development in for a mandatory staff workshop.

Older Kids

School buildings full of adolescents reek of hormones. Hundreds of students with testosterone or estrogen flowing through their bodies in quantities they have yet to assimilate prowl the hallways and fidget through classes. Experienced teachers learn to understand this peculiar developmental phase and figure out how to reach their students in spite of this monumental distraction. One of the strongest arguments for single-gender schools at this age is that adolescents may learn better without the distraction of being sexually attracted to each other. All of this social-sexual intrigue among kids this age is normal. One danger comes when the alpha male (or female) in the group happens to be a teacher or coach so drunk on the heady cocktail of adolescent sexuality that he abdicates his responsibility to set boundaries and enforce standards, and instead becomes a participant.

A young friend of mine only a few years out of school told me of a teacher who became involved with the social intrigue so common in high school—using his status to render opinions of which kids belonged in the more popular social group. This teacher crossed the line and was on his way down the slippery slope of entering the teens' peer group. As long as he kept his hands to himself, he was most likely not subject to formal sanctions at the school, though his behavior was still inappropriate. In a healthy sexual climate, other teachers might have intervened and reminded him to establish better boundaries between himself as the teacher and his students.

On the other end of the continuum, teachers can pollute the sexual climate of a school by abusing their authority. A terrible example of abuse of authority by a teacher is found in the story of Ohio high school health and gym teacher Stacey Schuler, found guilty on sixteen counts of sexual battery in 2011 because she decided to have sex with several members of the football team.[71] For a less blatant but hurtful example, I offer my vivid memory as a student attending a school where the dress code meant skirts or dresses only (no pants) for girls. An old male science teacher always chose the girl with the shortest skirt and had her walk to the blackboard, requiring that she stretch to fill in a blank at the top of the board. Lecherous and humiliating behavior of this kind is a major red flag that something is very wrong with the sexual climate at a school. This man taught hundreds if not thousands of students over several decades and no one ever called him out on this lewd and damaging behavior. If your child tells you about any behavior such as this happening in her classroom, be prepared to make a difficult but important phone call to the school principal or guidance counselor to discuss your child's perception of the teacher's behavior.

How students are allowed to treat each other is another vitally important component of a school's sexual climate. Are boys allowed to make catcalls at girls? Do girls feel safe from being rubbed up against in crowded hallways and stairwells? Is it tolerated if a girl purposely arouses a boy only to sneer at his discomfort?

It's important to remember that males are not exclusively the aggressors in these situations. A focus group member told me of the day her son came home from high school with a condom and a highly suggestive note that a girl had placed in his book bag. If a boy had written those words to a girl, he would have been classified as a sexual aggressor, or worse. Clearly, the sexual climate in this boy's school included a double standard that was offensive, outdated, and damaging to students of both genders.

Adults must pay attention and have patience with teens. You now know the brains of your young folks have not finished developing, particularly in the area responsible for risk taking and judgment. Girl brains become flooded with estrogen and oxytocin—the cuddle and nesting hormones. Boy brains become flooded with testosterone, the aggressor/orgasm-driven hormone. Neither boys nor girls have good judgment at this age because the frontal lobes of their brains are still developing. Both sexes lack empathy and the ability to fully comprehend the impact of their behaviors on others. This

---

71 See http://abcnews.go.com/US/ohio-gym-teacher-jailed-sex-student/
    story?id=14831933

creates an emotional and social minefield that parents, teachers, and anyone else whose life includes adolescents must understand. Schools have a responsibility to maintain an environment that respects these developmental phases but stops those behaviors that cause damage or leave emotional or social scars. And you, as the parent, have the responsibility to instill your values and expectations in your child so he or she can act appropriately and safely in an environment outside of the home.

Listen to your child to determine if she has stories of friends who share information that makes her uncomfortable, a counselor who jumps to conclusions, a teacher who objectifies students, or discrimination based on real or perceived sex roles. If so, gently steer the conversation to learn your child's perception of how the school responds. The best middle and high school administrators are vigilant about the sexual climate in their school and take steps to keep it safe and healthy for all students (and the staff as well).

Teachers and Students

Perhaps the most glaring example of a quietly poisonous sexual climate comes from the story of Monica Lewinsky. Let's see what she learned in high school:

Monica Lewinsky had a long-running affair with a married man—her high school drama teacher. It began just after Lewinsky's graduation in 1991, and ended in 1997, when his wife found out. During that time Lewinsky often babysat for their children.[72]

Does anyone even know this man's name? Every time someone cracks a Monica Lewinsky joke, stop and ask yourself why the man who taught her fellatio as a teen is not in jail. A young woman two years behind Monica in the same school reported that "I was subjected to his advances like many girls our age were at that school."[73] Then ask yourself how many people in her school knew and why it was tolerated for so long. That's what I mean about sexual climate—however we choose to describe the climate in her school, it basically just stunk. Could you recognize this same odor in your community? No

---

72   See http://www.nndb.com/people/588/000025513/.
73   *Monica in Black and White*. HBO TV Special Part 8. http://www.youtube.com/watch?v=JCZm1puUD3Y Accessed 11/6/11

parent wants her child in a school that tolerates sexual encounters between adults and children, even once the children turn eighteen.

Constantly working with teens can be difficult for teachers. Teens and preteens are trying out their new-found sexuality, and literally emanate hormonal signals. No matter how hard you try to monitor your child's dress and action, adolescents will find a way to express themselves, and for many teens that includes expressing their sexuality. Expressing their sexuality can include flirting with adults in school, particularly the younger adults who have the least experience. Many of today's young teachers grew up in the generation where oral sex was hardly considered to be a sexual act. These teachers and their colleagues need a constant reality check to deal with student crushes and flirtations. Teachers need to be constantly reminded of the biological facts of adolescence, and that this sexualized behavior is triggered by many things, which do *not* include the teacher's personal attractiveness. Younger teachers and those facing a midlife crisis are especially vulnerable to having their judgment clouded by sexual attraction to students. Maybe there should be a campaign started for high school teachers, "Remember: They're Just Kids," and signs posted in the teacher's lounge to help confused teachers maintain perspective.

Seven Questions to Ask to Assess Sexual Climate

In chapter 4, you learned how important it is for you to make conscious decisions about the norms you expect to operate in your family, and then model and communicate them to the other members of your family. Wouldn't it be great if the administrators of your child's school did that as well? Remember, norms are expectations, and people rise or sink to the level of what is expected of them. Just as you are encouraged to communicate your norms to your child at home, the formal and informal authorities in the school should also communicate to your child the kinds of behaviors that are expected, tolerated, or punished at the school. What follows is a list of questions for you to consider as you determine if the sexual climate in your child's school feels right to you.[74]

As you carry out your due diligence, look for both the existence of a formal policy—school culture—and the actual way the policy is carried out in

---

74 Based on Betty Tableman, Adrienne Herron, and Mike Muir's *Research Brief, The principals partnership*. 2004, 2006. Accessed at http://www.principalspartnership.com.

your child's school. If the formal policies exist, they are generally accessible from the superintendent's office or through the school's website, but it takes real parental interaction with your child and the school to assess the climate, or how these policies are actually put to work.

1) Is the school's physical environment welcoming and conducive to your child's learning?

To be sexually safe and healthy, kids need to feel physically safe. This is especially so in the places where they undress. Ask your child how much privacy is afforded in the bathrooms, locker rooms, and showers. Is there any adult supervision? If so, who is supervising? If bullying occurs in these places, would an authority know and be able to stop it in a timely manner?

Crowds in schools can also be a problem; halls and stairwells need to be supervised to prevent rubbing or groping. One colleague of mine recalled a "game" played in high school in the 1980s where points were scored for touching certain girls' breasts while moving through the hallway.

Graffiti can also be unsettling in a school, particularly if it is violent or sexually suggestive. If your school has this problem, gauge the reaction of the administration and what actions they are taking to combat the problem; no matter how scarce the resources may be, removing frightening or sexual graffiti needs to be a very high priority for any school authorities. Any graffiti with a child's name should be removed immediately. If you are in a district with few resources, you and other parents can form a volunteer team to help remove graffiti, but a long-term problem requires outside assistance to the school— perhaps from the community services officers in the local police department.

Basic safety issues should also be considered. Halls and parking lots should be well lit, and blind corners outfitted with mirrors. It's true that kids can't learn when they're scared. If using the restroom or moving between classes leaves your child feeling breathless with anxiety, the school climate is out of balance and it is your job as a parent to start taking action to making your (and other people's) children feel safe.

2) What is the school's policy and track record regarding bullying?

To be sexually safe and healthy, kids need to be in a school that does not tolerate bullying and responds with a strong disciplinary and educational program if it becomes a problem.

Bullying is one of the strongest indicators of a social environment that is off-balance. It's getting a lot of much-needed attention in the media now, and people are becoming aware of the emotional devastation it can bring to a child. Bullying has always existed (it was called "scapegoating" a generation ago), and the more fully we understand it, the more we know it often centers on sexual issues. As we consider bullying, remember that a fish rots from the head down; if you attend a school event and hear an administrator making jokes at the expense of staff or otherwise insulting them, take that as a warning signal that this environment tolerates bullying. If the staff work in an environment that disrespects or humiliates them, it is much more likely that they will respond in kind to your child. Contact the administrator privately and express your concern for the damaging behavior, including the fact that you believe she is setting a poor example for the bullies in the school.

Your state may have a formal policy on bullying, but if the staff have not been trained in effectively working to temper bullying, your children may see no programming or materials on the subject. And if no one at the district level monitors progress in the school, the climate may indeed tolerate bullying. Again, the formal policy may mean nothing if the actual climate of the individual school is poisoned by people who find bullying, intimidation, and humiliation to be tools of their trade.

3) What is your child's school's policy and track record regarding sexual harassment?

To be sexually safe and healthy, people of any age deserve to spend their days in an environment free of sexual harassment. Sexual harassment in schools has been against the law since the federal government passed Title IX of the Educational Amendments Act of 1972. A school is required to have and circulate a sexual harassment policy that includes a grievance procedure. Once again, though, the existence of a policy is not enough to stop sexual harassment. The school climate must also be intolerant of these behaviors, punish those who engage in them, *and* support those who make a report.

Your school district should offer periodic in-service training for all faculty and staff to ensure that they are aware of the sexual harassment policy and their responsibility to enforce it. Some schools also offer workshops for students; if taught by a sensitive teacher who understands how very important this topic is, this can be a great learning experience for any child. If, however, the school assigns a wise-cracking guy to teach the workshop, who smirks as he says, "'I wish someone would sexually harass me a little bit," you'll know that the climate in this school only allows for lip service on the policy and that your child may be at risk for being sexually harassed.

4) What is the school's policy and track record regarding teacher–student contact?

To be sexually safe and healthy, kids at school need to be protected from sexual advances from adults, and the policy must be zero-tolerance. A healthy sexual climate encourages interaction between students and faculty with age-appropriate boundaries. Use of first names between teachers and students requires careful consideration. In most schools it implies an artificial familiarity inconsistent with the roles each member plays in the school community.

Clear formal rules on out-of-school interaction between staff and students should exist and be enforced. This includes both actual interaction and virtual interaction such as e-mail, texting, and connecting on social networking sites. This is particularly important since the school's sexual climate can erode gradually and the impersonal nature of virtual communication makes it easier to slip across once-defined boundaries.

Many schools have rules prohibiting a teacher from being completely alone with a child; even when such rules aren't in place, many teachers won't take the risk of being vulnerable to accusations. If your child is going to be alone with a teacher, for example the last one dropped off after a team event of some sort, ask your child specifically how the ride was and what it was like being alone with Mr. or Ms. X.

With younger kids, you need to consider the dangers of a pedophile who may begin a relationship with your child as a friend or mentor; with older kids, you need to be concerned about predators and adults lacking the necessary self-control to manage their own attraction to a teen or to gently extricate themselves from an adolescent crush.

5) What is your child's school's policy on dress code, and how is it enforced?

If can you see belly buttons, breast cleavage, butt cleavage, or suggestive slogans on T-shirts on either students or staff at your child's school, the sexual climate is clearly off balance. It is perfectly natural for kids to push boundaries and show up to school wearing something that bends—if not actually breaks—the dress code rules. School staff should react firmly to any breaches in the rules, while not embarrassing or humiliating the student in any way.

Teachers are not immune from bad judgment in this case either. I certainly remember being a precocious twenty-one-year-old teaching college classes (human sexuality no less) in short cut-offs and a too-tight T-shirt. I sincerely hope someone would have called me out on that in a high school as it's an unprofessional and inappropriate way to dress in front of teenage students.

6) How are sexual issues handled in the classroom?

For your child to be sexually safe and healthy, you should expect that academically appropriate language about sexual issues will be used in context in art, literature, health, biology, social studies, or other classes your student attends. Sexual issues permeate through the arts, and it is disingenuous to pretend they don't. Sexual violence is a theme in many historical and current events, and sexual discrimination is a part of history. But can your child's teachers discuss this in an age-appropriate context? Is open discussion encouraged so students can ask questions and receive answers without feeling judged or unsafe?

In my concept of an ideal world, students would come to school with a clear understanding of their family's particular set of values and beliefs regarding sexuality. School classes would provide the opportunity to add solid information on anatomy, physiology, psychosexual development, and other related areas to the child's knowledge of the subject. Teachers would be able to integrate sexual issues into curriculum as appropriate and teach with confidence and without embarrassment. Parents would read what their children are reading and have family discussions about the content. Facts and opinions would be clearly labeled as such, and differences in opinions could be debated with mutual respect. What would it take to make that happen in your family and community? You can start the process at home by opening the lines of communication and continue this process into your community by working with your school.

7) What specific formal actions are being taken by your child's school to promote a sexually safe and healthy environment?

Throughout my career, I have heard many educators complain that every time a social issue comes up involving kids, the public looks to the schools to fix it. "How can we concentrate in reading and math scores when we're responsible for everything from nutrition to child abuse prevention?" some educators ask. They have a valid point and the competing demands on a school's time and resources must be respected, but never at the expense of the safety of children in the school. Kids can't learn if they're frightened, same as if they're hungry.

There are resources in many communities that can be useful for schools. One example is funding in each state by the U.S. Centers for Disease Control and Prevention for rape prevention and education;[75] most states direct these funds to support programs targeting young people. These funds support program models like the "Green Dot"[76] strategy, which provides the tools for developing and maintaining non-violent social norms in any given community. Schools throughout the country have taken the lead in bringing programs like Green Dot, The Developmental Assets Program of The Search Institute,[77] Every Person Influences Children (EPIC),[78] and others to their communities, involving students, faculty, staff, and parents in bringing about positive change. These are comprehensive programs offering multiple activities over the course of the school year. A one-shot assembly program may fulfill a requirement of some sort, but experts remind us that "dosage matters" and one-shot speeches have little lasting effect.[79] If your child's school can't find funding in its district budget or from another grant, think about collaborating with other parents and raising funds to bring a program like this to your school. It could make a world of difference for your child's sexual health and safety!

---

75 See www.cdc.gov/ViolencePrevention/RPE/.

76 See www.LiveTheGreenDot.com.

77 See www.search-institute.org/developmental-assets.

78 See www.epicforchildren.org/.

79 Regina Podhorin, Evaluator, CDC&P, EMPOWER Rape Prevention Education Project. Personal communication in August 2011.

Conclusion: What You Can Do

If you have real reason to believe there is an actual sexual relationship between an adult and your (or another) child, call the child protection agency in your state immediately. There are no two ways about this. Most states have a designated unit with specially trained staff to investigate cases in schools and other child-serving agencies. There should be no second thoughts on what to do if actual sexual contact is alleged.

The creepy, uncomfortable, or ambiguous situations are tougher to confront, though. A young teacher lacking experience may not have found the right balance between trying to be liked by the students and being an authority figure; accidental slips into inappropriateness can happen. More experienced teachers may have figured out how to flirt with danger by approaching being lewd without crossing into anything actionable. These teachers and staff members, however, also need to be stopped. This type of insidious behavior poisons the sexual climate of your child's school. And their actions may eventually go beyond this point and end up hurting a student—who could be your child.

Let's say that you overhear a conversation while you're driving carpool (keep taking advantage of the fact that drivers become invisible to fourteen-year-olds) that raises a concern about a sexual climate issue in your child's school. Stay calm and wait until you arrive home to bring the concern up with your child. Review your concern calmly. Begin with some clarifying statement, such as, "Did I hear correctly that Mr. X said . . . ?" Continue asking gently probing questions until you are comfortable that you have as much of the story as possible. If you can assure yourself that the children in the car were exaggerating about a particular situation, or that the action is acceptable in the right context, let it go but keep listening for follow-up conversations on the same topic. You may not be able to stop a creepy person from behaving as he does, but you'll gain a lot by opening the dialogue with your kids and reminding them of your family's values and norms.

Listening without showing judgment is key to being a grown-up kids can talk to if they are worried about one of their friends or if they're uncomfortable with the way an adult is acting in school or even at home. If you lose your cool when your child confides in you on a sensitive issue, odds are you won't be told the rest of the story—or at least not truthfully told. Practice keeping your cool with another adult before you find yourself in this conversation with your child. Counselors in training practice reacting calmly to unusual comments from clients, and you can learn from this example.

Do not fall into the trap of promising your child that you will keep a secret. If your child starts a conversation by saying, "If I tell you something, do you promise not to tell anyone?" an appropriate answer is, "If I think you or someone else needs help, I want to make sure they get it." If the child walks away, they will almost certainly be back later to confide in you. If they don't come back to you, gently pursue them by consistently expressing your concern.

Listen carefully to your child. Acknowledge that you find the behavior in question unacceptable, even if it is OK with your child. Don't start a culture war if your child is telling you something that he thinks is funny, such as repeating an off-color joke a coach told at practice. Remember that no adolescent wants to be the one who gets a popular teacher in trouble, but do be sure you tell your child that you think the remark was uncalled for and why.

In this post-Megan's Law era, there are very serious consequences of being labeled a sex offender of any sort. School officials know this and will rightfully work to protect their staff from unfounded complaints. Once again, if you believe that an adult is engaging in sex with a child, contact the police or local child protection agency. On the other hand, if you fear that your child has been exposed to inappropriate language or behavior by a teacher or school staff member, your first contact with the school should be made after gently confirming these circumstances with your child. In an initial meeting with school officials, just ask to be heard. Be prepared to describe the problematic circumstances in as much detail as possible. If you are seeking a remedy, be realistic. For example, it is not at all realistic to insist that someone who showed bad judgment or poor taste be fired. Acknowledge that you understand confidentiality and do not expect the details of any action that may be taken. Then, continue to monitor the situation through continued dialogue with your child.

Some of you may hesitate to ask these kinds of questions about your child's school—what can you really do if you don't like what you find? It's true that most of us can't afford to put our kids in a private school, and even then, what's to say your child won't encounter similar problems there? Study after study shows that parental involvement improves a child's academic performance. Those of you who know this show up for parent-teacher conferences, use your scarce vacation days to chaperone field trips, use your minimal spare time to monitor school electronic bulletin boards, to check homework, to proofread papers, and to find countless other ways to show your support for your child's academic performance. And now, here I am asking you to take on the affective environment, too. I know there are only so many hours in a day and only so many things you can do, but remember that a seed can't grow in contaminated soil. At best your child may not learn; at worst she may be in physical or emotional danger. Once your eyes are open, problems with the sexual climate surrounding your child will become obvious and you'll be able to start taking steps to remedy the problem and keep your and other children safe.

CHAPTER 10

What Are the Media Influences on Your Child's Sexuality?

To Find Out, Be a POS![80]

An adolescent will see 14,000 sexual images on TV in a typical year[81] **and** more than 40,000 commercial advertisements in a year.[82] A study by the Kaiser Family Foundation reports that two-thirds of all eight- to eighteen-year-olds own a cell phone and spend almost two hours each day sharing text messages with their friends.[83] And almost three quarters of all eight- to eighteen-year-olds olds have a personal TV in their bedroom, with the proportion increasing as kids get older.[84] Studies show that teens, particularly boys,

---

80   POS is text-speak for "Parent Over Shoulder."

81   American Academy of Pediatrics, Committee on Public Education Sexuality, Contraception, and the Media. 2001. Accessed at http://aappolicy.aappublications.org/cgi/reprint/pediatrics;107/1/191.pdf.

82   American Academy of Pediatrics, Committee on Communications. "Policy Statement on Children, Adolescents, and Advertising." Accessed on August 2011, at http://aappolicy.aappublications.org/cgi/reprint/pediatrics;118/6/2563.pdf.

83   Rideout, Victoria, Ulla G. Foehr, and Donald F. Roberts. "Generation M² Media in the lives of 8–18 year olds." The Kaiser Family Foundation, 2010: 18.

84   Ibid, p. 9.

spend between four and fifteen hours per week playing video games on a personal gaming device or online.[85]

Kids identify with similarly-aged kids they see on the big screen or on television and learn life lessons from movie or TV show plot lines. How do the residents of Sesame Street deal with a grouch? How does Miley handle a lunchroom bully? OMG! Sixteen and pregnant means seventeen and a mom! When the media provides kids with a seemingly practical solution to a problem that's real to them, they are only too happy to accept the lesson and to believe it as truth.

When the issue of kids and media is brought up, parents tend to link the words "sex and violence" into one category of things to cause concern. It's relatively easy to talk to kids about objections to violence, but it takes the courage to discuss the issues about sex that your child will see in the media. Researchers are fairly consistent in their reports that exposure to violence in the media is not related to increased violent behavior in healthy people; that's the good news. However, researchers find the opposite effect when they study sexuality as portrayed in media and its affect on children.

All healthy adolescents have natural urges for sexual gratification, while no healthy kids have urges to kill and maim. Since people scratched images on cave walls, it's been clear that kids will learn from media. War games and alien invaders exist in fantasy and play, but sex exists right there in their own bodies. So sexual content in the media is more relatable to children (maybe adults, too) than violence is.

Old forms of media are still undoubtedly an extraordinarily potent presence in a child's life, while at the same time new media options are also appearing with breathtaking speed. In this chapter, we will explore the messages young people receive and process from mainstream and new media, and offer actions you can take to neutralize the harmful influence on your child, no matter her age. Hopefully by the end of this chapter you'll understand the current media environment and will be able to use the ABC rule for all media, which is as follows:

Access what your children are accessing

OBserve what your child is doing/watching/hearing

Communicate about what you see and hear

---

85   See http://www.pewinternet.org/Reports/2003/Let-the-games-begin-Gaming-technology-and-college-students/2-Gaming-Comes-of-Age.aspx?view=all#footnote8.

Old School Media

Television

New advances in technology has not killed TV—it's just made it more accessible, and in many ways, more interesting. If you've had to wrestle the remote out of the hands of an MTV-watching child you know firsthand that kids still spend a great deal of time in front of the television. Given that the majority of kids report having a TV in their bedroom, the fight for the remote happens less frequently. However, kids who have personal TVs in their rooms have access to increased viewing time and, if they have a PC, also can watch Internet TV shows; that means you are less likely to know what your kids are watching at any given moment. Likewise, websites such as Hulu.com archive and stream a massive volume of television programming online. As a result, the show you've forbidden to be aired in your living room could be on your child's computer or other electronic device in his bedroom or even on the school bus.

The Kaiser Family Foundation conducts a major national survey of youth and media every five years, and their results tell us that television is still the most common type of media consumed by kids. In fact, their research shows that the amount of television content consumed by youth actually increased by almost 20 percent from 1999 to 2009—from 3 hours and 47 minutes daily in 1999 to 4 hours and 29 minutes in 2009.[86] The Kaiser researchers found that less than half of kids report that their parents set any limits on their television consumption. When parents do set limits, it's more likely to be restriction on content rather than on time. Parents of younger children are more likely to set limits on both, but it is reported that most parents give tweens and teens full freedom of choice with the TV.

The older your child gets, the more difficult it is to monitor his exposure to messages, images, and values foreign to your own. The Kaiser researchers found that a majority of parents don't set rules for media use for their children, but kids whose parents do set rules spend more time with real (as opposed to virtual) peers and get better grades. Remember that when they whine at your limits. With the freedom to choose their own content, adoles-

---

86   Rideout, Victoria, Ulla G. Foehr, and Donald F. Roberts. "Generation M² Media in the lives of 8–18 year olds." The Kaiser Family Foundation, 2010.

cent and teen boys are typically most likely to watch shows featuring aggression and violent content, while girls are drawn to dramas and soap operas with continuing plotlines created to appeal to their interests in love, sex, and fashion. For a child with a firm grip on reality, a little TV fantasy can be a great escape from the real world. In fact, there's a strong argument made by scholars like the perspective offered by Steven Johnson in his book *Everything Bad Is Good For You*[87] that watching highly complex television shows requiring concentration and analysis well beyond the challenges of real life actually helps kids develop analytical skills.

By the time your child hits adolescence, it is unreasonable to expect you to be able to stop your son or daughter from watching a show you find objectionable. If your child is set on seeing a particular TV program, be sure that he or she will find a way—a friend may save the episode on her DVR, your child might find it online, or some new technology will come along to make it even easier to access the "forbidden" program. Instead of trying to keep your child from watching an objectionable show, you should sit and watch the offending television show with your son or daughter, which is what I did as often as possible with my own son. Under the guise of folding laundry, my son and I spent many Sunday evenings sitting on his bed watching *Beavis and Butthead* or *Married with Children*, with me muttering under my breath, "You know people aren't really like that in real life," or "A real teenage girl wouldn't act like Kelly Bundy." I don't think this tactic will ever go out of style. As an added benefit, you'll also be able to start conversations with your child about the questionable material you see in the programs and make sure they understand how it goes against your family's values.

By the time my son was thirteen, he wanted no part of this arrangement, though, and I was faced with knowing that I could no longer monitor every show my son watched—a common parental dilemma with teenage children. One way to combat this is by asking your child what she watches or check out what is on the "Now Playing" list on the DVR in her bedroom, watch a few episodes yourself, and then discuss what's going on with the characters. You may be surprised at what you find out about your teen's favorite show. While the plotlines may contain objectionable materials, they may also be a great source of food for thought. Twenty-first-century dramas, with their convo-

---

87   Johnson, Steven. *Everything Bad Is Good for You*. New York: Riverhead Books, 2006.

luted and interconnected plotlines, require a lot more concentration and analysis than the sitcoms many of you watched as kids. Try watching one of your favorite shows from the 1980s—unless it was one of the Steven Boccho originals like *Hill Street Blues* or *St. Elsewhere*, you will probably be shocked at how boring it seems now. Today's more complex shows build concentration and sophisticated thinking in kids[88] and can be particularly helpful as a learning tool for boys, whose patterns of concentration can be very different than that of girls.

If you can untangle the multiple plot lines that characterize twenty-first-century television shows, you may be surprised to find that many of the shows your kids watch actually promote decent values. The honorable kid usually wins. Doing well in school means getting out of town and going off to college, where success is almost guaranteed. Violence is often the context of a battle of good versus evil, and good generally wins. It's quite possible that television shows watched by your child have redeeming qualities that are not immediately obvious. Finding those qualities and emphasizing them with your child is yet another reason to watch as well.

On the other hand, we have the twenty-first-century boom in reality television, with many shows focusing on sex as a subplot. This is a double-edged sword in a way; the American Academy of Pediatrics reports that "exposure to sexual content in music, movies, television, and magazines accelerates white adolescents' sexual activity and increases their risk of engaging in early sexual intercourse,"[89] an activity most parents would rather discourage in their adolescents. On the other hand, an example of what kids learn from exposure to sexual activity by teens via TV can be found in the report from The National Campaign to Prevent Teen and Unplanned Pregnancy who report that "among those teens who have watched MTV's *16 and Pregnant,* a reality show following the real lives of pregnant teens, 82 percent think the show helps teens better understand the challenges of teen pregnancy and parenthood and how to

---

88 Ibid.

89 Brown, Jane D., PhD, MA, Kelly Ladin L'Engle, PhD, MPH , Carol J. Pardun, PhD, MA, et al. "Sexy Media Matter: Exposure to Sexual Content in Music, Movies, Television, and Magazines Predicts Black and White Adolescents' Sexual Behavior." *Pediatrics*, Vol. 117, No. 4, April 1, 2006: 1,018–1,027.

avoid it."[90] Of course, remember that teens are not developmentally capable of realistically assessing risk and many have unprotected sex thinking that pregnancy just won't happen to them.

Observing sex in the media, particularly when it is being experienced and enjoyed by relatable characters, makes sexual activity seem normal to teens, which in some ways it is. Teen-oriented drama series and soaps often present characters whose everyday lives and situations may seem perfectly relevant to your child, and many of these shows portray sex as easy and risk-free, wherein lies the danger of such shows. You need to be the person to let your kids know that it is neither easy nor risk-free and be sure they have the accurate information about sex and how it can affect their lives for better or worse.

Use the News

You don't a need fictional plotline about an important issue relating to sex and media to start a conversation with your child. Sometimes the newspaper or TV news headlines are more than enough. During a single network morning news show I viewed, the program broadcast a story about a religious cult leader on trial for sexual abuse for marrying multiple underage girls, some as young as twelve. This was followed by an opinion piece about ten-year-old girls who were made-up and decked out for "glam shots."[91] And a few months earlier, CNN news anchor Don Lemon revealed his childhood sexual victimization on the air while he covered a story about an alleged sexual abuse case by a clergyman, who was described by a young member of his congregation as "known to be a mentor to young men."[92] In November 2011, alleged sexual harassment by a presidential candidate vied with a horrific sex abuse scandal for headlines. These news stories are the perfect lead-ins to speaking with your child about sex and related issues. You may ask your child what he thinks of the headline. Listen to your child's answer (or grunt if you're trying to communicate with an adolescent) and use the opportunity to tell him exactly what you think about the issue and why. You may be surprised how much your child listens and takes your thoughts to heart.

---

90   Albert, B. *With One Voice 2010: America's Adults and Teens sound Off About Teen Pregnancy.* Washington, D.C.: The National Campaign to Prevent Teen and Unplanned Pregnancy, 2010.

91   *Good Morning America*, August 4, 2011.

92   CNN air date September 25, 2010.

Public funding for reproductive health, funding for international HIV/ AIDS prevention, legal challenges to sex education or gay marriage, teachers being fired for blogging about their personal life, the abortion debate—news programs deliver a long list of issues ripe for conversation with your child. Little ones who hear or see a story on TV should be asked if they understand what they just heard, and, as with a commercial, should be given an age-appropriate explanation if they do not understand the message they have just received. Open the debate about sex on TV with your older kids; if your child replies with a groan of disagreement, keep talking and sharing your views— they are most likely listening!

Movies and Music

By the time your child is an adolescent, her taste in both movies and music are highly dependent on her peers; by adolescence, if not before, both movies and music are typically consumed by your child without you being present. Because of this, you have to work a little harder to know the content and context of the messages about sex, violence, and other topics that may conflict with your family's values. While movies are subject to a more detailed and easily-accessed rating system, music is also rated if it has "explicit" lyrics or content. And you should know what your child is drawn to and be prepared to talk about it.

Parents have been complaining about the younger generation's music at least since the early nineteenth century, when the introduction of the waltz created a scandal among the older generation. Kids identify with specific music as part of the process of developing an identity separate from their parents. Listening to music can be relaxing and serve as a unifying factor between adolescent peers—whether it be a song, musical genre, or musician. Like video games, kids don't necessarily learn overt behaviors from music, but they do pick up attitudes and language from the music they most hear. Most music consumed by adolescents has an accompanying visual; a rather thorough, scientific "content analysis" concluded that:

> . . . music videos across genres feature sexual portrayals, [and] certain genres feature more sex than others [hip-hop, rap, soul, and rhythm and blues videos tending to feature the most sexual content and country music videos tending to feature the least]. Also, music videos

are relatively unlikely to feature or reference explicit sexual behaviors such as intercourse, although such behaviors are certainly implied by acts such as pelvic thrusting, which are commonly depicted.[93]

Given that, watching music videos may well be an early source of sexual arousal for your kids, a substitution for the adult entertainment magazines kids used to hunt for under their fathers' beds. Be sure that your child has an age-appropriate understanding of autonomic sexual arousal—which they ought to have anyway—before they start watching music videos. Reference chapter 4 for help with this if you are unclear of how to give your child that information.

When choosing movies, you can rely on movie ratings for finding age-appropriate films; ratings are a good predictor of the amount of sex and violence depicted in a given film. The G rating seems to be the most predictable way to avoid sex in movies; the number and intensity of sex scenes increases as the rating scale increases from PG to PG-13 to R.[94] While there's no way you can deny that sexual content in movies is waiting as soon as your kids graduate from G-rated movies and the children's section of the video store, you can prepare for this transition by speaking with your child about sexual health and wellbeing before he begins viewing sexually suggestive or explicit content in films. Even PG films have the occasional sexual reference or brief nudity.

When you do allow your children to begin watching movies rated PG or higher, take the time to discuss the plot, particularly the roles of sex, violence, drugs, and alcohol, and emphasize that these things are exaggerated for enter-tainment's sake. You may have a conversation such as, "The producers who make movies know that people enjoy seeing this stuff on the screen—there's no consequences to watching but doing it is another story," or "This may look real, but it's as fake as the witch in *Snow White*; people who make movies make up things they think kids want to watch."

For assistance evaluating the content of music, the Recording Industry Association of America[95] offers their PAL program, an acronym for a "Parental

---

93   Wright, Paul J . "Sexual Socialization Messages in Mainstream Entertainment Mass Media." *Sexuality & Culture*, No. 13, 2009: 181–200.

94   Ibid, p. 190.

95   See http://www.riaa.com/.

Advisory Label." While movies are given a rating by an independent board applying a consistent set of standards, the PAL program is voluntary. The RIAA tells us that "the Parental Advisory is a notice to consumers that recordings identified by this logo may contain strong language or depictions of violence, sex, or substance abuse. Parental discretion is advised." A PAL notice is voluntarily placed on a product; in most cases "the decision that a particular sound recording should receive a PAL Notice is made by each record company in conjunction with the artist." The PAL program is designed to alert parents that they need to make a judgment about a particular song, album, or video and whether its content is age-appropriate for their children.

For most families, it is impractical to think about monitoring every bit of music or every video consumed by older teens and adolescents, so use the time until adolescence to teach your children your family values and to give them good information about sex. If you deny your child access to a particular movie or song, be sure to explain why: "That movie shows sex in a way that makes it seem like a game. It's not"; "That song encourages girls to be mean to boys"; "That song uses words that insult people—we don't use those words in this family." If your child continues to whine about your decision, be firm and keep your cool. And if you've explained more than three times why you've made your particular decision, feel free to resort to "Because I said so" to end the discussion. After all, you are the adult and the authority figure in the household, and it's both your right and responsibility to set and keep standards.

To go beyond industry ratings, you may choose to rely on independent media rating organizations like Common Sense Media[96] to help you make decisions on what media your child will be exposed to. Common Sense Media rates books, movies, music, websites, and television shows, and offers good guidelines and resources for both you and educators.

Advertising

In 1742, Benjamin Franklin printed what is considered to be the first paid ad in his magazine[97] and almost certainly could never have imagined that he was helping to create a new industry. As the industry matured, new technolo-

---

96   See CommonSenseMedia.org.
97   See http://adage.com/century/timeline/.

gies were integrated, from the printing press to the World Wide Web. Now, social and psychological sciences are used to craft messages appealing to the most fundamental human instincts and feelings. Advertisers have become remarkably skilled at associating their products with the need to satisfy basic human desire and to evoke the most pleasurable human emotions. Advertisers have built a multibillion dollar industry on their expertise in appealing to human drives including sexual instincts and the need for status and acceptance. Today, much of their communication is specifically directed towards kids, the next generation of consumers in our society.

Advertisers target young people for many reasons, including the fact that they know that teens often have their own disposable income and that reaching young people can mean cultivating a lifetime customer. Advertisers also know something that as a parent you must take to heart: **Young kids lack the ability to discriminate between real authorities, such as parents and teachers, and people who pose as an authority in a commercial**. By the time kids are old enough to understand this difference, they have another exploitable vulnerability; adolescents and teens are still developing their self-image and are exquisitely susceptible to messages for products that purport to make them more acceptable and desirable to their peers, particularly those of the opposite sex.

The images accompanying ads presented to kids can be as troublesome as the messages, if not more. It's a fact that all girls are not a perfect size 0 and all boys are not "cut" like an athlete. The fact that kids develop at their own individual pace exacerbates this issue; kids who develop physical signs of puberty later than others may be even more vulnerable to self-criticism from viewing these idealized images. Many of you probably remember your own adolescent angst, much of it revolving around worrying if you were normal. As back then, boys today wonder if they are muscular enough and worry over when the shadow on their upper lip will appear. Likewise, girls wonder when their breasts will develop or when the baby fat around their middle will finally disappear. Unrealistic advertising images of perfectly happy, physically flawless young people do nothing to ease the uncertainty of normal, everyday kids like yours. Be sure to remind your children that media messages are contrived to sell a product, find opportunities to point out your conception of real beauty, and to praise your child's appearance and speak to his or her self-worth.

Unless you have a media-free home, you know that twenty-first-century advertising is filled with products that *do* explicitly refer to sex, usually in cryptic ways but not always. Viewers of all ages see commercials for erectile dysfunction drugs (euphemistically called ED, presumably to shield delicate ears from the medically accurate term erection). Menstrual periods are referred to as "that time" in most ads, as if the word *menstruation* is unspeakable. Television networks air commercials for vaginal lubricants made by mainstream consumer product companies portraying sex as a leisure activity to be improved with science. And condom ads air without, surprisingly, ever quite describing what the product is for. These contrived attempts to avoid words that some might find objectionable result in ads that deliver only partial messages, leaving kids to fill in the blanks themselves—and you now know how that usually ends.

When an ad for a sexually-related product airs, ask your child if he or she knows what that the product is for. If the child says no, ask if he would like to know and respect a "no" answer from a child under age ten or eleven. Tell an older child that he is old enough that he should know and that you'd like to be the one who tells him. On the other hand, if the child says he does know what the commercial means, ask him to share his idea with you and be ready to *gently* correct any misinformation.

Books and Magazines

From *The Scarlet Letter* to Scarlett O'Hara, literature is filled with messages about life and love. The ABC rule (see p. 182) applies here as well as in visual media, but it takes a bit more effort to apply. If you are a busy parent, you may prefer to spend the rare quiet moment you have to read with a bestseller, but be sure to take some time to read the book that has your child's interest. If you have to choose which of your child's books to read, choose the books your child chose on her own. It's a pretty safe bet that if a book was assigned in school, the major storylines and themes will be discussed in class and so you shouldn't have to worry about the content as much. The Internet may provide some shortcuts to help you know more about the books your child may be choosing to read on her own; popular books have often websites where you can learn about characters and plotlines. You can also use your favorite search engine and find reviews of the books your child likes to read; find the reviews by experts like syndicated columnist Kendal A. Rautzhan, whose column "Books to Borrow, Books to Buy"[98] has been informing parents for decades on the books their kids are reading.

There are too many genres of books to generalize about the content and message within each, but teen magazines, unlike books, have certain consistent themes that you can come to know. Primarily directed towards girls, teen magazines are notorious for giving girls a double message—"be sexy enough to catch a boy, but then channel males' sexuality into relational and romantic endeavors."[99] Is this the future you have in mind for your daughter? If not, then send a consistent message that "this is not how things are in real life" and finish the conversation with your own values, maybe along the lines that "girls and boys need to be honest with each other about what they want in a relationship."

So What Can Parents Do?

- Set limits on both time and content for kids' media intake. When your adolescent screams at you about restricting the types of movies, music, or other media he consumes, repeat to yourself *children whose parents limit media exposure do better in school*. Hold your ground—consider your suffering through the tantrum as an investment in your kid's future, like paying for an SAT prep course.
- Choose your battles wisely; there seem to be fewer reasons to worry about healthy kids seeing fantasy violence on the screen than relatable sex.
- "Moderated media exposure" is a fancy term coined by sociologists for what parents might call sharing the media experience with their child. That means watch what your kid is watching, read what your kid is reading, listen to what your kid is listening to, and discuss, discuss, discuss.
- If it's not practical to watch your kid's favorite TV shows or Internet series, find the companion websites and follow the plotlines. Start a conversa-

---

98 See www.greatestbooksforkids.com.

99 Wright, Paul J. "Sexual Socialization Messages in Mainstream Entertainment Mass Media: A Review and Synthesis." *Sexuality & Culture*, No. 13, 2009: 181–200.

tion about the issues facing the characters, particularly how the situation deviates from reality.

- Watch commercials with your child and explain what the products are for, again starting with a question to see what the child already knows.

- Expose your kids to realistic images of beauty. One example is the "Dove Campaign for Real Beauty,"[100] an advertising campaign promoting the message that "real beauty comes in all shapes, sizes, and colors" to "free ourselves and the next generation of stereotypes about beauty."

- Pay attention to your son's body image, too; the trend of juvenile male body building reminds parents that boys are just as vulnerable to idealized imagery as girls and need to develop healthy habits and self-image as well.

- Be one of those parents who sends letters to companies with offensive advertising. Air your legitimate grievances online.

- Watch what you leave around the house. Women's magazines like *Cosmo* do as much to promote the sexual objectification of women and men as men's magazines, and neither does a great job presenting reality-based images of sex, bodies, or relationships.

- I'll repeat once more: Read what your kids are reading, watch what your kids are watching, listen to the music your kids are listening to, and share your opinion for better or worse about the content of each.

- Turn the TV off during meals and other family time. At other times, leave it on only if someone is really watching a show. Let your child become accustomed to the calming effect of silence.

New Media

No sooner do you have one technology figured out then the next generation comes along with more speed, power, connectivity, and electronic devices. You master your cell phone, then along comes a smart phone. You're hand-picking the video games you let your kids buy, then you have to figure out online gaming communities. The options available to your kids to see messages about sexuality and relationships are growing all the time, and you have no

---

100 See www.campaignforrealbeauty.com

choice but to keep up as well. When Marshall McLuhan famously said that the medium is the message, he was trying to tell us that the way a message is delivered changes its impact. Is it delivered on paper or TV? Is it received alone or in a group? The impact of media on the brain is a complicated subject, but producers of media messages know how their media works on our brains, and so should we.

There are two aspects to this media explosion that are particularly important for you as a parent. Most significant is the enormous increase in your kids' ability to access material on their own. Gone are the days when parents had to buy the book or video for their kids, or give them a ride to the mall if they wanted the latest music. The ubiquitous headphones may have quieted the fight to control the car radio, but they deprive you of knowing if the lyrics to the song your kid is playing dozens of times each day are objectionable. The second issue is two-way access. Not only can kids access media that you've never seen, but other people can now access your kids! The continuum of intruders ranges from benign but annoying marketers to bullies and sexual predators.

Some basic rules apply, and none is more important than keeping the home computer in a common location for as long as possible. Twenty years ago, my dad showed up one Sunday afternoon with a TV for my son's bedroom, surprising me and delighting my son; but I had to work a lot harder to know what my son was watching once he no longer needed to watch TV in the family room. A younger friend of mine shared how a gift of an iPad to her son in 2011 had the same effect on her ability to monitor his Internet usage. The expanding capabilities of smart phones give your kids even more privacy and options to send and receive information that you must help them learn how to handle and properly understand.

The generation of parents you fall into has more work to do to than ever before to protect and guide your kids. Each new media type presents its own challenges, but many offer golden opportunities for learning and life experiences you could have never imagined when you were a child. When you were writing letters to pen pals years ago, you could not have imagined chatting with them via a computer screen. But along with these new modes of communication come real dangers, such as cyberbullying, that when you were a child, you didn't need to worry about.

Websites, Social Networks, and Virtual Communities

The twenty-first century has brought the concept of virtual community into our lives and homes, and you need to keep up with this because your children certainly are. Which communities do your children claim to be a part of? Are they members of any virtual sports leagues or earning credits in Woogi-world? And what exactly are they doing on Facebook? What groups have they joined? What are their privacy settings? How many identities have they created on different networking sites? Why are they doing any of this at all?

Experts continue to debate how children incorporate what they learn and experience in virtual communities to real life. There's no definitive agreement of the age at which a child can truly appreciate that she is learning subconscious lessons from online experiences. How can you expect your children to understand that lessons they didn't even realize they were learning only apply to the virtual world? This requires some pretty sophisticated comprehension skills that are beyond the scope of all school-age children and most adolescents. There really is no substitute for parental monitoring of Internet activity and discussions about your child's experiences on these sites to help them process this onslaught of information.

You must develop and maintain rules for your children's participation in online communities. And rules are no good without enforcement. You can look for some assistance on this in COPPA, the Children's Online Privacy Protection Act.[101] COPPA was signed into law in 2000 and sets specific rules about the types of personal information that can be collected by child-oriented websites. The best thing for you to know is that COPPA requires a child-oriented site to post a prominent link to their privacy policy on their homepage and any secondary page that collects information from users. I've spent time on some of the most popular child-oriented websites and shockingly didn't see the privacy rules emphasized on many of them as the law intended. Once again, it is up to you to ensure your child knows never to enter real identifying information of any type on any site. And even if you have to look hard to find it, be sure to click through to the privacy link and read the privacy policy. If you don't agree with it, restrict your child from using that site all together.

---

101 http://business.ftc.gov/privacy-and-security/children%E2%80%99s-online-privacy

Restrict grade-school kids to online communities developed for kids and sponsored by reputable companies you recognize. Choose sites that have a parental control feature, where you can manage the modules you child uses, the areas your child can enter, and how long she can spend online at any given time.

Many of the poplar social networking sites set a minimum age to join but obviously can't check IDs to ensure their users are of an appropriate age. Countless younger children join social networking sites, many with the blessing of their parents, who succumb to the pleas that their child not be left out of their friends' groups. "All of the birthday party invitations come through Facebook!" a sixth grader groaned to her parents, who relented and allowed the eleven-year-old to set up her first Facebook page, vigilantly monitored by the mom. The mother also asked her adult friends and relatives to "friend" her daughter; now a community of loving grown-ups is participating in this child's early online experience.

Of course, a child who really wants to can get around formal and informal parental controls, and so can predators. Kids may establish multiple identities on social networking sites, using one you don't know about for unauthorized activities. I was able to set up both parent and child accounts to use the most popular online communities for children, and clearly, I am not a child. So never be lulled into thinking there is any substitute for real-time monitoring of your child's online activities.

The older your child becomes, the less she will appreciate your monitoring her online activities. Remind your child that privacy is a privilege to be earned, like driving the car alone. Allow your child to earn online privacy in small bits—consider by starting with easing up on checking your child's e-mail. Set an age, perhaps sixteen, when you will ease up on monitoring your child online, providing he demonstrates good judgment along the way and maintains a password that you have access to. Always insist on being a member of every social network he joins, and learn to consider the label "stalker," in this context, to be a compliment.

So What Can a Parent Do?

- Follow the ABC Rule: **A**ssess the site, O**B**serve your child's use, and **C**ommunicate about the experience. The ABC rule also applies to schools and childcare settings that increasingly use online tools for recreational and educational purposes. Some free sites with high-quality educational activities bombard kids with ads or offer games that you might find objectionable.

- Use every type of technology available, including SPAM filters, pop-up blockers, browser filters, parental controls on child-oriented websites, and whatever is invented in the coming years to moderate your child's exposure to media messages online.

- Monitor your child's e-mail accounts, check the browser to see where they've been, and discuss what you found if you do find something questionable. If you don't feel tech-savvy enough to do this, check with the information technology (IT) manager at your child's school, or the local children's librarian, to find help.

- Monitor the "communities" that your child claims to be part of, both real and virtual. For the same reasons that we want to know if her dance club is mean to non-members of if his sports team denigrates girls, we want to know if the virtual community includes games that reward violence or attacks on weaker opponents. Chances are that gaming sites promote sex role stereotyping, so discuss the characters with your kids in a conversation, not by lecturing.

- Check to see if the site your child wants to use complies with the Children's Online Privacy Protection Act (COPPA). The most important feature of this law is a requirement that a child-oriented site post a prominent link to its privacy policy on the homepage and any page that collects information from users. Find the link and read the policy, and admonish your child to not fill out any online forms without you watching.

- Find virtual communities designed to promote values that fit with yours, such as communities that enable kids to sample different careers or experience world-class museums, or those sponsored by parent-approved TV shows. Sites with names ending in ".edu" are generally sponsored by educational institutions and may be a good place to start.

- Discuss the difference between real friends and virtual ones. Focus on the fact that virtual friends can pretend to be anyone and may not even be another child; and emphasize how little effort is required to be an online friend compared to a real friend.

- Encourage your real-life friends to become online friends with your child.

- Encourage a community that you know and approve of, such as your school district or religious congregation, to set up a monitored online community for kids.

- Keep the family computer in a central location for as long as possible. Be aware than once a child gets a cell phone, she can send and receive content anyway, so the central location may not provide the safety net you assume it does. Allow your child to use the home computer under the condition that parents receive the password to each of your child's accounts. If your child says no, cut off Internet access to his PC.

- Knowing the password to every one of your child's accounts gives you the responsibility to log on periodically and monitor what your child is doing online. Keep your child's privacy settings at the most restrictive level. If you find an objectionable post of some sort feel free to remove it, but (I'm about to yell here) **never post anything on your child's site that appears to be posted by them!** This is exactly the type of dishonesty that we're trying to discourage, and you will instantly lose their trust and potentially lose the ability to have productive talks with them about sex and safety issues.

- Be a POS often enough to stay informed.

Gaming

More than half of American teens play electronic games, and they spend a lot of time doing so. Experts estimate that kids spend between four and fifteen hours per week gaming, but if you have an adolescent, you don't have to look at statistical reports to know that many teens seem obsessed with their favorite games. Online and self-contained video games are a major part of the lives of kids, especially adolescent boys. On average, boys spend almost an hour and a half per day playing console or online video games, while on average girls spend just over twenty minutes per day at the same activity.[102] Many online games involve collaboration or competition with other players, providing a virtual community for your teens.

102　The Kaiser Family Foundation. "Generation M²: Media in the Lives of 8- to 18-Year-Olds." Accessed at www.Kff.org.

There are some very important reasons to be optimistic about kids and gaming. Well-designed games can be great for learning; in fact, most young kids are introduced to gaming by parents or educators. Specially designed games can also promote civic involvement[103] or help kids recover from medical conditions; the Make a Wish Foundation even offers a game designed to help kids with cancer cope with treatment. Clearly games are a powerful way to reach kids and hold their attention.

The content and intention of games can vary widely given the subject matter and overall effect, however, so you need to be aware of what games your children are exposed to and playing. The content of some video games can be so objectionable that individual states have sought to restrict the sale of especially violent games to minors. Game makers sued over what they considered censorship. The case went all the way to the Supreme Court, which ruled in 2011 that banning the sale of games is unconstitutional; games are, after all, protected by the First Amendment. So, you are almost on your own in regards to monitoring what games your child plays, and you need to use every resource available to assess and evaluate the appropriateness of your child's games. Video games are rated by the Entertainment Software Rating Board (ESRB), a self-regulatory organization established by the videogame industry.[104]

The ESRB ratings for video games suggest the appropriate age of players, from EC for "early childhood" all the way up to AO for "adults only." They also offer "content descriptors" that describe the content that triggered a specific rating, such as the language or the depiction of sex or violence. The Board suggests to parents that "to take full advantage of the ESRB rating system, it's important to check both the rating symbol (on the front of the box) and the content descriptors (on the back)."[105] Read the ratings carefully and use them as a guide. No child under the age of seventeen should be playing a game rated M (for "mature") or AO.

There is some good news here; an undercover study by the Federal Trade Commission found that retailers refused to sell underage customers M-rated

---

103 http://www.pewinternet.org/Press-Releases/2008/Major-new-study-shatters-stereo-types-about-teens-and-video-games.aspx

104 See http://www.esrb.org/about/index.jsp

105 Accessed on August 10, 2011, at http://www.ESRB.org.

games 87 percent of the time.[106] Resourceful kids will try to find other ways around this, of course, so still check what games are holding your child's interest and be prepared to discuss your feelings about them and also ask questions about the content. Be sure to note the game's disclaimer that once a child joins an online group to play a game, ratings clearly can't offer any assurance of what might be said, sent, or shown to your child through interactions with other gamers.

It's important to note that new media carry messages that are often less visible to parents. Even the most ardent supporters of the video-gaming industry agree that video games present sexist stereotyping. Some games now being developed specifically to be marketed to girls show more balanced roles, but boys are still being exposed to the standard fare of female characters being both ravaged and rescued by male characters—make sure your children understand what these roles are implying and what your values are for real-world interactions between the sexes.

So What Can You Do?

- Remember the ABC rule: Access the site or game, OBserve what your child does, and Communicate about what you saw.
- Set time limits for gaming and keep to them. Turn off your PDA to set the tone and example in your home.
- Really pay attention to ratings. Parents are usually proud when their four-year-old masters a toy rated for kids aged six to eight, but when it comes to websites and gaming, don't second guess the rating. Find the entertainment rating software rating board at ESRB.com, or turn to Common Sense Media at CommonSenseMedia.org, and pay attention to what they offer.
- If you have a daughter, find games that do not promote sexist stereotyping and build critical thinking skills designed especially for girls.
- Be an occasional POS and watch the game. Present this to your child with a focus on your interest in the game as opposed to checking up on your kid or second-guessing his judgment.

106 http://www.ftc.gov/opa/2011/04/violentkidsent.shtm

Cell phones

At least three quarters of American kids have a cell phone that they use for entertainment and communication, primarily with their peers. The age at which a child received her first phone declined over the past decade, but has leveled off; the most common age for a child to receive her first cell phone is between twelve and thirteen, coinciding with her entrance to middle school.[107]

A remarkably high number of cell phone owning kids—84 percent— sleep with their phone by their bed.[108] Some, particularly boys, cite the alarm clock function as the reason for this, but for many kids it is all about leaving open the channel for communication. Clearly, having a personal phone next to a child's bed can interrupt their sleep patterns; what's more, their friends are now able to reach them any time of day or night, increasing the potential for kids sending careless messages or images while half asleep. And kids rarely use cell phones to talk to each other; rather, they spend hours each day texting away on teeny little keyboards or touch screens.

Text messaging has become the primary way that teens reach their friends, surpassing face-to-face contact, email, instant messaging, and voice calling as the go-to daily communication tool for this age group. According to a major national study, seventh through twelfth graders report spending an average of ninety-five minutes a day sending or receiving texts.[109] And texting can be done solely in private; young kids rarely allow their phones to ring and consequently you have no idea when or with whom your child is conversing. A man in his twenties told me that when a cell phone rings in public you can bet it belongs to someone well over thirty; young folks prefer privacy and discretion and set their personal devices on "silent." Another sign of the digital generation gap is that for most teens, voice calling is still the preferred mode for reaching parents.[110] Many teens lament that their parents text too slowly, so

107 Lenhart, Amanda. "Is the age at which kids get cell phones getting younger?" December 1, 2010. Accessed at www.pewinternet.org/Commentary/2010/December/Is-the-age-at-which-kids-get-cell-phones-getting-younger.aspx.

108 Lenhart Amanda, Rich Ling, Scott Campbell, and Kristen Purcell. "Teens and Mobile Phones." April 20, 2010.

109 The Kaiser Family Foundation. "Generation M^2: Media in the Lives of 8- to 18-Year-Olds." Accessed at www.Kff.org.

110 Lenhart, Amanda, Rich Ling, Scott Campbell, and Kristen Purcell. "Teens and Mobile Phones." Pew Internet & American Life Project, April 2010. Accessed at http://pewinternet.org/Reports/2010/Teens-and-Mobile-Phones.aspx.

that's why they prefer to call. But you better believe that with their peers, your children are solely texting.

Sexting

Texting is a microcosm of adolescent communications, and most of these messages are routine or innocuous. But when the cell phone is used as a tool on the rocky road to young love, things can go terribly awry.

As if learning to navigate sex, love, lust, affection, relationships, honor, morality, and trust weren't already difficult enough for a teen to do in private, kids now have to do all that living in a world where one stupid text message or email can become public, permanent, and prosecutable. Between 4 percent and 20 percent of youth have engaged in a behavior experts are now referring to as "youth produced sexual images,"[111] a term designed to highlight the huge variations in motivation, outcome, and actors in situations involving kids creating or receiving sexually suggestive pictures electronically—commonly known as "sexting."

When the federal government sponsored a study of sexting incidents reported to law enforcement authorities, its researchers found huge variations in the circumstances surrounding particular cases.[112] These cases ranged from one part of a loving adult couple accidently sending an explicit photo to the wrong number, to adolescent squabbles uploaded to cyberspace, to pedophiles and pornography mongers targeting adolescents whose social networking profiles showed exploitable vulnerabilities.

In past generations, preteen girls might have looked at each others' breasts in the locker room and discussed who was developing faster; now they can take cell phone shots of each other that have the potential to become socially toxic weapons when and if a spat occurs. A snooping brother might find the images and be unable to resist the urge to share them with his friends—and as a result, people's personal lives and bodies are transmitted into the ether.

Since time immemorial, testosterone-fueled teenage boys seeking sexual gratification have been urging oxytocin-driven teenage girls, who are seeking

---

111 Wolak, Janis and David Finkelhor. *Sexting: A Typology*. University of New Hampshire Crimes Against Children Research Center Bulletin, March 2011. Accessed at http://www.unh.edu/ccrc/pdf/CV231_Sexting%20Typology%20Bulletin_4-6-11_revised.pdf 8/7/2011.

112 Ibid.

loving relationships, to take the next sexual step. Kids speak of sexual relationships in term of what "base" the boy got to, as if the adolescent sexual relationship were a baseball game and the boys were the team at bat and the girls shortstops playing defensively. However, with the advent of texting and teens owning cell phones, getting to second base can now be recorded for posterity—and with potentially devastating legal and social consequences.

Author and psychologist David Walsh explains sexting this way:

> When developing a relationship, adolescent boys and girls are interested in both the relational and physical components, but the balance is completely different. The developing brain of the adolescent male is wired to emphasize the physical side, with the interpersonal relationship secondary. Girls, brains are wired to emphasize the interpersonal relationship, with the physical relationship secondary. If a boy asks a girl to send a naked or provocative picture, she hears the request in the context of a loving, trusting relationship, and makes her decision in that context. When our researchers ask a girl if she understands the risks, girls say that they do, but that "my boyfriend would never do anything like that to me."[113]

If a boy shares the photo, the girl will be devastated by the betrayal, and the typical teenage boy, yet to develop empathy, has no conception of the depth of the pain he could cause by making the photo go public. He also has a miserable surprise in store if the laws in his state define the picture he shared as child pornography. You must be aware of this as a parent of either a son or daughter and be sure to speak with your child about the senseless risk of taking or receiving nude photos before something awful and irreversible happens.

In just about every case reported to the authorities, the illicit photo was found by a parent checking her child's cell phone. There's an important lesson in this and that is to **check your child's cell phone**! Check the actual phone for photos or troublesome text messages, and if you find any, immediately speak with your child about what you've found. Explain the social, emotional,

113 Dr. David Walsh, personal communication, August 8, 2011. See also David Walsh's *Why Do They Act That Way? A Survival Guide to the Adolescent Brain* (Free Press, 2004).

and legal consequences of the photo being shared without their knowledge or permission.

You should never think that the contents of your child's cell phone are private, though you may be inclined to believe so at first. Even if your child has a job and pays her own phone bill, you still have the right and obligation to check in on your child and her phone activity. One parent who I pushed on this point in an interview said, "If your child earned enough money to buy drugs, or a gun, you'd intervene wouldn't you?" View this as one more opportunity to remind yourself how teens can try to intimidate parents into allowing them more freedom than they are developmentally capable of managing. Just picture them as a screaming three-year-old and hold your ground on the cell phone rules you set for them.

In addition, don't just stop with looking. Choose to receive the most detailed bill your cell-phone carrier offers and actually look each month to see if there is an unfamiliar number showing up frequently. Be particularly interested if the number is from a distant area code, although keep in mind that cell phone numbers are portable when someone moves from one state to another. Discretely call that number and determine who is on the receiving end. If you need some incentive to prepare for your child's protestations, go online and use your search engine to find the report I reference in note 110 a few pages ago (p. 204); the case studies will give you all the motivation you need to be vigilant about your child's phone safety.

So What Can a Parent Do?

- Model responsible cell phone behavior of your own.
- Be respectful but not intimidated when your child protests your monitoring his calls and text messages.
- Choose the most detailed bill you can get from your cell-service carrier and really read it!
- Take full advantage of the parental control technology offered by your carrier. Take a lesson from the dad of a teen who refused to return his parent's calls for several hours. This dad used his cell carrier's online account management feature and turned off his son's cell service, and kept it off for two weeks as punishment and a good life lesson .

Conclusion

You're probably exhausted just reading the list of things you might do to moderate the influence of media on your child's sexual health and safety. Setting limits sounds easy, but the personalities of some kids and some parents just make that seem impossible. No matter how loud your child's protestations, though, you can't simply relinquish your rights and responsibilities to your child when it comes to media and technology. Choose your battles wisely, learn to negotiate, and be clear that you have the final say. If you have to choose between limiting your child's access to content including sex and content including violence, hold tighter to the line on sex. The experts believe that viewing sex is related to earlier sexual activity, while this has not been demonstrated to be true for healthy kids viewing violence.

Kids whose families limit media consumption do better in school and spend more time with their peers. Setting this limit is good for your child, although it may feel like pulling teeth at times. With or without limits, one thing you can do without your child's acquiescence is to stay in contact with the media your children experience and discuss your thoughts with your child. "I can't believe you watched my show!" your fourteen-year-old may scream at you. "You bet I did," you should reply. "It's part of my job as a parent and I want to do my job well, and I expect the same from you." If your child protests that he doesn't have a job, you should look him straight in the eye and tell him, "Oh yes you do. Your job is to turn into a healthy, successful adult." An exchange like that could set the stage for speaking with your child about why you set these rules and why you expect them to be followed.

PART 4

What to Do if Problems Arise

CHAPTER 11

Kids' Sexual Health and Safety

Children act out sexually for the same reasons they do anything else— because it feels good at the time. The motivation to act out sexually is different at different ages, but regardless of age, how you react is critical. Given this, you need to know what is developmentally normal and how to spot a problem. Does your toddler have her hands in her diaper too often? Are your school-aged kids playing hide and seek naked? Is your adolescent viewing pornography online? Does your teenager's relationship seem inappropriate for his age? Can you ever figure out, for example, how much affection is normal for fourteen-year-olds?

In this chapter, you'll receive advice on dealing with typical sexual issues that arise while raising your children, learn how to understand the sexual or sexualized behaviors of your children at various developmental stages, as well as sexual health issues and tools to gauge your child's relationships with her peers and other adults.

The Youngest Kids

Learning All about Their World

Infants come into this world in a fog of new experiences, and their senses need to develop to process these accurately. Different senses learn to respond to stimuli at different times, but the sense of touch and bodily comfort comes very quickly for newborns. Babies need to be held, touched, cuddled, and comforted—this, in turn, teaches them that, at a primal level, the world is a safe place. Developing this sense is fundamental to healthy personality development and strong relations with a child's parents or other caregivers. Remember: You can never cuddle an infant too much; this nurturing, sensitive touch is a baby's first lesson that human touch can mean love. Understanding this is one of the most important components to a human being becoming a sexually safe and healthy adult.

Many moms choose to breastfeed their infant. Most medical professionals strongly encourage this practice as a physical health benefit for the child—from the documented nutritional power of breast milk—as well as the strengthening of the bond between the mother and baby. As discussed in chapter 5, when a baby sucks on her mother's nipple, the hormone oxytocin is released to stimulate the milk glands to contract and secrete milk. Oxytocin is a multipurpose hormone—it is responsible for the strong contractions of the uterus during child birth and the milder contractions of various parts of the sexual anatomy during sexual arousal and orgasm. When a baby's sucking stimulates the release of oxytocin, it may cause uterine contractions that help the mother's body recover from child birth; it may also cause genital contractions mimicking sexual arousal, which can frighten and confuse a new mom unaware of the phenomenon. The most fortunate of you learned all about this early on from a lactation specialist at the birthing center or hospital maternity ward; if not, a nursing support group can help both you and your spouse understand exactly how normal this is.

Sometime during their first year, babies may discover their genitalia. It means no more or less to them than any other body part. It is important that an infant is allowed to maintain this perspective; an infant is not developmentally capable of understanding nuances of context; for them, something is either all right or it's not. As the infant becomes a toddler—particularly as he develops language or starts potty training—he can be directed to limit self-play to his private time. One mom of three boys under the age of five reported that their house rule was, "When the Big One comes out, take it to your room!"

Health

Babies of either gender can suffer from diaper rash or other skin irritations in and around the diaper area. Good old-fashioned cleanliness is a simple and effective cure. You may not be comfortable washing your babies' genitalia, especially if you see a little baby erection, hear a happy little coo, or have another indication that the cleaning process feels good to the baby. But you know discomfort is no excuse to neglect this task. Urine, fecal material, shedding skin cells, and garden-variety dirt can all collect in the folds of the skin around the thighs, buttocks, and genitalia and may cause irritation to sensitive baby skin. Discuss proper baby bathing techniques with your medical provider and don't skip any body parts during bath time. There is a world of difference between a baby having a pleasant reaction to a sensitive touch and a grownup purposely stimulating a child for his or her own gratification. The former is a natural phenomenon and the latter selfish, immoral, dangerous, and illegal for a very good reason.

Some babies are born with physical issues affecting their genitalia. During fetal development, about 1 out of 300 boy babies develop a condition called hypospadias,[114] where the penis develops with the opening of the urethra on the underside of the penis instead of the tip. Generally, if the birth occurs in the hospital, the condition is noted at that time, but it can be missed and so occasionally a parent will notice the anomaly once the child is home.

Surgery to repair this condition generally takes place while the child is still in diapers and once a pediatrician believes the baby has developed enough to reduce the risk of general anesthesia. Medical opinions differ about the best age for this surgery; if your child has hypospadias, your pediatrician will recommend a pediatric urologist and the decision about surgery should be made as a parent-doctor team. If there are other children in your home who may notice that one sibling's penis looks or works differently, just treat the situation in a matter-of-fact way. The goal is for the whole issue to be absolutely no big deal, and the trip to the hospital for repair as eventful as a tonsillectomy.

Between 3 and 5 percent of all boys are born with one testicle undescended, a condition known as cryptorchidism. In chapter 4 we discussed how the reproductive organs develop before birth, so you know that the

---

114 Choi, James, Kimberly L. Cooper, Terry W. Hensle, and Harry Fisch. "Incidence and Surgical Repair Rates of Hyposoadiasis in New York State." *Pediatric Urology*, 2001: 151–153.

testicles develop internally in the same way as ovaries. A hormonal signal sends the testes on their journey down and out to the scrotal sac, and in these very rare occasions, one testicle does not completely descend. The timing and specific treatment for the undescended testicle will depend on exactly how much of the journey was completed pre-birth; this is another time to team up with your pediatrician and a pediatric urologist to determine what is best for your child and when.

Pre-birth issues that affect female genitalia are very rare; the incidence is estimated to be 1 in 15,000 births. Occasionally the hormonal signals that stimulate genital development go awry, and a chromosomal female may be born with genitals that appear male or ambiguous; it is also possible that a chromosomal male may have ambiguous genitals. After many hard lessons learned in the last half of the twentieth century, physicians now know that gender identity (the gender a child really believes he or she is) is more closely related to the chromosomal gender than the appearance of the genitalia; no treatment decisions should be made without a chromosomal analysis and consultation with experts. This is a time to find the best medical experts in the country; it's out of the league of your neighborhood pediatrician or pediatric urologist. Their role is to help you find the state of the art medical researchers and practitioners.

Dealing with Others

Peers

For more than a century, developmental psychologists have been studying how and why children play. One of the most widely accepted schools of thought describes children going through three stages of play: *solitary,* or playing by themselves; *parallel,* or playing near other children but not necessarily with them; and *group play,* where the children are clearly interacting with each other. The speed at which children pass through these stages is highly variable, depending on such factors as the child's personality, the number of siblings in her household, or her exposure to other children. You should take note that most children are not capable of true group play until well into their preschool years.

As a parent, you may wonder about sex play between kids. There are certain issues that differ with the ages of children, for example touching between two-year-olds is very different than touching between twelve-year-olds, but there is one universal indication for your concern: if coercion of any kind was used by either child to gain compliance from the other, you must intervene. There is also one universal rule for parental reaction: regardless of what you see, stay calm and *think* before you say anything to your child or another parent. If you display a shocked exclamation or scream, this can stay with the children involved long after any memory of the activities that caused this reaction.

Recognizing the harmlessness of parallel play with or without clothes, many families allow full nudity among their kids, for example bathing the younger kids all together. A child will let you know when she's outgrown this, and then you must honor a request for privacy from siblings.

Toddlers who are still in the solitary or parallel phase of development would be highly unlikely to be interested in a game like naked doctor or you-show-me-yours-and-I'll-show-you-mine. Toddlers may glance at one another or maybe even reach out in curiosity to touch another child's genitals, but this behavior should most likely be ignored by you and other parents.

It is not uncommon for an older child to decide that he or she is curious and wants to inspect a younger child. The younger child may not mind at all. If you come upon this situation, you should calmly announce that playtime is over and then speak with the older child in private. That conversation should be a lesson in respecting the personal boundaries of others, and offering to answer their questions about body parts. Doing this without shaming the older child is crucial. If your conversation leads you to conclude that the older child used any kind of force or coercion, try to determine the motivation and where your child came up with this idea. If the answers trouble you, it may be time to seek the support of a qualified child development specialist.

ADULTS

The youngest children rarely comes into contact with strangers without her parents present. Some parents I interviewed reported a general fear of their children being abducted by a stranger; several even talked specifically about places where they felt particularly vulnerable, such as public restrooms or airports. Infants and toddlers are developmentally incapable of protecting themselves in any circumstance and so you must develop a healthy sense of vigilance in order to keep them safe. If a stranger stops to admire your beautiful baby, thank her and keep walking. Never allow a stranger to hold your baby, unless he is your seatmate on an airplane and can't possibly go anywhere. Just explain that you're a germ freak and end the conversation.

Kids may also come into contact with people you don't know when you've left them under the supervision of a childcare provider (choosing safe programs for kids was discussed in chapter 8). As a parent, you may rely on teenage babysitters to watch your children—this is a staple of countless American communities. Author Ken Singer offers the following food for thought in his book about recovering from childhood sexual abuse:

> Because adolescents are frequently sexually aroused, normal behaviors they used to do without any sexual intent, such as horseplay and wrestling, may inadvertently or deliberately become a means to achieve sexual gratification.[115]

Singer also makes a strong point that adolescents hired to babysit, or who are otherwise given control over smaller children, require careful consideration before trusting them with your child. We've discussed the need to interview caregivers and check references, but Singers' point reminds us that the adolescent watching your kids for a few hours on a Saturday night must also be thoroughly vetted prior to hiring. Arousal coupled with the naturally poor impulse control of adolescence can be a powerfully difficult combination for a teenager left alone with your children.

Make sure your teenage babysitter knows that her guests are not welcome while she's caring for your children; if you really know the sitter and the proposed guest, you may choose to disagree with me, but again I have to say that adolescence is a time of remarkably poor judgment and even the "best" kids are capable of doing stupid things when in the presence and influence of their peers.

If your child expresses any displeasure at the thought of spending time with a particular grownup or teenager, ask why. Separation anxiety can be expected in toddlers, so do your best to determine if your child is upset

---

115 Singer, Ken. *Evicting the Perpetrator*. 2010, p. 72.

because she doesn't want to leave you or because she doesn't want to spend time with the babysitter or caregiver. If your child is going through a stage in which leaving him with anyone makes him upset, he is most likely missing you, but pay very close attention if only one person or place brings this reaction out in your child. If a preverbal child cries hysterically when a particular person arrives at your house, or when you arrive at the home of another person, speak frankly to the other adult to determine what might be going on and what has happened while you've been away at other times.

School-aged Kids

Driven to Discover Themselves

School-aged kids are working on the answer to a uniquely and universally human question that some people ponder their entire lifetime: "Who am I in relation to the rest of the world?" Curiosity and wonder are earmarks of this age—this is one reason why kids going through this state are generally quite delightful to be around. They want to know everything and still think you, their parent, knows all the answers.

The unprecedented stream of images available to our children makes some of today's parents worry about helping their kids understand the context of things that may seem innocuous to them. One focus group mom told of being angry when her ten-year-old daughter "snuck and bought skinny jeans" (considered a sexualized garment in her frame of reference) while shopping with a loving but clueless relative; another wondered how to tell her seven-year-old daughter that the child's favorite dance move copied from a music video looks like simulated intercourse. At this age, kids are forming their sense of self while incorporating messages from all around, many of which are unintelligible to school-aged kids. So they rely on you to provide them proper information and guidance on these confusing messages and images.

When I was a camp counselor decades ago, kids and staff shared a locker room to change for swimming. I clearly recall that my "bunk" of eight- and nine-year-old girls could barely take their eyes off of the bodies of us, their teenage counselors, as we all changed. Luckily, our young staff had been prepared for the kids' reactions by an exceptionally good pre-camp orientation session; we were taught that kids are naturally curious. Even if the campers had seen their parents unclothed, we camp counselors most likely looked very different. It was a normal part of camp life and our supervisors made it clear that it was the counselors' responsibility to calmly and maturely accept the natural curiosity of children and to not make a big deal out of this normal behavior.

Decades later, I had a very close girlfriend whose body type was very different than mine. When we went clothes shopping, her school-aged daughter often stared at my partially clothed body in the fitting room. My early training as a summer camp counselor kicked right back in and I accepted her curiosity in context. Yet, when a strange child poked his head under the fitting room partition while I was trying on bathing suits, I felt totally violated and was ready to scream at his mother! It is perfectly acceptable for an adult to passively acquiesce to being a visual aid in the development of a child that is part of his or her life; yet, it is equally important to teach your kids to respect the privacy of others. Intimate interactions with loving, caring adults are crucial to helping kids make sense of the messages they receive—but should not be allowed to overstep social boundaries for personal privacy and proper behavior.

Curiosity arises in kids from trying to make sense of the world and their place in it. It is healthier to have this curiosity fulfilled by loving family members or others prepared for this role. Many kids seek to satisfy their curiosity with their peers, and we'll spend more time on that later in the chapter.

Maturation Is Not a Race

Kids mature at speeds as diverse as their unique personalities; visit a fifth- or sixth-grade classroom and you're likely to see an eleven-year-old girl who looks fourteen and an eleven-year-old boy who looks nine. Girls tend to mature more quickly than boys during this stage. Variations in genetics, diet, environment, and other factors make it impossible to say exactly when your child will mature physically. Even two siblings of the same gender in the same home may develop at different speeds. Answering the question, "Is my child normal?" can be most perplexing for any parent during these years. The overwhelming majority of the time the answer is a resounding "yes," but continuing regular examinations as suggested by your medical care provider and keeping lines of communications open with your kids are key for your reassurance as well as your child's.

As children move through this stage, you must prepare them for the bodily changes of adolescence. Children may start to show signs of puberty as young as seven or eight and need to be reassured that their bodily changes are healthy, normal milestones on their road to growing up. Refresh your own understanding of anatomy and physiology (chapter 4 is a good place to start) and share certain concepts with your child in language he can understand. Kids worry about their bodily changes at these times, and you have an opportunity that is rare in a child's journey to adulthood to inform, relieve anxiety, and build trust with them by providing the facts in a safe and loving manner.

Health and Safety

Pay attention if your child reports any type of pain or discomfort in his or her genitalia or surrounding areas. Ask general questions of your child to find out the source of the pain: "Does it hurt more when you pee or poop?" "Have you seen blood on the toilet paper?" "Do you remember hurting your butt/tushy/pee-pee/vagina?" "Has anyone touched your butt/tushy/pee-pee/vagina?" Use the same tone you would use if you were asking about a sore throat; read the section in chapter 13 on questioning and avoid planting ideas in your child's mind before you start asking these types of questions.

A child can hurt his or her genitalia the same ways he or she can hurt other parts of his or her body. A wipe-out on a bike might actually cause bruising on the upper thighs. Urinary tract infections can happen when germs from the rectum occasionally make their way to the urethra, the tube that carries urine outside of the body from the bladder. But pay attention and remember the story I heard from a convicted pedophile, who told me of being able to convince the mother of his victim that her son's complaint about an irritated penis was due to a new brand of toilet paper, when the child's penis was really irritated from an act of sexual abuse.

Vaginal discharge is normal under many circumstances, but if your child seems to have itching or the discharge has an odor, contact your medical care provider. Make sure you learn from the doctor the exact nature of the condition causing the discharge and specifically ask how your child developed it.

See chapter 4 to be reminded of the non-sexual ways that girls can develop vaginal infections, but make sure your medical professional is able to answer all of your questions about how your child developed the condition before you rule out any foul play.

Dealing with Peers

Kids are well into the stage of "group play" by elementary school and interact with others kids in many ways. Occasionally, those interactions cross into areas that appear to be sexualized, and parents I've interviewed frequently want guidance on differentiating between play and trouble, but unfortunately there is no single answer to this.

Play that appears sexualized to adults may start as early as preschool and should stop well before puberty. By puberty, the exquisite shyness that accompanies bodily changes sets in, and consensual sex play becomes more unusual. But some elementary school kids are curious and will figure out how to satisfy their curiosity on this topic. Satisfying curiosity is miles away from satisfying sexual needs, though, which most school-aged kids have not yet developed, so keep this in mind when trying to determine if a behavior is really problematic.

A certain amount of play that adults may interpret as sexualized can be expected at this age. Two curious, similarly aged kids looking at each other's bodies presents little to worry about. Let's go back to the two basic standards mentioned for the youngest kids: there is always a cause for parental concern if coercion of any kind was used by either child to gain compliance from the other, and regardless of what you see, stay calm and *think* before you say anything to your child about sexual play.

Kelly, the mother of a seven-year-old girl, shared in an interview the story of one of her daughter's friends, also aged seven, who regularly wanted to play sexualized games with her daughter when visiting. The imaginary games of "prince and princess get married" moved from cute to disturbing when the visiting friend wanted the prince and princess to make a baby by imitating simulated intercourse. The mom learned about the girl's special game when, after a visit from this friend, her daughter asked her how that kind of hugging made a baby. Kelly learned that her daughter didn't particularly like that part of the game, but her friend would let her pick the next video they watched if she went along with it. Kelly was lucky to catch her daughter's vulnerability to this type of subtle coercion. Her child was old enough to hear the message from her mother that real friends don't try to make you do things you don't like to do; real friends can hear you say "no" and will still be your friend. Although hesitant to do so, Kelly contacted the mother of the other child and expressed her concern about the sexualized play, and monitored future visits from this little girl.

Another focus group mom wondered what a parent should do if she finds two school-aged boys masturbating together. The longer we discussed this, the more complex her question became. Our two basic rules still applied: try to determine if there was any coercion and calmly announce that play time is over and prepare to talk to your kids. But there are other areas of concern that require specific sensitivity and thought in regards to this issue. Look back to Rosenzweig's Rule # 2 and bear in mind that your immediate reaction to your child's behavior may cause feelings that your child may continue to associate with his or her sexuality. An expression of anger or disgust on your part may leave your child vulnerable to associating anger or disgust with sexual arousal. This is also time to recall a lesson I learned from the convicted pedophile I interviewed for this book: He believed that his lifelong attraction to children may have begun during group sex play with the first group of peers that accepted him as a friend.

So is this a problem? Maybe, but the last thing you want to do is to let your reaction make it worse. If you witness overtly sexual behavior among your and other kids and instinctually show a shocked or negative reaction, clear the air when you talk to the children. Explain your shock by saying this is a private behavior that is not meant to be shared until people grow up, and you didn't expect to see it happening with kids. Let your child know that you expect him not to share sexual behavior like mutual masturbation and remind him that every child has the privacy of his room or the bathroom to explore this by himself. I suggest your goal should be to avoid negative messages—don't make your child feel as though he is bad or that sex or sexual arousal is bad. Rather your message should be that it's not OK to share his arousal with anyone while still a child. This is a complex message but one worth thinking about and even practicing discussing with a partner or friend. Kids understand that there are things that grownups can do that kids can't, such as driving a car or having a bunch of money in their wallet. Your message should be that sharing sexual behaviors is also a grownup behavior and something that kids are not allowed to do until they mature.

As a general rule, it is a good idea to speak with the parent of the other child involved in any school-aged sexual play. Be very careful how you approach the topic, though, and be sure to avoid any appearance of blame. Once again, use I-statements such as, "I was surprised to find our kids playing with their clothes off. I spoke to my kid about modesty and privacy, and thought you might want to know." This is far more effective in starting a conversation with another parent than seeming to make an accusation or place blame. You might want to consider trying this message out with your partner or a friend first before approaching the other parent. If the other parent responds with anger or harsh words, think twice before allowing your child to visit that home without an adult chaperone.

Your reaction to your child's sexualized play should depend on her age and the circumstances surrounding the incident. Your task as a parent is to try to determine if there is any kind of coercion involved or a power differential among the kids involved. The oldest or biggest child may not always have the most power, either, so keep this in mind. Threats like "I'll tell Dad you broke his iPad" or "I'll tell Sue what you said about her" can sometimes carry more force than being physically overpowered, and are much easier for kids to hide from their parents.

If you have reason to believe your kids have been playing doctor or naked dancing with friends, or have participated in some other made-up game that is little more than an excuse to look at each other's bodies, it's time for you to have a talk. Acknowledge that curiosity is normal and gently seek to find out how the game started with an ear towards learning if one child had to work hard to convince the others or used any kind of power to get the other kids to go along. If it appears that power *was* involved, spend time alone time with the instigator, find out what was on his or her mind, and be emphatic that it is not acceptable for kids to talk to other kids into things they don't want to do. If the troubling behavior continues, consider seeking help from a professional with specialized training in child development.

Things change as kids move closer to and enter adolescence. In the previous section, you read about how easily adolescents may become sexually aroused while engaging in non-sexual behavior. You can communicate with your adolescent to ensure that he or she understands that arousal is normal and should be dealt with alone; on the other hand, younger kids should be taught that older kids, even if they are in charge in a certain situation, don't automatically have the right to make the younger ones do anything that they think is wrong.

Many of you will also recognize the huge variations in the speed of development of pre-adolescents and may worry that your more naive child will be taken advantage of or otherwise harmed by the "fast kids" in the neighborhood or classroom. Some of you may worry that your kids will be drawn into a seemingly innocent game that gradually turns sexual and potentially harmful for your child. These situations are certainly possible and are best dealt with through the open communications still relatively easy for you with your pre-teens or younger children. In fact, these years are the best times to strengthen the foundation you've built for trusting communication, which is necessary to get you (and your child) through the teenage years. Watch your kids with their friends, express your positive thoughts as well as any concerns you may have, and have lots of conversations about what your child did during any given day and if she enjoyed it or not.

Adults

FEAR OF PEDOPHILES

Parents I've interviewed consistently admit, "I'm always scared of pedophiles," and "I won't leave my kids alone anywhere anymore, not even church." On the other hand, one mom reported that the last time she chaperoned an activity at her son's school, a distressed little girl sought comfort from her: "This girl was in my lap for hours—and I can bet her mother has no idea!"

School-aged children are at the highest risk of being pulled into a potentially harmful relationship with a pedophile. Most pedophiles report attraction to children of a particular pre-pubescent body type that appeals to them; the onset of secondary sex characteristics like pubic hair diminishes the child's attractiveness to many pedophiles. Because school-aged children are in the latency stage of their psychosexual development, things of a sexual nature are not in their primary frame of reference. A manipulative adult can thus introduce a game to an elementary school-aged child that subtly becomes sexual over time, and a latency-aged child may miss all of the cues until the relationship is completely sexualized. The pedophile then uses the child's autonomic sexual response to convince her that she really likes the sexual activities. With that in mind, this is the time to be particularly vigilant about the adults in your child's life.

Many parents report "fear of a creepy neighbor" in terms of ensuring their children's safety, and even *Modern Family* explored this issue in a 2011 episode entitled "Boys Night."[116] An older male neighbor invited their son over to watch movies and the parents (Claire and Phil) decided to go meet him first. When they shared the reason for their visit, the neighbor yelled, "Are you saying I'm some kind of pervert?" and eventually told the parents to mind their own business. "Ultimately our son is our business," Claire replies. In this fictional setting, there were no hard feelings, and these TV parents had the right idea. Most of us don't have professional writers providing dialogue for us, but this is one line I don't think anyone would mind if you borrowed: ultimately, who your child spends time with *is* your business, and it's your right and responsibility to make sure your child will be safe with other people.

Adolescence

Finding Where They Want to Fit into the World

SENSE OF SELF

Adolescence is filled with the experience of trying out different identities. Kids may change their look, hobbies, sports, and friends repeatedly during this age; this need to try new things may frighten you as a parent, who will question your child's judgment and find it difficult to keep track of all of the new influences in your child's life. As a child works to separate himself from his family and find his place in his community, parenting becomes particularly challenging. But your continued vigilance is crucial, even if made more difficult by the fact that a characteristic of this period of separation is a child's strong desire to avoid spending time with his parents. It can be tough keeping track of what's happening in your teenager's life.

---

116 Modern Family, Season 2, Episode 18, original air date March 23, 2011.

Kids this age want privacy, but privacy should be a privilege your child can earn as he or she matures. This implies that you have a right to see what your child has in her room or on the computer—and you as the parent have a responsibility to check until your child has earned the privilege of privacy. You may find cigarettes, drugs, condoms, explicit pictures, or other question-able materials that your child is hiding from you. These clues can help you to know what is going on with your child and are a cue to engage your child in a conversation about the meaning of what you've found. The actual items you've found may not necessarily be a problem; you need to consider the meaning they hold for your child, however. Your job, for example, is to deter-mine if your fourteen-year-old has a condom in his wallet as a status symbol or an accessory for a weekend date.

Parents have been finding sexualized images in their adolescents' posses-sion since long before the Internet started delivering them for free. All explicit materials are not equally problematic, though; if the images are of naked bodies, or adults enjoying what appears to be consensual sex, you may choose not to say anything at all about them. Images of any type of violence are always cause for a serious discussion. What does your child think is going on in the photo? How does he think the victim feels? Who does he think actually took the picture? Again, remember that adolescents are still in the process of developing the capacity for empathy and discussing such images with you can help that process. Shaming your child for lacking empathy at this point will just make the problem worse.

Finding images of people being hurt could merely mean that your child is curious. You have a teachable moment if you find these types of images, pointing out that real people were forced to commit the acts in those images and how awful it must feel to be the victim.

It is appropriate to tell your child that you want his sexual thoughts and feelings to be associated with happy and pleasant loving images, and not pain and violence. Your family values do not place sex and violence together under any circumstances and you should make this explicitly known to your child.

Finding images of child pornography is definitely cause for a very serious discussion with your child, starting with the issue of empathy. Explain that sexual acts with children are wrong under any circumstance, even if the images are from another culture and the purveyor alleges that sex with those kids is acceptable. The truth is that children are not capable of consenting to sex, period. Move on to the fact that possessing child pornography is a criminal offense that could have lifelong consequences for your child, and possibly other members of your household. Your child should know that certain websites showing illegal sexual behaviors are monitored by law enforcement authorities and that your child's web surfing may open your household to legal sanctions, which you will not tolerate.

Ideally, you want to know as soon as possible if your child is sexually aroused by children. It is possible that your child experienced involuntary sexual arousal while engaging in otherwise innocent play with a child and for the moment, his arousal has become associated with children, but make it clear that this is neither healthy nor acceptable, and encourage him to find age-appropriate sexual images to help satisfy his sexual arousal. Psychologists teach us that "knowledge about sex is acquired in multiple ways: through one's own experience of it, once the rewards of sexual stimulation induce pleasure; and through other sources, including the media, education programs, and peers."[117] If your child has somehow correlated sexual arousal with images of children, smart, careful, loving intervention on your part to redirect the sexual energy may spare you and your child a great deal of pain in the future.

Learning where your child found any questionable images is also important. Did an adult give them to your child? Pedophiles often show kids pornography as part of the seduction; most are too smart to chance letting a child take it home, though. If an older child or adult gave your child the images, talk to that person immediately and determine from your child if there is any coercion happening between her and the adult or child. Even if your child accepted the images willingly, let him know his relationship with the person who provided the pornographic material is now either prohibited or subject to your supervision. If the images were provided to your child by an adult (especially if you don't know the person), contact the police. If the images were provided by another child, contact his or her parents and decide together how to proceed.

Perhaps the direst situation would be finding an explicit image of *your* child on the web, a computer, or cell phone. You should ask your child who

117 Everaerd, Walter, Stephanie Both, and Ellen Laan. "The Experience of Sexual Emotions." *Annual Review of Sex Research*, Vol. 17, 2006: 183–199.

took the photo and why. If your child is younger than thirteen, suspect that an older person is involved, then brush up on the issues around questioning children described in chapter 13 and try to determine who the perpetrator is. Do not hesitate to take legal action if any adult was involved in any way—call the police! If you find that another child took the photo, use the same standards to determine the seriousness of the situation—such as the age of the child and the degrees of coercion.[118] By adolescence, it is possible that judgment-challenged teens made this stupid decision without coercion; the photo may just be the result of a bad case of adolescent "group think."

Poor adolescent judgment can really be put to the test by the presence of a webcam. Webcams and kids are a volatile mix. Disconnect webcams in your home and only allow their use in an open, supervised family setting. Sad stories have surfaced of lonely kids being seduced online by pedophiles, who after receiving the initial suggestive photos blackmail the child into sending more photos with threats of broadcasting the ones they have on the Internet. Smart phones are generally equipped with a camera and you should consider restricting younger kids to phones lacking Internet access.

SEXUAL HEALTH

You can find a lot to be concerned about regarding the health of your adolescent child. Growth spurts, taking more naps than a toddler, skin eruptions, out-of-nowhere tears, or tantrums can all be symptoms of adolescent growth. A strong relationship with a medical provider is very important at this point, particularly one who can answer questions for both your child and you. Many pediatricians end your child's annual exam by asking you to leave and by spending time alone with your child; if your medical provider doesn't do this, try suggesting it when you schedule the next exam. Pediatricians should provide "anticipatory guidance" for you to help you know what's coming next in your child's development; by the time your child hits adolescence, he or she will need guidance from a health professional too. You'll just be an ostrich with your head in the sand if you fail to anticipate that adolescents will become sexually active; knowing as much, you need to provide guidance to them

---

118 It is possible that some states may consider the act a crime even if everyone involved was a minor. New technologies are presenting new challenges to law enforcement authorities.

(whether on your own or with the help of a doctor) to keep your child sexually safe and healthy.

Adolescents need to know about sexually transmitted diseases and sexually transmitted infections, that safe sex includes contraception, and that protection from disease and infections is best provided by a condom and a conversation with their sexual partner. Adolescents, particularly testosterone-driven males, may find it easier to have an orgasm than a conversation with a partner; frank talk with a potential sexual partner is difficult for kids, and they know it. You must be willing to speak with your kids, providing opportunities for them to become comfortable with sexual language before your child finds himself confronted with the possibility of sex and need to speak frankly about sex with a partner.

In June 2011, NPR was among the media outlets covering the thirtieth anniversary of the first cases of HIV/AIDS in the United States. They assigned a teen reporter from Youth Radio to talk to her peers about HIV and AIDS.[119] The narrator shared that she'd had decent sex education in school and that her mother had provided a particularly helpful book to her, but most of the kids she interviewed weren't so fortunate. While today's generation of teens can search Google for answers to a variety of questions, the teen reporter observed that "no amount of research can prepare a young person to ask their partner if they were tested for AIDS."[120] Other young people she interviewed echoed her sentiments. One young man said that "no matter how uncomfortable you are, you have to ask"[121] a new partner about their HIV status. Adolescents must be able to determine if their partner is a risk for other sexually transmitted infections as well.

Long before adolescents were counseled on the importance on being able to ask a potential sexual partner for verification of his or her HIV status, sex educators like me encouraged people to take specific steps to determine if a potential sexual partner was healthy. One tried and true method is to look closely at your partner's genitals, and stop the sexual contact immediately if you see anything that looks like a sore. Herpes can look like a blister, HPV

---

119 National Public Radio. Youth Radio, June 3, 2011. Accessed at
http://www.npr.org/2011/06/03/136930347/young-people-talk-about-aids.
120 Ibid.
121 Ibid.

(human papillomavirus) can look like a wart, and other infections can cause a discharge from the urethra or vagina. When offering workshops for college students, I used to remind students that they would never put food in their bodies without looking at it first; the same standard should apply to sex partners. Share with your child that being too uncomfortable to look at the genitals of a potential partner is a clear sign that he or she is not fully ready to have sexual intercourse with that partner.

We also had a circa-1976 pamphlet entitled "VD—What a little soap and water can do" that encouraged people to wash thoroughly before sex. While the term VD is now obsolete, the concept of cleansing genitals before sexual contact in a non-monogamous relationship still makes sense. It is no substitute for condom use, but may help reduce risks of transmitting certain germs.

Sharing these tips for helping your child to avoid sexually transmitted infections could save your child's life. What a compelling reason for you to model your courage to be uncomfortable by discussing sex with your kids!

Adolescents may also have independent access to professional services to support their sexual health. All fifty states and the District of Columbia explicitly allow minors to consent to sexually transmitted infections (STI) services without parental involvement, although eleven states require that a minor be of a certain age (generally twelve or fourteen) to do so. Thirty-one states explicitly include HIV testing and treatment in the package of STI services to which minors may consent.[122] You may want to check for your state's services and be sure they are made known to your adolescent child. Or, you may prefer to let your child know that her health is so important to you that you'll help her get medical attention for any reason and withhold judgment until the medical problem has been resolved.

One STI is now preventable with a vaccine. That STI is HPV, or human papillomavirus, the most common sexually transmitted infection in the United States. Nearly 40 percent of American adults carry this virus. Some infected people have absolutely no symptoms while others experience diseases from venereal warts to cervical cancer. The U.S. Centers for Disease Control and Prevention and the American Academy of Pediatrics both recommend vaccinating young girls for HPV between the ages of nine and twelve, long before

---

122 Guttmacher Institute. "Facts on American Teens' Sexual and Reproductive Health." January 2011.

they become sexually active. The vaccination is most effective before a person is exposed to any of the multiple strains of the HPV virus. The CDC&P recommends the series of three shots for young women; while the vaccination is also effective in males, it is not yet on the CDC&P list of recommended vaccination for young men "because studies suggest that the best way to prevent the most disease due to HPV is to vaccinate as many girls and women as possible. Parents of boys can decide if the vaccine is right for their sons by talking with their sons' health care providers. Young men and their parents can also discuss this vaccine with their doctors."[123]

PEERS

With adolescence, sex play can actually be real sex, with the "play" part ending when the hormones make sexual arousal a real force in adolescent life. This thought frightens most parents, but you can use this fear as motivation to make your plan to support and talk to your kids.

A very common fear expressed by parents of adolescent boys is that their son will impregnate a girl. Since the ultimate decision about handling an unexpected pregnancy usually lies with the girl, parents of boys fear the loss of control over their sons' future in this circumstance. This fear leads many parents (and could lead you) to having a very minimal sex talk with your child that amounts to "just don't do it." However, researchers have learned that this advice is practically useless for teens who have decided to have sex. One focus group member recalled his parents providing him a gentle explanation of why not to have sex as a teen. They told him that he may meet a girl who seems to be very sexually attracted to him and invites him to be her sexual partner. If she suggests unprotected sex, it may be possible that she sees her future as a mom. His parents told him that if he didn't see himself as a dad in nine months and had a vision of a different future for himself then he should not accept this invitation. Along with appropriate and considerate talks about sex, remind your adolescent children that drinking or doing drugs may make such an invitation to have unprotected sex more difficult to turn down.

Parents of teenage girls worry that their daughters will be taken advantage of sexually. One focus group member recalled her father's unique method of inoculating his daughters against boys' attempts to make them feel as if they

---

123 The United States Centers for Disease Control and Prevention, 2011.

owed a sexual favor after a date. This father took each daughter to an expensive restaurant and insisted that she order anything she wanted. In fact, he encouraged his girls to order the most expensive thing on the menu, even when they knew family finances were tight. "He wanted us to know that we deserved the best, with no strings attached," the focus-group member told me, and apparently this lesson lasted a lifetime. Throughout her dating life, she never once felt obligated to thank a man for dinner with anything more than a gracious smile!

ADULTS

Many adolescents, particularly females, appear to be sexually mature adults years before their social, emotional, and intellectual development catches up to their bodies. While many of you know about school-girl crushes that teens develop on adults, you must also consider that adults develop crushes on kids. For instance, a smart female social worker sought support from her clinical supervisor to maintain a treatment relationship with a particularly handsome seventeen-year-old-boy, and a male teacher knew to make sure he was never alone with the teen who he found attractive. However, not all professionals bother to do the work necessary to process their very human reactions to a person they find particularly attractive or charming. Chapter 9 discussed the sexual climate of your child's school, but this is a good time to remember the statistic published by the U.S. Department of Education on this topic: at least 5 percent of all kids reported a sexual contact with a school employee sometime during their school experience.[124] Whether it's the male teacher living out his midlife crisis with a crush on a young girl or the young, plain-jane teacher responding to her first experience of male adoration, there are a surprisingly large number of possibilities for indiscretions where teens and adults mingle. By the time our kids become teens, we are less worried about pedophiles and more worried about manipulative adults of either gender. Pay close attention to all relationships your teen has with adults and be sure to check in with him or her regularly about their daily interactions with their teachers, coaches, and other adults.

---

124 Shakeshaft, Carol. *Educator Sexual Misconduct: A Synthesis of Existing Literature.* 2004.

Considerations for Unmarried Parents

It can be terribly disconcerting to realize that you don't know everything your child experiences for the extended periods of time he or she spends with the other parent. Sometimes, kids come home with language, clothes, toys, music, and the like that does not match your personal values. Calmly bring your concern to the attention of your child. As always, use I-statements rather than accusations, such as, "I'm concerned because I've never seen you do that before"; this is a much better way to start a conversation with your teen than, "What the heck is that all about?"

If there are additional kids in the other partner's home, be sensitive to where your child fits into the age and gender order, and make sure your child is comfortable with the sleeping arrangements and her ability to maintain privacy while away from your house.

Ideally, if you live apart from your spouse or former partner, you will continue to communicate and determine together how to handle your child's sexual issues. If this is not possible, be sensitive to the fact that your child cannot control the behavior of the other parent. You may have to settle for enforcing rules or standards in your home and know that different rules apply with the other parent. Compromise over music, curfew, and dress may be necessary to keep the peace. But compromise does not work if you believe that your child is at any risk in the other home. Share your concern with the other parent in a calm and non-accusing manner, presenting your worries and asking for cooperation to work out a solution that has your child's interest at heart. If you've had a contentious divorce, you may be tempted to use a child's discomfort with the other parent or some aspect of their home as a way to limit that parent's access to your child. Resist that temptation. A calm, rational exploration of the reasons for your child's discomfort will be much more fruitful than a knee-jerk reaction to stop visitation all together—a decision that will also, inevitably, affect your child and may make him or her angry and defiant toward your rules and values.

A Special Note to Adults Victimized as Kids

If you come into parenthood with unresolved issues regarding sexual victimization of any kind, you may have an even longer list of fears about potential harm to your child. You may bring a victim's perspective to interpreting or misinterpreting your child's behaviors as well. When trying to figure out if a situation is problematic, though, it is particularly important for you to remain calm and seek the perspective of a trusted confidante or clinician. Bear in mind that there is much individual variation in a child's response to a behavior by another person. Your goal is to get to the bottom of the questionable situation by carefully learning more about what happened without jumping to incorrect conclusions or upsetting your child or yourself. With some forethought and support, you can help your child and family remain sexually healthy and safe.

CHAPTER 12

Variations in Sexuality

Human sexuality is richly complex. Some aspects are culturally defined, some are learned while maturing, and still others are wired into the brain before birth. These diverse influences of nature and nurture interact to influence how an individual experiences his or her own sexuality throughout life. There are many ways to define the dimensions of sexuality, but the one I find particularly helpful describes the difference between gender role (a set of behaviors), sexual orientation (who people are attracted to as potential sexual partners), and gender identity (the sex or gender people believe they are— usually, but not always, the one that matches their body).

There is a wide range in the ways that people experience sexual development. At least one in twenty kids will experience divergence from the typical or expected path in their sexual development. Myths, misinformation, and confusion can overwhelm a child and his entire family. Poor societal treatment can place sexually atypical kids at a higher risk than other kids for mental and physical health issues. Having a supportive family has been clearly identified as *the* factor for a child that reduces the damage caused by the heightened stress of not being completely accepted in school or her community, so if your child is expressing her sexuality in an unexpected way, resist any urge to shy away; this child needs even more thoughtful parenting. You need to clearly understand the differences between gender identity, gender role and behaviors, and most importantly that sexual orientation is neither a choice nor a mental disorder. All kids need informed, patient, and supportive parents to nurture them through the tumultuous changes of childhood and adolescence, and sexual minority kids need this even more.

Sexual Orientation

Sexual orientation refers to the gender of the people one is sexually attracted to as a potential sex partner. When men prefer exclusively women and women prefer exclusively men, their sexual orientation is described as heterosexual. When men prefer exclusively men and women prefer exclusively women, their orientation is described as homosexual. When either men or women prefer either men or women, their sexual orientation is referred to bisexual. Heterosexuality, homosexuality, and bisexuality describe relations between mutually attracted, consenting partners.

Gay and Lesbian

"Gay" is the American vernacular for being sexually attracted to a member of your own gender. In some communities, gay may refer to men attracted to other men only, while "lesbian" refers to women attracted to other women. The scientific term "homosexual" is derived from the Latin root *homo*, meaning same, as in homogeneous. The Latin root *hetero* means "different," as in heterogeneous. We live in a heterogeneous society, and it is crucial that we as a society understand and respect these differences—and this includes sexual orientation.

Every culture and most species have members who become coupled with same-sex partners. Estimates of the prevalence of gay people in the United States range from 1 in 10 to 1 in 20. Current estimates are that there are close to one million households where both adult partners are the same sex.

There is no single factor that determines if a person will become a homosexual adult. Rather, this is determined by a complex mix of social, psychological, biological, and, most likely, genetic factors. Myths and misinformation abound about homosexuality, such as boys raised in homes with all women are more likely to grow up gay—but this is just inaccurate. So too is the myth that girls who like short hair and contact sports are more likely to grow up gay. The most important myth to dispel, however, is that being gay is a *choice*. It is not. Healthy gay people feel an instinctual attraction to a member of their own gender in the same way that healthy heterosexual people experience attraction to the other gender.

Many gay adults report that they knew there were gay by junior high school or sometimes earlier. Others took much longer to recognize this. Bob, a focus group member in his forties, recalled that the meanest kid in grade school used to sneer and call him a homo. "I had no idea what that meant," Bob recalled. "I was nine or ten and didn't know anything at all about sex, and *I* certainly didn't know I was gay for years!"

Imagine Bob as a young man on the path to discovering his sexuality and having the word "homo" programmed into his brain as something to be sneered about. How would this affect his ability to recognize and accept his own sexual preference? This is a typical example of the obstacles faced by sexual minority youths as they mature and learn to understand their own sexuality.

Most likely, we all know someone who is gay or lesbian, either in our communities or perhaps in our families. Marginalizing or victimizing people of any age based on perceptions of some notion of their sexuality should have no place in our society—and you can start combating that by teaching tolerance and acceptance to your children as they begin to mature sexually and even before.

Young people who are in a sexual minority who endure poor treatment by their peers, family, and community members are put at risk for low self-esteem, poor academic performance, and a host of mental health issues, including higher than average rates of suicide attempts, substance abuse, and depression.[125] The U.S. Centers for Disease Control and Prevention reports that 6 out of 10 sexual minority students feel unsafe at school, 8 out of 10 have been verbally harassed, and 1 out of 5 have been physically assaulted.[126]

While gender discrimination places females on the losing end of the equation in many important areas like earning power, girls may actually have a slightly easier time in our culture when it comes to their sexual orientation and gender roles. It is generally acceptable for a girl to take on stereotypically male behaviors—in fact this rarely attracts unwanted or hostile attention from those around them. Western cultures are also much more accepting of girls showing affection toward each other. Girls routinely hug or kiss their BFFs;

---

125 The United States Centers for Disease Control and Prevention. Accessed on July 30, 2011 at http://www.cdc.gov/lgbthealth/youth.htm.
126 Ibid.

conversely, I recall being a camp counselor for a group of sixth-grade boys who would rather miss a field trip than hold hands with a buddy as per our safe-travel procedures.

Discomfort with things that have any connotation of "gayness" is not restricted to young boys. Discrimination still exists, some of it covert and some of it advertised by hate-mongering organizations. Some parents feel uncomfortable if they or their kids are in the company of gay adults; the term for this is homophobia.

The dictionary defines homophobia as an "irrational fear or aversion to or discrimination against homosexuals or homosexuality."[127] The expression of this irrational fear and the resulting discrimination is a major contributor to the harmful social, physical, and mental health problems experienced by sexual minority youth and adults. Peruse anti-gay websites and you'll find that irrational justifications for homophobia are often based on some notion about gay adults and children.[128] But the fact of the matter is, healthy gay people, just like healthy straight people, have no sexual interest in kids. Pedophiles have interest in children, and their sexual preference has nothing to do with being gay or not. It's imperative that you understand this. Buying into irrational stereotypes may lead you into a false sense of security; keeping your children away from openly gay people is not by any means a strategy to keep kids safe from sexual predators. Furthermore, belief in these negative and inaccurate stereotypes is damaging to the thousands of gay people who are forced to live in communities where anti-gay bullying and discrimination are socially accepted.

There is hope now for creating tolerance as understanding and acceptance of homosexuals are increasing. A 2010 Gallup poll reported on "a gradual cultural shift underway in Americans' views toward gay individuals and gay rights . . . the shift is apparent in a record-high level of the public seeing gay and lesbian relations as morally acceptable."[129] Homophobia is also on the

---

127 *Merriam-Webster Dictionary*. Accessed on August 30, 2011 at http://www.merriam-webster.com/dictionary/homophobia.

128 See, for example, Evelyn Schlatter's *18 Anti-Gay Groups and Their Propaganda*. Online, http://www.splcenter.org/get-informed/intelligence-report/browse-all-issues/2010/winter/the-hard-liners

129 Saad, Lydia. "Americans' Acceptance of Gay Relations Crosses 50% Threshold." Gallop.com, 2010. Accessed on September 5, 2011, at http://www.gallup.com/poll/135764/americans-acceptance-gay-relations-crosses-threshold.aspx.

decline due in some part to new media images offered through mainstream sources. Network television now offers mainstream gay characters living in suburbia as part of loving families, a pop superstar sings an anthem to tolerance, an openly gay American Idol finalist is flanked by loving parents who banter about their son's sexual orientation, and a film star receives an academy award nomination for playing half of a lesbian couple parenting two teens. These images serve to make lesbians and gay men less mysterious to others and are very important to the mental health and wellbeing of sexual minority youths. A gay man approaching age seventy shared with me that he had no idea how gay people were supposed to live when he came of age in the 1960s and "now gays have their own cable TV shows. A young guy today has his choice of gay role models." The same can be said for lesbians, so it's true that the popular culture references to gays and lesbians have an unanticipated benefit— the appearance of more gay role models in the media may help reduce the stress for young people going through the process called "coming out."

What exactly is meant by the phrase "coming out"? It generally refers to the decision a homosexual person makes to be public about his or her sexual orientation. Like the other psychosexual developmental tasks we described in chapter 5, coming out also proceeds in stages. Different experts offer variations on the process, but a most basic sequence starts with the person questioning his or her sexual orientation and then these steps follow: self-recognition as gay, disclosure to a small group of people deemed safe and accepting, socializing with other gay people, broader disclosure, and positive self-acceptance. The beginning stages of questioning and self-recognition generally occur early in life, such as in adolescence or young adulthood. Stages can overlap and the entire process can be very difficult and painful for a young person. Researchers report that the coming-out process is currently beginning at younger ages than in prior generations. One major study identified the mean age of coming out to others as just under seventeen years old for people aged eighteen to twenty-seven, an age more than ten years younger than the age of the process of coming out to others reported by gay adults over age fifty-five.[130]

---

130 Grov, Christian, David S. Bimbi, Jose E. Nanin, and Jeffrey T. Parsons. "Race, Ethnicity, Gender, and Generational Factors Associated With the Coming-Out Process Among Gay, Lesbian, and Bisexual Individuals." *The Journal of Sex Research*, Volume 43, Number 2, May 2006: 115–121.

The U.S. Centers for Disease Control and Prevention (CDC&P) offer insights into the public health issues associated with gay and lesbian youth.[131] As expected, HIV/AIDS is on their list, but there are many more common concerns. Sexual minority youths are at an extraordinarily high risk of being bullied at school, of experiencing suicidal thoughts or actions, of getting involved in substance abuse, and of engaging in unsafe sexual practices. Safe, supportive, emotional relationships with family members are crucial for these teens. Many adolescents require the skills of a counselor or therapist to navigate the turbulent teen years; the added turmoil of sexual questioning may make professional support all the more important. If your child seems to be struggling with issues of sexuality, offer him or her the option of working with a counselor or therapist specializing in teens. Your local United Way may be able to help identify an appropriate, affordable counseling service for your child.

Kids rejected by their families are at a high risk of homelessness, being runaways, and becoming exploited. Supportive parenting can make a world of difference, and community support counts. The CDC&P recommends that "going to a school that creates a safe and supportive learning environment for all students and having caring and accepting parents are especially important"[132] for sexual minority children. Try searching "GLBTQ" (Gay Lesbian Bisexual Transgender Questioning) on the Internet and you will find GLBTQ alliances at many U.S. colleges but few in high schools. Why is it that kids are made to wait until they are away from home to find the comfort and support of a peer group on this issue? Even the CDC&P recommends that high schools consider developing Gay-Straight Alliances to encourage tolerance, reduce alienation and isolation of gay students, and minimize bullying and stigmatization of teens struggling with their sexual preferences.[133]

Devastating things can happen to people who live in a culture that stigmatizes homosexuality. Victims of a same-sex attack may keep the offense to themselves to avoid being labeled gay by community members. The medical

---

131 The United States Centers for Disease Control and Prevention. Accessed in July 2011 at http://www.cdc.gov/lgbthealth/youth.htm.

132 Ibid.

133 See the U.S. Centers for Disease Control and Prevention at http://www.cdc.gov/lgbthealth/youth.htm.

and mental health consequences of holding that secret can be awful for the victims. Some researchers report that gays can be at a higher risk for inter-partner violence when internal conflict over a socially stigmatized, same-sex attraction fuels conflicts in a relationship. Forcing anyone to live a lie can take its toll on that person's mental health. In order for your child to live in a sexually safe and healthy community, is enormously important that you teach your children that intolerance and victimization of any minority—especially when sex is the focus—is unacceptable.

Parenting a Gay Child

A gay focus group member was incredulous when I asked if his parents ever spoke to him about sex. "Why would they?" he asked me. "My father must have had some notion that I wouldn't be making love to women, wouldn't be making any babies." If his dad really was thinking this way, he was very short-sighted and missed an important opportunity to support his son. If you have a gay child, whether or not you are concerned with procreation, you must speak with him about safe and healthy sexual relationships. All adolescents need to understand safe, respectful, loving sex and the risks involved with any sexual interactions that may or may not be about procreation.

Some feminist writers and researchers have gone to great lengths to point out that we live in a "hetero-dominant" culture. Fairy tales that tell little girls that if they're lucky when they grow up they can marry a prince, or that boys will only want to dance with the pretty girls, do little to help socialize a female child or to instill in her a personal sense of value and self-esteem—and this is particularly true if the female is lesbian. Illustrating this, lesbian poet Adrienne Rich wrote:

> When those who have the power to name and to socially construct reality choose not to see you or hear you, whether you are dark-skinned, old, disabled, female, or speak with a different accent or dialect than theirs, when someone with the authority of a teacher, say, describes the world and you are not in it, there is a moment of psychic disequilibrium, as if you looked into a mirror and saw nothing. [134]

---

134 Adrienne Rich, poet. Quoted in *The Feminist Classroom* by Frances A. Maher and Mary Kay Thompson Tetreault. Oxford: Rowman and Littlefield, 2001.

Many parents choose not to see much about their children's sexuality, regardless of sexual orientation. Yet, no loving parents wish to make their child feel as if they are staring into a blank mirror. The father of a gay daughter shared with me that he was completely taken by surprise when his daughter came out: "I had no idea . . . she dated boys all through high school"; this child's sexuality was invisible to her dad. As a parent, you should consider how you can transmit your values and communicate your principles in ways that do not assume that your child will lead an adult social or sexual life just like yours. But experts recommend that you don't ask your child outright if he or she is gay. The "coming out" process is developmental, and like all developmental processes, children go through it at a highly individualized pace. Do take every opportunity to illustrate to your child your love for him and support his interest in social or educational groups, even if it is logistically difficult for you. And, of course, ban all homophobic comments from your home. Showing loving support will let your child know that you'll be receptive to any information when he or she is ready to share it.

It is understandable that some of you may feel disappointed when you learn your child is gay. For some parents, it may mean that their specific picture of their child's future won't be realized. If you feel this way, know you are not alone but, like other parents, you must face this fact and continue to support your child. Parents longing to raise a doctor may also be disappointed if their daughter becomes an artist instead; the founders of a family business may be stunned when their son wants nothing to do with the empire; the fashionista can't stand it that her daughter will wear only jeans. So if you learn that your child is gay, remember that anger is an unreasonable reaction—unlike education, careers, or appearance, sexual orientation is *not* a choice.

Take your lead from the American Academy of Pediatrics, which offers the following advice to parents:

> Sexual orientation cannot be changed. A child's heterosexuality or homosexuality is deeply ingrained as part of them. As a parent, your most important role is to offer understanding, respect, and support to your child. A non-judgmental approach will gain your child's trust and put you in a better position to help him or her through these

difficult times. You need to be supportive and helpful, no matter what your youngster's sexual orientation may be.[135]

Gays and Sexual Abuse

I have a vivid memory from my days as a young social worker for a sexual abuse project of a father whose five-year-old son had been victimized by a man. "He's ruined," the dad sobbed into the phone. "He'll never be right." This father's comments during that call expressed his belief that his son was now *destined* to be gay—and that this was a huge problem.

But is there a link between boys who've being sexually abused by a male and their becoming gay because of the experience? The answer is no. Sexual orientation motivated by real, loving attraction is much more complex than that. Some researchers describe certain types of sexual behavior as being driven by "imprinted arousal patterns," as the victim "continues to be eroticized by stimulation that covertly or overtly resembles the abuse circumstances."[136] Early sexual experiences can certainly set the patterns for how the brain interprets sex. When the victimization is long-term, when the child is convinced by the pedophile that he was a willing, indeed orgasmic partner, a child's sexual self-image may potentially develop around same-sex behaviors. Given this, it is possible that a victim of sexual assault may act out sexually if left with unresolved issues around the assault, particularly if they are lacking the insight into the fact that their experience of physical arousal was purely autonomic. But this in no way means that sexual assault of a child by a same-gendered adult will influence a child's sexual preference. Likewise, sexual victimization may have the exact *opposite* effect on some victims; victims of either gender may never want to see or deal with genitalia that resemble their molester's ever again, but this also does not define their sexual orientation.

---

135 See the American Academy of Pediatrics at http://www.healthychildren.org/English/ages-stages/gradeschool/Pages/Gender-Identity-and-Gender-Confusion-In-Children.aspx.

136 King, Neal. "Childhood Sexual Trauma in Gay Men: Social Context and the Imprinted Arousal Pattern." Copublished simultaneously in *Journal of Gay & Lesbian Social Services* (Harrington Park Press, an imprint of The Haworth Press, Inc.) Vol. 12, No. 1/2, 2000: 19–35.

However, a same sex assault can place an additional layer of conflict on gay victims. Some gay male survivors of same-sex abuse describe their ambivalence to the gay community, in some way associating their molester with all gay men. Closeted gays may be hindered in accepting their sexuality because of the belief that the abuse "made them this way" (as expressed by that distraught father mentioned earlier seeking services for his son victimized by a man).

No matter a person's sexual orientation, all victims of sexual assault require care, compassion, and optimism that with support and qualified professional help they will be able to recover from the assault and grow into a sexually safe and healthy adult. See chapter 13 for specific considerations if you believe abuse has occurred to your child.

Gender Identity

Gender identity is defined as the gender a person identifies with—what gender he or she really believes to be. For the overwhelming majority of people, this is ridiculously simple—our body matches who we think we are psychologically, and we are generally at ease with many of the gender expectations that society has of us. But a small number of people don't feel the comfort of a match between their physical and psychological selves. In very rare situations, a young child may declare the "mistake" to their parents; in others, as a person progresses through life they may come to identify as "transgender."

The concept of transgender is a complicated one for many people to grasp because it requires us to rethink a belief in the absolute differences between male and female. Many people still incorrectly use the terms "transgender" and "transsexual" as synonyms, but this ignores the very many ways that being transgender is felt and expressed by an individual. "While 'transsexual' is a medical term developed by psychiatrists and psychologists, 'transgender' describes a social movement. Transgender refers to the spectrum of gender ambiguity—the various ways in which our gendered behavior, activities, dress, and identities do not match up neatly with the assumption that there are two biological categories: 'male' and 'female.'"[137] Another expert explains that "a person who is convinced that their bodies do not match their gender

---

137 Sarah Wilcox, as quoted in 2004 by Beth Rankin on http://fusion.kent.edu/archives/spring04/trans/transprint.html.

identities and feel that they need to change that are identified as transsexual. Some, but not all, seek medical interception to change their body."[138]

The important concept to grasp is that there is wide variation in how people experience being transgender and it is not at all the same as being gay. A gay focus group member highlighted this when he said, "This can be a particularly challenging area even for the gay and lesbian community. Many gay men are not comfortable around those who are transgendered. It's a learning process for almost all of us."

There are few models of transgender individuals in the mainstream media. A transgender fashion model received media attention when she competed in a popular televised modeling competition. The protagonist in the Pulitzer Prize-winning novel *Middlesex*[139]grows into an adult who lives alternately as a man and a woman. Transsexuals have been more prominent in media; Renee Richards made waves as one of the first prominent male-to-female transsexuals, and Chaz Bono, born as the daughter named Chastity to Sonny and Cher, received extensive media coverage when he came out publicly as a male in 2010. The differences are more than nuance and need to be understood by you if your child questions his or her gender identity.

Experts offer wide variations in their estimates of transgender and transsexuality, from as common as 1 on 500 to as rare as 1 in 30,000. This wide range of estimates may be due to inconsistencies in the definitions of the two terms. None of these numbers matter to a parent, however, whose son insists she's really a girl, or whose daughter insists he's a boy. A very small number of young children eventually become absolutely sure that they are in a body of the wrong gender. If a toddler sincerely wants to know when her penis is going to fall off so she can look like the other girls, or wants to know when his penis will grow in, this child may truly believe that they are not the same gender in their brains as they are in their bodies, and you should be prepared to explore this further as your child matures. In the words of little Jazz, a transgendered child interviewed in the national media, "I got a girl brain and a boy body."[140]

---

138 Dr. Patricia Barthalow Koch. Personal communication on September 7, 2011.
139 Eugenides, Jeffrey. *Middlesex*. New York: Picador, 2002.
140 See, for example, http://abcnews.go.com/2020/story?id=3088298&page=1.

Remember that this is not the same as a child wanting to play with toys of the other gender, or wanting to play games with children of another gender. If a child communicates in no uncertain terms that he or she *is* the other gender, ask your pediatrician to help you find the experts who can help, or contact a university-based children's hospital with specialists in this area. It is important that you show support for your child as early as possible if he or she feels of a different gender.

The experience of being transgender while still a small child is a highly unusual scenario; most children develop the various aspects of their sexuality in later childhood before or during adolescence. Like any other developmental issues, there are many individual variations. While some kids realize they are transgender during adolescence, others may interpret their feelings to mean they are gay (which is a gender orientation) and proceed through the stages of coming out and then explore their gender identity as young adults. While mainstream media offers few messages on this topic, kids questioning their sexuality who are old enough to surf the Internet will find plenty to read about transgender issues. Like any other topic, the quality and accuracy of the information varies tremendously. If you sense that your adolescent is questioning her sexuality, help steer her and yourself to reputable sources of information, like the American Psychological Association.[141] Regardless of how your child presents a gender issue to you and your partner, your response has to be calm, thoughtful, supportive, and loving, and guided by the best professional help available.

Intersex and Disorders of Sex Development (DSD)

One of about every 2,000 births may be intersex, which means a baby who has physical, hormonal, or chromosomal characteristics that are both male and female. The old term for this group of conditions was *hermaphroditism*, a term combining the names of a Greek god Hermes and goddess Aphrodite. Although the term *intersex* is still widely used in the popular media, the National Institute of Health recommends adopting the term "disorders of sex development," or DSD.[142]

---

141 http://www.apa.org/topics/sexuality/transgender.aspx
142 See the website for the United States National Library of Medicine at http://www.nlm.nih.gov/medlineplus/ency/article/001669.htm.

Prenatal conditions, environmental conditions, and genetics are among the contributing factors identified for DSDs. As discussed in detail in chapter 11, if you notice any anomalies with your child's genitalia at birth or shortly after, you should work with your pediatrician to find the best possible experts to deal with the problem. Most importantly, you should not rush to judgment and assign a gender to your child. Children with ambiguous genitalia used to be assigned the role of female because it was easier for physicians to surgically construct female genitals. Long-term studies show that labia and dresses are not enough to change a male's gender identity to female. If your child is born with one of these conditions, you need patience, an open heart, and a university-affiliated children's hospital staffed with experts who are in no rush to the surgical suite and who can help you and your child through this confusing time.

Gender Roles

Gender roles refer to the behaviors a culture ascribes to a particular gender. Boys play football, girls play with dolls, and other stereotyped behaviors describe gender roles, but these definitions and beliefs change over time and place. While scientists believe that gender-specific hormones influence certain behavior—such as the role of estrogen with bonding and the role of testosterone with certain types of aggression—gender roles are generally culturally-defined behaviors.

The changing status of women in sports over the past four decades provides a great example of how gender roles can change. President Nixon signed Title IX of the Education Amendments of 1972, prohibiting discrimination in educational activities on the basis of gender. One of the greatest results of Title IX was the development of sports programs for girls that equaled those for boys.

In 1972 my large, well-funded high school was typical of most in that it offered no extracurricular athletic activities for girls (unless you consider cheerleading athletic—it certainly was competitive). It was inconceivable then to think of girls on the soccer field or on the basketball court. But ten years later, it was almost as easy to find athletic clubs, teams, and leagues for girls as it was for boys. Decades later, the country cheered as the U.S. Women's Soccer Team made it to the World Cup finals. Clearly, gender role expectations for girls and sports have changed over the course of the last generation, thanks in some part to Title IX.

Title IX brought young women more than a chance to develop athletic abilities, however. Social skills like teamwork, negotiation, safe and healthy competition among peers, and respect for a coach are life-long lessons garnered from team sports. Not all girls want to play a sport, and neither do all boys, but a sexually safe and healthy community, like a sports team, offers choices that are not based on gender alone; broad definitions of gender roles are encouraged and accepted, allowing all people to develop any of their talents to their full potential.

Yet another shift in gender roles is illustrated through census data informing us that the number of married couples with a breadwinner mom and stay-at home dad is on the rise. The economic crisis of 2010 hit male-dominated industries like construction and finance harder than most other industries, meaning that men have been disproportionally affected with unemployment. Not all men miss the daily grind, and not all women want to be home as the primary caregiver. Economic conditions have caused changes in gender roles, and you can help reduce the stress on affected families by ensuring that your extended family and community supports gender role options and choice, for whatever reason a family makes it.

If you think your kids aren't paying attention to the gender roles in your home, you should think again. One focus group mom gave a great example when she shared how cool she thought it was when her five-year-old son reacted to his dad's comment that he'd be home late because of a meeting. Her son replied, "I thought only moms had late meetings." Kids absorb messages about gender roles from a very early age. In many families, kids learn from a very young age to bring certain issues to mom and others to dad without a second thought. It's important to be thoughtful about the messages your family promotes

Dress and Gender Role

American cinema culture is filled with examples of men dressing like women, from *Some Like it Hot* in the 1950s to *Tootsie* in the 1980s to Tyler Perry's twenty-first century *Madea's Big Happy Family*. Whether men do it for a movie role, for personal comfort, or to perform in a drag show, cross-dressing is not the same as being gay. Dressing is a behavior and consequently a component of gender roles. Dress is not a de facto predicator of sexual orientation or gender identity. There may be as many as a million straight men who enjoy dressing in women's clothing; some find it sexually arousing, others find it comforting, still others find it just plain fun. Enough heterosexual men cross dress that there are even support groups for the wives married to cross-dressing men!

In American culture, cross-dressing seems to be primarily an issue for males who choose to dress as females; it is generally considered socially acceptable for a woman to wear men's clothing without being labeled as a cross-dresser. Female celebrities sometimes show up on the red carpet in tuxedos, and most consider this a fashion statement. It is entirely possible that there are straight women who meet emotional needs, such as being comforted or erotically aroused, by dressing as a man, but it is not widely studied or reported.

Many therapists and researchers believe that a desire for a male to cross-dress starts when a boy is very young. Perhaps the boy learns to feel deep comfort and relief from stress when he cuddles with a special article of women's clothing. Cuddling or handling women's clothing may progress to occasionally wearing women's clothing at home, then to wearing women's clothing in public and passing as a female. Cross dressing can become a life-long behavior for a straight man. There are gay people and transsexuals who cross-dress too, but cross dressing alone is not an absolute indicator of sexual orientation.

So what do you do if you find your son in his mother's nightgown? The first rule of any reaction to a surprising behavior from your child is to stop and *think* before you utter a word. Remember, your child will continue to associate your reaction with the behavior in question. You will frighten and confuse your child by showing a strong, negative reaction to something he thinks is routine play. Being frightened and confused will make it more difficult for your child to respond to the message from you that is most helpful—a message of concern and support.

If your son is a preschooler, the nightgown probably means no more to him than any other costume. If that style of dress-up continues as your child ages, talk to your child gently and without blame to determine the circumstances that make him want to dress up. For some kids, the clothes can become like a security blanket; they look, smell, or feel like someone who brings or brought them comfort. Giving your son permission to openly cuddle the articles of clothing or maybe sleep with them under his pillow may be all the comfort he needs. A calm, inquisitive, and supportive response can help make these objects eventually lose any special meaning or value, unlike an upsetting outburst from you, which can well have the opposite effect. Your calm reaction may help your child outgrow the attachment, like sleeping with a favorite blanket or stuffed animal. Certainly punishment, insults, and denigration will do nothing good for your child's self-image or psychosexual development and has not been shown to permanently stop a behavior. Harsh treatment may actually heighten the stress that your child seeks to resolve through the comforting object.

Cross-dressing in adults whose gender identity matches their body can be considered a "fetish." A fetish is a sexually pleasing or arousing activity that is not typically associated with sexual behavior. Experts have documented a large array of fetishes, such as focusing on feet or inflicting pain on a partner. Adults form social groups dedicated to specific fetishes, such as "plushies," who dress as stuffed animals for social or erotic experiences. There have been textbooks and journal articles written by learned analysts about how fetishes develop, and most concur that childhood experiences play a role, principally in that the behavior developed in response to a stressor during childhood.

It is common for young children, particularly between the ages of two and four, to become very attached to an object such as a blanket or special stuffed animal. Psychologists refer to these as "transitional objects" and report that they are important in helping a child develop solitary sleeping habits and independence from infantile attachment to caretakers. Relinquishing any transitional object can be difficult for a child, and you need to gently support your child through this loss. If your young child becomes attached to an article of female clothing, shaming him and removing it harshly is unadvisable. Consider cutting the garment into another shape that is pleasing to this child but is no longer recognizable to preschool classmates as an article of clothing. Recall the same tactics you used to get your child to give up his bottle—a reward for going a day or night without it—or any other loving, supporting, educational tactic that works in your family. The key is to avoid adding stress to your child; it's the stress that makes him need his transitional object in the first place.

The idea of letting your son gain comfort from female clothing can be incredibly tough for you as a parent. You may even be dubious of the suggestion to avoid punishing or shaming a boy who is dressing like a girl. But this is one situation where you have no choice but to learn a lesson that you must come to understand sooner or later—that you do not have absolute control over your child's behavior or future.

Cross-dressing in and of itself is not necessarily a problem, but it can certainly lead to conflict or other issues. Being caught cross-dressing in the wrong place or by the wrong people can make a boy a target of violence; too many males, especially adolescent males with their testosterone-fueled, still-developing brains, become disgusted or enraged at the site of a male dressed like a woman. Instant availability of cameras and the technology to broadcast photographs now elevate this invasion of privacy to a tortuous public event. Being caught by immature peers can lead to violent aggression or public humiliation, which are incredibly damaging experiences for anyone.

Straight cross-dressers who marry often keep their behavior a secret from their wives for years, and otherwise-strong marriages can crumble from the strain of this deception. Suggesting that gentle support without judgment to help a boy outgrow the behavior is not a denigration of men for whom cross-dressing is a considered choice. Adults have the right and responsibility to make choices. Being gay or being transgender are not behavioral choices; for a straight young man, cross-dressing may well be. If it is possible for you to use gentle intervention to support a child to wean himself off the progressive path towards a behavior that can make adolescence and adulthood more difficult, I say proceed with love and understanding.

A Special Call-out to Straight Parents

As many as 10 million American children have a gay parent or are being raised in a household with same-sex parents. Odds are your child will meet at least one such family during his or her school years. This is a great opportunity for you to model tolerance and acceptance.

Even if you hold moral or religious values that are not accepting of homosexuality, religions rarely condone harsh treatment of a child based on a characteristic of his or her parents. There is no evidence that children raised by gays are more likely to grow up gay, and we have already established that having a sexual orientation for a same-sex adult partner is not at all the same as being attracted to children. Gay is not contagious and healthy gays have no sexual interest in children—theirs, yours, or anyone else's. Your child's developing a friendship with a child of same-sex parents offers a great opportunity to share your thoughts and values with your child. This is an opportunity to find an age-appropriate book to help your child understand gay families, so ask your local youth librarian for suggestions.

If your child wants to plan a visit to this family's home, exercise the same cautions with visits to this family that you would with visits to any home, as discussed in chapter 8. Know which adults will be in the house, know if any older kids will be there, speak to the parents, and learn their house rules and share yours. And be nice to the same-sex couple raising your child's friend; it's a great contribution to promoting a tolerant and sexually safe and healthy community!

So What Can a Parent Do?

- Be observant and supportive as your child develops.
- Understand that certain behaviors of young kids can be redirected, but that sexual orientation and gender identity cannot.
- Do not tolerate anti-gay slang in your house or from your children.
- Model tolerance while expressing your own values.
- Teach your kids tolerance for differences and respect for themselves.
- Understand that you as the parents will not be the ultimate factor in a child's sexual orientation or gender identity. And if it's not the one you want or expected, support your child's mental health and development by helping make your community a safe and accepting place for all sexual minorities. Learn all you can from organizations like PFLAG (Parents, Families and Friends of Lesbians and Gays)[143] and the Gay Straight Alliance Network.[144] Use these resources to support your family learning about others and help make yours a sexually safe and healthy community.

---

143 See www.PFLAG.org.
144 See www.GSAnetwork.org.

CHAPTER 13

Be Prepared

It *Can* Happen Here

Each year, at least 65,000 families deal with the public systems for inves-tigating and treating child sexual abuse,[145] but it's also known that twice that many cases go unreported.[146]

If you have suspicions that your child or teen has been touched or violated sexually, should you call the police? Your lawyer? Child protection authorities? Your initial response will have long-term implications for yourself, your child, and your community, so it's important you are able to think through the situation carefully and make the best decisions possible for your child and family.

In the following cases drawn from people I've known as friends, colleagues, clients, and others who wanted to share their story to help other parents, you'll find large variations in parental response to child sex abuse issues.

I learned Brenda's story when she was in her late fifties. Brenda was a neighbor who learned that I was working on a sexual abuse helpline and she shared with me that as an adolescent, she told her mother that her mother's boyfriend touched her sexually whenever they were left alone. Her mother confronted the man, who said they were all being prudes. The adults' relation-

---

145 See the U.S. Department of Health and Human Services table 3-13, page 47, at http://www.acf.hhs.gov/programs/cb/pubs/cm09/cm09.pdf.

146 According to a report to Congress entitled the "Fourth National Incidence Study of Child Abuse and Neglect (NIS-4)," more than 180,00 children experienced a sexual abuse incident that met the study definition during the NIS-4 study year (2005-2006).

ship ended, and so did Brenda's abuse, but the predatory boyfriend remained free to pursue kids in other relationships.

I learned Rich's story while having dinner with him and another friend when the conversation turned to the then highly-publicized clergy sexual abuse scandals. Rich shared the memory of telling his very devout parents back in the 1960s that their parish priest had touched him in a sexual manner. His father smacked him for speaking badly of the priest and that blow stopped Rich from speaking of the abuse again for decades.

Jill joined one of my focus groups and shared that she and her husband were parents of seven-year-old Ben. Ben was approached in the locker room at summer camp by a junior life guard, a teen who asked Ben to touch his penis. Jill noticed that Ben had not been swimming at camp for a few days and when she asked him why he told her that he didn't like the lifeguard anymore. She pressed him and he finally told her about the locker room situation. She waited until morning then called the camp. The camp's first call was to a lawyer, who advised them not to talk to anyone. Jill and her husband weighed their options and decided that they did not want their son to go through what they thought would be a difficult ordeal if they called the police. Instead, they threatened the camp by saying they would tell every parent in the program if the suspect lifeguard was not fired. Once the lifeguard was dismissed, Jill and her husband had no additional follow-up and dropped the issue.

In these situations, the parents chose to handle their specific crisis without going to the authorities or a public source of assistance. We may not agree with these parents but cannot judge their responses under excruciating circumstances. But their inaction in this regard can offer a lesson. Rich, Brenda, and Ben each faced a scarring and troubling violation; they did not receive counseling and suffered alone with their memories. In each case a predator remained loose in the community. Public systems often seem confusing and frightening to families, and some are. By avoiding them, kids are denied help and abusers remain free to attack other children. But many communities have placed a strong priority on services for child sexual abuse and really can offer your family help if you suspect sexual abuse.

Sally, a friend of a friend, shared very different experience. Sally's wealthy family responded to her allegation of sexual abuse by a member of her extended family by sending her to a private, in-patient mental health treatment facility. Sally's parents may have thought they made the best decision at the time, but she would later explain that in her mind, she had been punished, torn from her home and community and denied the teenage years she'd been longing for. To her it didn't seem fair that she had been sent away, and it still doesn't decades later. In her case as well, the predator remained loose in her community.

Before a tragedy strikes, decide now that you will never pursue a course of action that leaves a child molester free to pursue other victims, and that you will find the best possible help for your child.

You may feel isolated if you find yourself in the dreadful position of planning an appropriate course of action if you fear that your child was sexually assaulted. Will you be strong enough to get the police or other people involved? In this chapter, you'll find an approach for parents, caregivers, and concerned adults who want to provide effective responses for kids who may have been violated. By considering these suggestions, you can improve the odds of finding out what really occurred with your child, potentially minimize stress for your child, and increase the odds of getting the best services your community has to offer to cope with the abuse. To start, you should learn the three Cs of responding: Stay Calm, Keep Your Child First, and Maintain Control of the Situation. Let's start with the first C on the list.

Step 1: Stay Calm

This is a hard but crucial step. Should you suspect that someone is victimizing your child, you need to take one careful step at a time without revealing your fears to your child. It is entirely possible that the signs you see may not be abuse. Your obvious distress may upset your child; if you start questioning him without a plan, you may well wind up with useless information.

Not all parents whose kids have been at risk get a heart-stopping phone call like the one I received from my son's preschool, informing me that a teacher had been arrested for molesting another child. Brenda's mom had a daughter who was articulate, brave, and trusting enough to tell her mom about her concerns. Ben's mom noticed that her pool-loving son was coming home from camp with an unused swim suit. Other parents just "get the feeling" that something is "off." They can't quite put their finger on it, but their child is just not herself or himself.

It could be anything or nothing, but you should trust your instincts and gently follow up on the suspicion as soon as you are calm. The rush to question your child while you are still obviously frightened, angry, or shocked is one of the biggest mistakes you can make and may have long-term consequences in an investigation. Take a few hours or even a day to compose yourself, while keeping your child out of the suspect situation; give yourself the opportunity to proceed calmly. Your initial sense of rage could be about seeking vengeance toward the person who you believe hurt your child, or it might be misplaced guilt; there will be plenty of time to resolve that later. Just remember that your state of mind will clearly influence your child's decision to inform you about what's going on. The very best interviewers trained to elicit accurate information from kids are advised to appear completely neutral and stay even, warm, and supportive[147] no matter what the child says. You should do the same, but it may be hard, as unlike a professional interviewer with no personal relationship with the child, you are clearly emotionally involved. [148] It's much better to say nothing at first rather than plant your ideas or fears into your child's mind; that's almost certain to cause trouble later as your child integrates your fears into his thoughts.

How Would You Know That Something Might Have Happened to Your Child?

Somewhere between a phone call with a direct message and an inkling, we can find some helpful signals to determining whether or not your child has been abused. The American Academy of Child and Adolescent Psychiatry suggests the following as possible warning signs:

- unusual interest in or avoidance of all things of a sexual nature
- sleep problems or nightmares
- depression or withdrawal from friends or family
- seductiveness

---

147 Faller, Ann Coulborn. *Interviewing Children Abuse Sexual Abuse*. New York: Oxford University Press, 2007.

148 Annon, Jack. "Recommended Guidelines for Interviewing Children in Cases of Alleged Sexual Abuse."

- statements that their bodies are dirty or damaged, or fear that there is something wrong with them in the genital area
- refusal to go to school
- delinquency/conduct problems
- secretiveness
- aspects of sexual molestation in drawings, games, fantasies
- unusual aggressiveness
- suicidal behavior[149]

From my experience, I also suggest being alert for the following signs:

- extreme changes in weight
- "cutting" or self-mutilation, particularly in adolescents
- a sudden refusal to spend time with a particular person or at a specific place
- a newly developed refusal to change clothes in front of others such as in a fitting room while shopping or a locker room at camp or school
- knowledge of sexual language beyond their maturity level, especially in children too young to read or access the Internet
- simulated sex acts as part of play, again especially in children too young to read or access the Internet
- sexualized interactions with other children that are aggressive rather than curious.

A child exhibiting *any* of the items in this list needs your attention or possibly professional help. If you see these symptoms, all you know is that a child is experiencing a problem. More important, **every single symptom on these lists could really be caused by something other than sexual abuse!** Think of this as you try to stay calm. Every child is an individual. Every experience is unique. Checklists are a highly imperfect resource. Any one of these symptoms alone does not indicate abuse, but they all mean it is time for some

---

149 The American Academy of Child And Adolescent Psychiatry. "Facts for Families # 9." Accessed on March 11, 2011, at http://www.aacap.org/galleries/FactsForFamilies/09_child_sexual_abuse.pdf.

serious thought on your part and a talk with your child. Whatever problem you find will require a clear head and skillful parenting.

Part of staying calm is making sure all of the adults in the home are on the same page. If there are two adults in the household, strongly consider developing a plan together. The thought that your child has been sexually victimized is awful for any loving parent. Many may have an initial response of anger, rage, or revenge, which is only made worse by the unrealistic sense that they should have done a better job protecting their child. These are terrible and powerful feelings *that must not be shared with the child* in this initial phase. Adults may want to blame each other; I recall being beyond angry at my husband for being late to pick up our son from the daycare center, leaving him in the care of the staff member who was later indicted. Jill's husband was initially angry at her for not keeping better tabs on their son at camp. You and your partner may blame yourselves for any number of reasons and **these feelings are absolutely normal but acting on them is absolutely useless.**

You and your partner can be a great help to each other during this time. Share your thoughts and fears with each other. Role play talking to your child and see which one can do a better job at keeping a game-face when it's time to have the real talk.

Your game plan will be entirely different if there is any chance that the other adult in the home may be the abuser. Step-parents and other parental partners in the home present a statistical risk to children, and as much as you may hate the thought of that, you must face that fact and be prepared to take the appropriate actions if you find your child is being abused by an in-home perpetrator.

Step 2: Keep Your Child First

How do you know when you're prepared to speak with your child, and where can you begin? First, you must truly understand the way children experience the world and the way they communicate about it. Their brains do not work the way adult brains do; this was burned into the American consciousness and translated in American law as one result of the now infamous McMartin case.

In 1983, a California parent reported to the police that she thought that her child had been abused by a relative and an employee at a local preschool.

The police responded by sending a letter to every parent with a child in that school urging them to question their children. Dozens of frightened, angry parents heard amazing and bizarre stories from their very young children. These stories led to additional questioning of kids by authorities using questioning techniques now known to be completely mismatched to the age of the children. The law enforcement system concluded that the stories were true. Following the most expensive criminal trial in California history, multiple appeals, retractions, and ruined lives, these stories are now widely believed to have come from the imaginations of children trying to please adults who were following the police direction and diligently looking for answers. This legal calamity was initiated based on information gathered by terrified parents and culminated in six years of criminal trials and not a single conviction.

We now know that the police request for parents to question their children made as much sense as asking a parent to conduct their child's annual medical exam. The spectacular failure of this case inspired linguists, developmental psychologists, and other experts on children's learning and language to share their expertise with professionals working in law enforcement and child protection services. Their work can offer some important lessons for you as you seek to keep your child first in the process of seeking information if you suspect possible abuse.

Children and Language Development

A bright ten-year-old was speaking with her aunt about the menu for an anniversary dinner they were making for her parents. The aunt expected to discuss what they would be cooking together; in the mind of the child, a menu was something a waiter put on the table in a restaurant, so she was thinking about what color marker to use and how to spell spaghetti. When the conversation is about food, toys, or a book, we all can chuckle at the misapplied definition for a commonly used word, such as menu. But this misunderstanding stops being cute when you are worried or scared that your child may be at risk and this is when parents need to keep the child first by concentrating on the child's feelings and status of their developing skills with language. Lacking specific skills in linguistics, you may try really hard to get answers from your child in a manner analogous to speaking louder to someone who doesn't understand English. Your child will sense your desperation, may become desperate to please you, and will struggle to provide the answer he or she thinks you want. Questioning your child and getting good information requires preparation in grasping the developmental stage of your child's communication and comprehension skills. Most American kids may seem to have full language capacity by around age five, but this is an illusion.[150] Children still lack the ability to cope with complex and sophisticated communications at this age. Ambiguity, embedded questions, double negatives, and circuitous or multi-message questions that adults find hard to follow will certainly confound even the brightest child. Linguists believe that a child is still developing comprehensive linguistic skills until "well into the teen years"[151] so keep that in mind as you prepare to speak with your child about your concern regarding abuse.

Once you've identified the signs that something is not quite right with your child and you've taken twenty-four hours to calm down and consider the possibility that there has been no abuse, you are ready to find a quiet time to have a discussion with your child. Experts advise professional interviewers to spend some time establishing rapport with a child; while you are certainly not a stranger to your child, you should consider this advice to ease into the conversation about the abuse. When ready to move into the real topic, start with a question that requires more than a yes-or-no answer; these types of open-ended questions generally yield better information. "How do you like hanging out with Joe at school?" or, "You hardly talked to me on the ride home—what's bothering you?" are much better opening questions than asking, "Do you still like Joe?" or, "Is anything wrong?" So-called "closed-ended" questions can lead to a very short, useless conversation. A broad, open-ended question offers another advantage besides allowing you to gain more information off the bat—it avoids the risk of planting ideas in your child's young, impressionable mind.

What Good is a Question Without an Answer?

There are many reasons why young children feel required to provide an answer when presented with a question by an adult. The answer may not be

---

150 Walker, Anne Graffam. *Handbook on Questioning Children*. Washington, D.C.: American Bar Association Center of Children and the Law, 1999.

151 Ibid.

accurate from an adult's point of view, but it will make sense to the child from her different viewpoint. Children often believe that if the adult is asking a question of them, the adult is smart enough to know that they must have the answer. Even if an adult softens a question with phrasing such as "it's OK if you don't know," experts believe this may only confuse a child. A child will then wonder why in the world are you asking the question if you don't think the child has the answer. As you can see, getting information that is accurate and helpful can be tricky business!

Younger kids interpret a question as existing as half of a pair—shoes go with socks, pants go with shirts, milk goes with cookies, and questions go with answers. That means that your child will make sure he has an answer if you present a question. Children have a very strong need to please grownups, at least until adolescence. Grownups are the child's anchor to their universe; it's a basic survival instinct to stay on the good side of the adult responsible for taking care of them. Even when going through the "terrible twos" or "obstinate threes," a child's behavior is really all about redefining his or her relationship with the parent or caretaker. In order to please you, your child will want to supply you with an answer to any question you propose to him or her, even if the answer is completely made up.

Children also have different perceptions of time, space, and size than do adults. The word "big" to a child can mean size, age, or birth order, as in "big sister." Perception of time is not developed until late elementary school; therefore, it's unrealistic to expect a young child to tell you the exact time something may have happened. Law enforcement may need that level of specific detail to consider bringing a criminal charge against a perpetrator, but you don't. Specially trained interviewers may use time landmarks such as a holiday or birthday or the start of school to help a child anchor the time of an offense. For your purposes, though, you're not trying to do the cops' job; you just need to know if your child feels as if he or she has been victimized.

Young children can also be literal with their answers. When asked, "Did the babysitter touch you?" a child may say no. Later we find that the babysitter "washed" his penis. If asked, "Did Joe ever hurt you?" a child might well answer no but remember, being rubbed on the genitals may not have physically hurt your child at all. Once again, open-ended questions are most helpful in gleaning information from your young child.

Asking your child to repeat a story is also problematic. If you tell your child, "Tell Detective John what you told Mommy about Joe," this can confuse your child as she may not remember exactly what she told you just moments before. Adding "didn't you say that the babysitter washed your penis?" adds another problem. Children typically defer to adults to inform them of what's going on in their world. If you seem to think your child said something, then it must be so to him or her.

WORDS WITH MULTIPLE MEANINGS

When I received the call about the teacher arrested at my son's preschool for molesting another child, I knew enough to avoid questioning my son until I had time to speak with a trusted colleague. I believed it was safe to let my son go back to school because the alleged abuser was in police custody, but I was delirious with rage at this man, the school, and even my husband, who one day had been unable to leave work to pick up our son. So when I arrived to pick him up, he was the last child left and was sitting on the front step at school with the suspect teacher's arm around his shoulder. That image was (and still is!) burned into my brain. But with coaching from a colleague, I carefully questioned my son about the teacher. I am incredibly relieved to report that my questioning of my son, then about four years old, revealed absolutely no indication that he had been victimized by the teacher. When I finally shared that there was a report that "Joe had hurt a child at his school," he thought for a minute and asked if maybe there was another person named Joe at his school that he didn't know. I still feel that sigh of relief decades later! Thank goodness I didn't open with "Has Joe ever touched you?" My son may well have said yes, referring to any interaction, such as the one I observed at pick-up time when the teacher had his arm around him.

A final reminder before you start questioning your child: It is entirely conceivable that a skilled pedophile can engage a child in a way that was not unpleasant to the child and in fact may have been interpreted by the child as affection. Remember Rosenzweig's Rule #1, that sexual arousal is an autonomic response by the body in response to specific stimuli. A behavior that you find abhorrent, that the police would define as a crime, may not be experienced as such by your child. So wait until you can stay calm, think of any possible answer your child may give you, and practice your reaction to it. If you get openly upset, your child will most certainly also become upset and the conversation may end abruptly or fail to lead to any useful information.

A Call to Adults Victimized as Children

Any inkling that your child is at risk can be an awful experience for you as a loving parent. *Please* be especially cautious if you are one of the millions of adults who experienced some sort of sexual victimization as a child. Even if you are a member of the minority lucky enough to have benefited from good clinical support, child sexual abuse may well continue to be a highly sensitive topic for you. The thought that your child is feeling the same pain you experienced may be overwhelming to think about. Sexual abuse can happen in a million different ways and your experience as a victim may limit your perceptions to your own awful experience. This limitation is the exact opposite of the neutral, open-minded position so important in the first questions presented to a child. Mobilize your own support system first and then proceed with care—for yourself and your child.

Step 3: Maintain Control of the Situation

Throughout the time you are talking to your child about your suspicions, maintaining control is vital. Remember, as you engage your child in a conversation asking open-ended questions, let him do the talking and ask him to expand on any topic that is not crystal clear to you. Watch for new physical or behavioral signs in the days that follow your suspicion. Avoid projecting your own perceptions and fears onto your child. **And if you think something happened, find the experts in your community to help you.** You really can't manage this alone even if you're thinking the following:

- I can handle this myself with the perpetrator;
- I'll help my child myself, keeping him away from the perpetrator and without calling anyone;
- The shame that would come from bringing this to light is more than my family or I can bear;
- My child must have done something to provoke the perpetrator; or
- The person I love and need could never have hurt my child.

These thoughts are all normal but non-productive. In fact, they can be downright damaging. If someone has molested your child, you owe it to your child and the other children in your community to work to remove the threat as quickly as possible. And millions of parents and step-parents have had to face the sad truth that someone they love and need did indeed hurt their child. Even with the limitations of finding good data on sexual abuse, the best researchers agree that the most common relationship between a sexual abuse victim and the abuser is a family acquaintance, followed by a family member.[152] The non-offending parent's support is critical. If your child has already been betrayed by one loved and trusted adult, betrayal by a second who refuses to help is sheer torture.

In order to maintain control, it helps to understand the public systems in place to deal with child sex abusers as systems have changed dramatically since the first child protection agencies were developed four decades ago. I remember when I was working in the trenches of child protection during the 1970s, my colleagues and I often lamented that the public system for intervention was more dysfunctional than any family we were charged with serving. That's because the law enforcement community cares about catching bad guys; workers in child protection services are charged with acting in the best interests of the child, while medical and mental health professionals tend to think their perspective is most important in all cases.

When Brenda and Rich were molested in the 1940s and 1960s, child protection services did not exist; in fact some people believed that reports of sexual abuse from children were developmentally "normal" fantasies! When Sally was sent off to a mental health facility in the 1970s, most states were not prosecuting people for failure to report child abuse, a crime then and now in almost every state. And when Ben was approached by the lifeguard in the 1980s, few communities had coordinated response teams or specialized services for youth who were sexually acting out, such as the lifeguard. But many (not all!) communities now have top-notch and well coordinated services, bringing law enforcement, public child protection, and treatment professionals together to investigate and intervene in a manner that considers the child first.

---

152 See Douglas and Finkelhor at http://www.unh.edu/ccrc/factsheet/pdf/childhoodSexualAbuseFactSheet.pdf.

To stay in control of the situation, you must turn to the experts. Recognizing the complexity of responding to a suspicion of child sexual abuse, many communities have special resources to coordinate the initial investigation. Communities variously call these services "Child Advocacy Centers" or "Child Friendly Centers," and they include representatives from law enforcement, Child Protection Services, and treatment professionals who coordinate the investigation. The name "Child Advocacy Center" may not mean the same thing in every community, so it's not a guarantee that you've found the right service; a call to the local United Way or another social service referral service should help you find the experts in your community.

As the parent, your job is to deal with these people in a way that will protect your child and help your family address what happened in the healthiest way. And the most important first step you can take is to find a good interviewer. To do that, call your local Child Protection Services (CPS) department. Even if your child's situation doesn't fall under their authority, CPS agencies are more likely than police departments to have staff specifically trained in interviewing children. They can most likely help you find a good interviewer to work with the appropriate law enforcement agency to get the necessary information about the abuse from your child, no matter his or her age.

Child Protection Services

Since the 1970s, every state in the United States is required to have a Child Protection Services (CPS) system charged with investigating all reports of child abuse, operated by either state or local government. Different states use different names for this service, such as the Department of Human Services, the Division of Youth and Family Services, the Office for Family Services, and so on, but they are all the designated CPS agencies for the state. A list of the CPS agency for each state and its contact information can be found in Appendix 1.

In most states, the CPS agency gets involved *only* in situations where the alleged abuser has some role as a caretaker of the child—i.e., parent, stepparent, teacher, childcare employee—and the exact relations are spelled out in each state's laws. If CPS investigates, the results of its investigation will most likely be processed through the family or civil court. A CPS case will be declared "founded" or "substantiated" if the investigators find evidence that abuse occurred or that the family needs services. In court, a judge or her staff may work with the CPS worker and you to order various services to help your family. The family court may order the child removed from the home if the case is substantiated and the alleged abuser lives there. If the court believes that another adult in the home is capable of protecting the child, the suspected abuser may be ordered to leave. Creative judges working in the best interests of the child can come up with many alternatives to support a child and family after a finding of sexual abuse.

Because sexually abusing a child is also a crime, CPS will inform the appropriate law enforcement authority of the case. Many communities have formal protocols to govern what happens next, particularly around interviewing the child in a manner that requires subjecting the child to the fewest number of interviews and gets the best possible information to use in court.

If you watch courtroom dramas on TV, you know that a criminal charge has to be proven "beyond a reasonable doubt" for a party to be convicted of a crime. That's a pretty high standard and can be difficult to achieve in the absence of physical evidence or a confession, but it's not impossible. Many criminal courts will offer the accused the option to "plea bargain," or to plead guilty to a lesser offense. The theory is that everyone wins—the prosecutor gets a guilty verdict, the perpetrator receives some punishment, the child is spared the trauma of testifying at a trial, and the taxpayers are spared the expense of a long, drawn out trial. This may all sound like a big win-win, and in some ways it is, but next time you come across an organization that relies on criminal background checks alone to ensure that someone is safe to work with children, remember that many sex-offense charges are pled down to other offenses. The absence of a conviction does not mean the absence of the act.

A criminal investigation will be carried out by a representative of the law enforcement system. In smaller communities, this will most likely be the police department or the district attorney's staff. Ensuring that the investigator has been trained in interviewing children is important. If that's not the case, suggest bringing in a trained investigator from CPS, even if your case does not involve a parent or caretaker. Mentioning the McMartin Case and six years of trials with no convictions may get their attention.

If the law enforcement investigation indicates that sexual abuse occurred, the police will bring their charges through the criminal court. Remember, CPS takes its case to the civil or family court, so a family involved with child sexual abuse can be involved with both the civil and criminal justice systems. This means two court processes and the possibility of a civil "finding" or "substantiation" without a criminal conviction. This can be confusing for a child and family. Some families consider retaining their own lawyer just to be their guide through this complicated process. If you choose to do so, find a lawyer familiar with child protection or family court; this is too complicated for the neighborhood lawyer who drew up your will.

I cannot stress this enough: having an experienced, fully credentialed professional interview your child is vitally important. A poorly conducted interview will provide a defense attorney with a large amount of ammunition in his efforts to discredit the charge brought against his client. There are certain nationally recognized credentials, such as completion of the ChildFirst curriculum (formerly widely known as Finding Words)[153] or training courses offered by the National Child Advocacy Center.[154] Finding an investigator who helps your child confirm your suspicions is worthless if the investigator is using questionable techniques, so do your research carefully and don't settle for just anyone.

A medical examination may also be in order; once again special training is key. Some communities have designated sexual abuse diagnostic centers where the medical and social work staff have had specialized training. CPS will know if your community has such a resource. If you turn to your own pediatrician, ask if she has received special training in medical evaluation of child sexual abuse. At the very least, she should have conducted examinations of other children, know the procedures for collecting evidence, and have read Dr. Martin Finkel's landmark text, *Medical Evaluation of Child Sexual Abuse*.[155] If the physician finds evidence of abuse, she is required by law to notify CPS. She may find other health issues that don't necessarily indicate abuse, though, so refer back to chapter 4 for a reminder of how, as an example, girls can develop certain vaginal infections that have nothing to do sexual contact.

---

153 See http://www.ncptc.org/.
154 See http://www.nationalcac.org/.
155 Published by the American Academy of Pediatrics, February 2009.

There are tools available to an experienced investigator that go beyond interviewing a child. Many use "collateral" interviews, meaning that he will interview as many people as possible who he thinks can provide additional information about the suspected abuse. The investigator will almost certainly interview the alleged perpetrator at some point as well.

If the above information has aroused your curiosity about the resources in your community, a great civics project for a high school or college student is to research the system for responding to charges of child sexual abuse, including the existence of interview protocols and the credentials of professionals charged with completing forensic interviews of children.

Is Your Community Prepared?

A fully prepared community has professional staff with appropriate training, formal coordination among systems, and sufficient resources to serve a child and family in crisis. Use this checklist to assess your own community:

Staff Training

1. Have any Child Protection Services staff completed specialized training in human sexuality and child sexual abuse?

   ____ yes   ____ no

2. Are workers with this training the only ones assigned to investigate sexual abuse cases?

   ____ yes   ____ no

3. Do law enforcement investigators have specialized training in human sexuality and forensic interviewing of children?

   ____ yes   ____ no

4. Do the treatment professionals who purport to specialize in child sexual abuse have specialized training in child development, human sexuality, and child sexual abuse?

   ____ yes   ____ no

5. Have the medical professionals assigned to provide crisis intervention and forensic medical examinations completed specialized training in child sexual abuse?

   ____ yes   ____ no

Coordinated Professional Systems

1. Do investigation protocols exist between CPS and Law Enforcement to minimize the number of times child victims are interviewed?

   _____ yes   _____ no

2. Is there a liaison between the family/civil court and the criminal court to coordinate services?

   _____ yes   _____ no

3. Have professionals in your community formed a multi-disciplinary team comprised of a minimum of law enforcement, medical, child protection services, and treatment professionals to plan an intervention to protect the child, sanction the offender, and support the recovery of the victim and family?

   _____ yes   _____ no

Adequate Resources

1. Are there enough investigators with specialized training in child sexual abuse so that one is always available to respond to a call for an investigation?

   _____ yes   _____ no

2. Is there a pediatric forensic medical examination facility in your community?

   _____ yes   _____ no

3. If no, are there arrangements to use a child-friendly medical facility in a nearby community?

   _____ yes   _____ no

4. Are treatment services affordable without regard to income or health insurance status?

   _____ yes   _____ no

5. Are treatment services available in a location accessible by public transportation?

   _____ yes   _____ no

6. Are treatment services provided outside of the 9-5 workday?

   _____ yes   _____ no

Prevention Efforts

1. Does your community support any comprehensive prevention programs such as those described in chapter 9?

Child Assault Prevention	____ yes	____ no
Darkness to Light	____ yes	____ no
Enough Abuse Campaign	____ yes	____ no
Every Person Influences Children	____ yes	____ no
The Green Dot	____ yes	____ no
Prevent Child Abuse America	____ yes	____ no
Stop It Now!	____ yes	____ no
Others?	____ yes	____ no

    _____

2. Do prevention programs move beyond targeting children to involve the entire community?

    ____ yes   ____ no

3. Do your educational, faith-based, or other community institutions offer support for parents to become both skilled and comfortable speaking with their children about sexuality?

    ____ yes   ____ no

    If you have more than one "No," contact your local elected officials and find a champion for the cause!

_____

Back to Your Family

There are so many questions to consider if you find your family in this terrible position. How should you deal with the other children, if you have any? Do you tell the grandparents? My suggestion is to involve as few people as possible, especially in the beginning stages of suspicion and investigation. Everyone who loves your child will feel the same rage that you felt if you tell them about the suspected abuse. However, their anger and sense of helplessness may get in the way of their support for you and your child. If you have a trusted friend who has had related professional experience, consider them a possible confidant or support person, but think really carefully about who you talk to about the situation before all of the facts are known. The last thing you need at this time is gossip, rumors, and misinformation spreading among your extended family or community, or a well-meaning relative saying something to your child that poisons the investigation.

It may become more difficult to keep things confidential if a criminal charge is filed. While a child protection complaint is confidential, a criminal charge is a public matter, and the story could be considered news to local reporters. Most credible news organizations follow the journalistic standard of withholding the name or identifying information of young victims, as well as the names of perpetrators if that will help identify the victim. If your local news outlet routinely breaches this standard, you might consider asking your attorney to call the editor and publisher when the charge is filed and express your concern over the impact of identifying your child.

When you discuss with your child the need to keep this issue to himself, you can avoid shaming him by keeping the focus on catching the abuser. With an older child, offer a strong but gentle reminder that mishandled information can interfere with a case. And in the twenty-first century, you cannot ignore the potential damage of a child confiding in an untrustworthy friend, which can be monumental in this era of cyberbullying. Immature adolescents can mishandle sensitive information, and you don't want your child to feel threatened or shamed by her alleged abuse making its way onto someone's Facebook status or Twitter feed.

The other kids in your family deserve an explanation about the situation as they will know something is up. Younger kids can be satisfied with an explanation as simple as, "We're worried about your brother and want to make sure he's OK." Older kids may want to know more, and if you choose to share, remember that the siblings need the same admonition to keep the information in the family or they'll risk interfering with the investigation.

Your responsibility to your child and family is to exercise as much control as possible during this difficult and confusing time. Learn your local systems and resources and obtain access to the very best as you seek to help your child recover and reclaim justice for your family and community.

Bob held a grudge and a secret for decades and can now talk about how that smack from his dad emotionally alienated him from his family permanently. Sally found peace in therapy as an adult but still has strained relations with her parents. And Brenda confided that she was unable to comfortably enjoy sexual arousal until well into her adult life due to the abuse and her family's handling the situation. If your child is unfortunate enough to encounter a predator, a calm, controlled response on your part and a plan that considers your child's feelings and developmental stage will demonstrate to your child that his world has not been shattered. And this clearly is a first step toward recovery. Everyone has the right to enjoy sexual health and safety.

Reporting Child Abuse

A State-by-State List[156]

Here is a list of state toll-free numbers and/or websites for specific agencies designated to receive and investigate reports of suspected child abuse and neglect, provided by The United States Department of Health and Human Services, Administration for Children and Families, Child Welfare Information Gateway.*

Alabama

Local Phone: (334) 242-9500
Website: http://dhr.alabama.gov/services/Child_Protective_Services/
Abuse_Neglect_Reporting.aspx
Check the website for information on reporting or call Childhelp®
(800-422-4453) for assistance.

Alaska

Toll-Free Phone: (800) 478-4444
Website: http://www.hss.state.ak.us/ocs/default.htm

---

156 List accessed on September 21, 2011, at http://www.childwelfare.gov/pubs/reslist/rl_
dsp.cfm?rs_id=5&rate_chno=11-11172.

Arizona

Toll-Free Phone: (888) SOS-CHILD (888-767-2445)
Website: https://www.azdes.gov/dcyf/cps/reporting.asp

Arkansas

Toll-Free Phone: (800) 482-5964
Website: http://www.state.ar.us/dhs/chilnfam/child_protective_services.
htm

California

Website: http://www.dss.cahwnet.gov/cdssweb/PG20.htm
Check out the website for information on reporting or call Childhelp®
(800-422-4453) for assistance.

Colorado

Local Phone: (303) 866-5932
Website: http://www.cdhs.state.co.us/childwelfare/FAQ.htm
Check out the website for information on reporting or call Childhelp®
(800-422-4453) for assistance.

Connecticut

TDD Phone: (800) 624-5518
Toll-Free Phone: (800) 842-2288
Website: http://www.state.ct.us/dcf/HOTLINE.htm

Delaware

Toll-Free Phone: (800) 292-9582
Website: http://kids.delaware.gov/services/crisis.shtml

District of Columbia

Local Phone: (202) 671-SAFE (202-671-7233)
Website: http://cfsa.dc.gov/DC/CFSA/Support+the+Safety+Net/
Report+Child+Abuse+and+Neglect

Florida

Toll-Free Phone: (800) 96-ABUSE (800-962-2873)
Website: http://www.dcf.state.fl.us/abuse/

Georgia

Website: http://dfcs.dhr.georgia.gov/portal/site/DHRDFCS/menuitem.5d
32235bb09bde9a50c8798dd03036a0/?vgnextoid=733a2b48d9a4ff00Vg
nVCM100000bf01010aRCRD
Check out the website for information on reporting or call Childhelp®
(800-422-4453) for assistance.

Hawaii

Local Phone: (808) 832-5300
Website: http://www.hawaii.gov/dhs/protection/social_services/child_
welfare/

Idaho

TDD Phone: (208) 332-7205
Toll-Free Phone: (800) 926-2588
Website: http://healthandwelfare.idaho.gov/Children/AbuseNeglect/
ChildProtectionContactPhoneNumbers/tabid/475/Default.aspx

Illinois

Local Phone: (217) 524-2606
Toll-Free Phone: (800) 252-2873
Website: http://www.state.il.us/dcfs/child/index.shtml

Indiana

Toll-Free Phone: (800) 800-5556
Website: http://www.in.gov/dcs/protection/dfcchi.html

Iowa

Toll-Free Phone: (800) 362-2178
Website: http://www.dhs.state.ia.us/dhs2005/dhs_homepage/children_
family/abuse_reporting/child_abuse.html

Kansas

Toll-Free Phone: (800) 922-5330
Website: http://www.srskansas.org/services/child_protective_services.
htm

Kentucky

Toll-Free Phone: (877) 597-2331
Website: http://chfs.ky.gov/dcbs/dpp/childsafety.htm

Louisiana

Toll-Free Phone: (855) 452-5437
Website: http://dss.louisiana.gov/index.cfm?md=pagebuilder&tmp=hom
e&pid=109

Maine

TTY Phone: (800) 963-9490
Toll-Free Phone: (800) 452-1999
Website: http://www.maine.gov/dhhs/ocfs/hotlines.htm

Maryland

Website: http://www.dhr.state.md.us/cps/report.htm
Check the website for information on reporting or call Childhelp®
(800-422-4453) for assistance.

Massachusetts

Toll-Free Phone: (800) 792-5200
Website: http://www.mass.gov/?pageID=eohhs2terminal&L=4&L0=Hom
e&L1=Consumer&L2=Family+Services&L3=Child+Abuse+and+Neglect
&sid=Eeohhs2&b=terminalcontent&f=dss_c_can_
reporting&csid=Eeohhs2

Michigan

Toll-Free Phone: (800) 942-4357
Website: http://www.michigan.gov/dhs/0,1607,7-124-5452_7119—-
,00.html

Minnesota

Website: http://www.dhs.state.mn.us/main/idcplg?IdcService=GET_
DYNAMIC_CONVERSION&RevisionSelectionMethod=LatestReleased&
dDocName=id_000152
Check out the website for information on reporting or call Childhelp®
(800-422-4453) for assistance.

Mississippi

Local Phone: (601) 359-4991
Toll-Free Phone: (800) 222-8000
Website: http://www.mdhs.state.ms.us/fcs_prot.html

Missouri

Toll-Free Phone: (800) 392-3738
Website: http://www.dss.mo.gov/cd/rptcan.htm

Montana

Toll-Free Phone: (866) 820-5437
Website: http://www.dphhs.mt.gov/cfsd/index.shtml

Nebraska

Toll-Free Phone: (800) 652-1999
Website: http://www.hhs.state.ne.us/cha/chaindex.htm

Nevada

Toll-Free Phone: (800) 992-5757
Website: http://dcfs.state.nv.us/DCFS_ReportSuspectedChildAbuse.htm

New Hampshire

Local Phone (603) 271-6556
Toll-Free Phone: (800) 894-5533
Website: http://www.dhhs.state.nh.us/dcyf/cps/contact.htm

New Jersey

TTY Phone: (800) 835-5510
Toll-Free Phone: (877) 652-2873
Website: http://www.state.nj.us/dcf/abuse/how/

New Mexico

Toll-Free Phone: (855) 333-7233
Website: http://www.cyfd.org/content/reporting-abuse-or-neglect

New York

Local Phone: (518) 474-8740
TDD Phone: (800) 369-2437
Toll-Free Phone: (800) 342-3720
Website: http://www.ocfs.state.ny.us/main/cps/

North Carolina

Website: http://www.dhhs.state.nc.us/dss/cps/index.htm
Check out the website for information on reporting or call Childhelp®
(800-422-4453) for assistance.

North Dakota

Website: http://www.nd.gov/dhs/services/childfamily/cps/#reporting
Check out the website for information on reporting or call Childhelp®
(800-422-4453) for assistance.

Ohio

Website: http://jfs.ohio.gov/county/cntydir.stm
Contact the county Public Children Services Agency using the list on the
website or call Childhelp® (800-422-4453) for assistance.

Oklahoma

Toll-Free Phone: (800) 522-3511
Website: http://www.okdhs.org/programsandservices/cps/default.htm

Oregon

Website: http://www.oregon.gov/DHS/children/abuse/cps/report.shtml
Check out the website for information on reporting or call Childhelp®
(800-422-4453) for assistance.

Pennsylvania

TDD Phone: (866) 872-1677
Toll-Free Phone: (800) 932-0313
Website: http://www.dpw.state.pa.us/forchildren/childwelfareservices/
calltoreportchildabuse!/index.htm

Puerto Rico

Local Phone: (787) 749-1333
Toll-Free Phone: (800) 981-8333
Spanish-language Website: http://www.gobierno.pr/GPRPortal/Stan-
dAlone/AgencyInformation.aspx?Filter=177

Rhode Island

Toll-Free Phone: (800) RI-CHILD (800-742-4453)
Website: http://www.dcyf.ri.gov/child_welfare/index.php

South Carolina

Local Phone: (803) 898-7318
Website: http://dss.sc.gov/content/customers/protection/cps/index.aspx
Check out the website for information on reporting or call Childhelp®
(800-422-4453) for assistance.

South Dakota

Website: http://dss.sd.gov/cps/protective/reporting.asp
Check out the website for information on reporting or call Childhelp®
(800-422-4453) for assistance.

Tennessee

Toll-Free Phone: (877) 237-0004

Website: http://tennessee.gov/youth/childsafety/whatisabuse.htm

Texas

Toll-Free Phone: (800) 252-5400

Website: https://www.dfps.state.tx.us/Child_Protection/About_Child_
Protective_Services/reportChildAbuse.asp

Utah

Toll-Free Phone: (800) 678-9399

Website: http://www.hsdcfs.utah.gov

Vermont

Toll-Free Phone (after hours only): (800) 649-5285

Website: http://www.dcf.state.vt.us/fsd/reporting_child_abuse

Virginia

Local Phone: (804) 786-8536

Toll-Free Phone: (800) 552-7096

Website: http://www.dss.virginia.gov/family/cps/index.html

Washington

TTY Phone: (800) 624-6186

Toll-Free Phone: (800) 562-5624

(866) END-HARM (866-363-4276)[157]

Website: http://www1.dshs.wa.gov/ca/safety/abuseReport.asp?2

West Virginia

Toll-Free Phone: (800) 352-6513

Website: http://www.wvdhhr.org/bcf/children_adult/cps/report.asp

---

157 1-866-363-4276 is Washington state's toll-free, twenty-four-hour, seven-days-a-week
hotline that will connect you directly to the appropriate local office to report suspected
child abuse or neglect.

Wisconsin

Website: http://dcf.wisconsin.gov/children/CPS/cpswimap.HTM
Check out the website for information on reporting or call Childhelp®
(800-422-4453) for assistance.

Wyoming

Website: http://dfsweb.state.wy.us/protective-services/cps/index.html
Check out the website for information on reporting or call Childhelp®
(800-422-4453) for assistance.

Resources for Parents

Resources with Information about Child Development

The American Academy of Child and Adolescent Psychiatry, www.aacap.org

The American Academy of Pediatrics, www.HealthyChildren.org

The American Psychological Association, www.apa.org/pi/families/resources/develop.pdf

Bright Futures, a national maternal and child health promotion initiative, www.BrightFutures.org

Zero to Three, www.zerotothree.org

Resources with Information about Youth and Media

Common Sense Media, www.CommonSenseMedia.org

Entertainment Software Ratings Board, www.esrb.org

Greatest Books for Kids, www.GreatestBooksForKids.com

Motion Picture Association of America Ratings System, www.mpaa.org/ratings

Resources with Sexuality Information

Advocates for Youth, Parents Sex Ed Center, www.advocatesforyouth.org/

Gay Straight Alliance Netowrk, www.gsanetwork.org/

The National Campaign to Prevent Teen and Unplanned Pregnancy,
www.thenationalcampaign.org

Parents and Friends of Gays and Lesbians, http://community.pflag.org

The Sexuality Information and Education Council of the United States,
www.SIECUS.org

Sex Ed, Honestly, www.Rutgers.answer.edu

The United States Centers for Disease Control and Prevention,
www.cdc.gov/lgbthealth/youth.htm
www.cdc.gov/std/
www.cdc.gov/vaccines/
www.cdc.gov/ViolencePrevention/RPE
www.cdc.gov/Features/TeenPregnancy/

Resources for Programs to Bring to Your Community

Child Assault Protection, www.childassaultprevention.org/

Darkness to Light, www.d2l.org

The Enough Abuse Campaign, www.EnoughAbuse.org

Every Person Influences Children, www.epicforchildren.org

The Green Dot Violence Prevention Program, www.LiveTheGreenDot.com

Healthy Families America, www.HealthyFamiliesAmerica.org

Prevent Child Abuse America, www.PreventChildAbuse.org

The Search Institute, www.search-institute.org/developmental-assets

Stop it Now!, www.StopitNow.org

Resources for Policymakers

The Guttmacher Institute, www.guttmacher.org

The Kaiser Family Foundation, www.kff.org

The National Child Advocacy Center, www.nationalcac.org

The National Child Protection Training Center, www.ncptc.org

The National Sexual Violence Resource Center, www.nsvrc.org

The Pew Internet and American Life Project, www.pewinternet.org

References

Chapter 1:

Bridges, Todd, with Sarah Tomlinson. *Killing Willis*. New York: Touchstone, 2010.

CFDA, Catalog of Federal Domestic Assistance. Community-Based Abstinence Education Program Number: 93.010. Accessed on August 6 , 2011, at https://www.cfda.gov/.

Dailard, Cynthia. "Sex Education: Politicians, Parents, Teachers and Teens." *The Guttmacher Report on Public Policy*, February 2001. Accessed at http://www.guttmacher.org/pubs/tgr/04/1/gr040109.html.

Devaney, Barbara, Amy Johnson, Rebecca Maynard, and Chris Trenholm. "The Evaluation of Abstinence Education Programs Funded Under Title V Section 510 Interim Report." *Evaluation Interim Report*. Princeton, NJ: Mathematica Policy Research, Inc., 2002.

Trenholm, Christopher, Barbara Devaney, Ken Fortson, Lisa Quay, Justin Wheeler, and Melissa Clark. *Impacts of Four Title V Section 510 Abstinence Only Education Programs, Final Report*. Princeton NJ: Mathmatica Policy Rresearch, 2007. Accessed at http://mathematica-mpr.net/publications/pdfs/impactabstinence.pdf.

Ventura, Stephanie J., T. J. Mathews, Brady E. Hamilton, Paul D. Sutton, and Joyce C. Abma. "Adolescent Pregnancy and Childbirth—United States, 1991–2008." *Morbidity and Mortality Weekly*, January 14, 2011: 1–3.

Chapter 2:

Fleischhauer-Hardt, Helga, and Will McBride. *Show Me! A Picture Book of Sex for Children and Parents*. New York: St. Martin's Press, 1975.

Guttmacher Institute. "State Policies in Brief." Sex and HIV Education, August, 2011. Accessed at www.guttmacher.org/pubs/FB-ATSRH. html.

Smith, Keith. *The Men in My Town*. Charleston, SC: BookSurge Publishing, 2009.

Chapter 3:

American Psychological Association. *Developing Adolescents: A Reference for Professionals*. Washington, D.C.: The American Psychological Assocation, 2002. Accessed at http://www.apa.org/pi/families/resources/develop.pdf 6/2011.

Guttmacher Institute. "State Policies in Brief." *Sex and HIV Education*, August, 2011. Accessed at http://www.guttmacher.org/statecenter/spibs/spib_SE. pdf.

Kaye, Kelleen, Katherine Suellentrop, and Corinna Sloup. *The Fog Zone: How misperceptions, magical thinking and ambivalance put young adults at risk for unplanned pregnancy*. Washington, D.C.: The National Campaign to Prevent Teen and Unplanned Pregnancy, 2009. Accessed at http://www. thenationalcampaign.org/fogzone/.

Kirby, Douglas. *Emerging Answers: Research Findings on Programs to Reduce Teen Pregnancy*. Washington, D.C.: National Campaign to Prevent Teen Pregnancy , 2001. Accessed at http://www.sexedlibrary.org/index. cfm?fuseaction=page.viewpage&pageid=877.

Markham, Christine M., Melissa F. Peskin, Robert C. Addy, Elizabeth R. Baumler, and Susan Tartolero. "Patterns of vaginal, oral and anal intercourse in an urban seventh-grade population." *Journal of School Health*, April 2009: 193–200.

Chapter 4:

The American Academy of Pediatrics. "HPV (Gardasil): What You Need to Know." 2011. Last updated May 31, 2011. Accessed on August, 23, 2011, at http://www.healthychildren.org/English/safety-prevention/immunizations/Pages/Human-Papilomavirus-HPV-Vaccine-What-You-Need-to-Know.aspx.

The American Cancer Society. "How to do testicular self-exam." 2011. Last updated January 19, 2011. Accessed on August 30, 2011, at http://www.cancer.org/Cancer/TesticularCancer/MoreInformation/DoIHaveTesticularCancer/do-i-have-testicular-cancer-self-exam.

Katchadourian, Herant A. and Donald T. Lunde. *Fundamentals of Human Sexuality*. New York: Holt Reinhart and Winston, 1975.

Levin, Roy Jerome. "Critically revisiting aspects of the human sexual response cycle of Masters and Johnson: correcting errors and suggesting modifications." *Sexual and Relationship Therapy*, Vol. 23, No. 4, November 2008: 393–399.

Masters, William and Virginia Johnson. *Human Sexual Response*. New York: Bantam Books, 1966.

Sex, etc. Sex Education by Teens, for Teens. Accessed on August 20, 2011 at http://www.sexetc.org/.

Strong, Bryan, Christine Devault, Barbara W. Sayad, and William Yarber. *Human Sexuality: Diversity in Contemporary America*. New York: McGraw-Hill, 2005.

The United States Centers for Disease Control and Prevention. "Trichomoniasis—CDC Fact Sheet." 2007. Last updated December 17, 2007. Accessed on August 24, 2011, at http://www.cdc.gov/std/trichomonas/.

The United States National Institutes of Health, National Cancer Institute . "SEER Stat Fact Sheets: Testis." Accessed on August 24, 2011, at http://seer.cancer.gov/statfacts/html/testis.html.

Chapter 5:

The American Academy of Pediatrics. *Bright Futures.* Accessed on October 21, 2011, at www.aap.org.

Breger, Louis. *From Instinct to Identity: The Development of Personality.* New Jersey: Prentiss Hall, 1974.

Guttmacher Institute. "Facts on American Teens' Sexual and Reproductive Health." January 2011. Accessed at http://www.guttmacher.org/pubs/FB-ATSRH.html.

Irwin, Charles E. Jr, Sally H. Adams, M. Jane Park, and Paul W. Newacheck. "Preventive Care for Adolescents: Few Get Visits and Fewer Get Services." *Pediatrics*, 2009: Vol. 123, 565–572.

Markham, Christine M, Melissa Fleschler Peskin, Robert C. Addy, Elizabeth R. Baumler, and Susan R. Tortolero. "Patterns of Vaginal, Oral, and Anal Sexual Intercourse in an Urban Seventh-Grade Population." *Journal of School Health*, 79.4 (April 2009): 193(8).

National Scientific Council on the Developing Child. *Young Children Develop in an Environment of Relationships: Working Paper No. 1*, 2004: 1. Accessed at http://developingchild.harvard.edu/index.php/resources/reports_and_working_papers/working_papers/wp1/.

Perry, Bruce. *Bonding and Attachment in Maltreated Children.* The Child Trauma Academy, 2001. Accessed on August 12, 2011, at http://www.childtrauma.org/.

Tolma, Eleni L, Roy F. Oman, Sara K. Velesy, Cheryl B. Aspy, Sharon Rodine, LaDonna Marshall, and Janene Fluhr. "Adolesent Sexuality Related Beliefs and Differences by Sexual Experience Status." *The Health Educator*, 2009: Volume 39, Number 1: 3–9.

The United States Centers for Disease Control and Prevention. *Cohabitation, Marriage, Divorce, and Remarriage in the United States.* June 2002: 17. Accessed at http://www.cdc.gov/nchs/data/series/sr_23/sr23_022.pdf.

Upchurch, Dawn M., Lene Levy-Storms, Clea A. Sucoff, and Carol S. Aneshensel. "Gender and Ethnic Differences in the Timing of First Sexual Intercourse." *Family Planning Perspectives*, 1998. Accessed at http://www.guttmacher.org/pubs/journals/3012198.html.

Walsh, David. *Why Do They Act That Way?* New York: Free Press, 2004.

"Zero to Three." *Early Experiences Matter*. Washington, D.C.: 2009. Accessed at http://main.zerotothree.org/site/DocServer/Policy_Guide.pdf?docID=8401.

Chapter 6:

The United States Consumer Product Safety Commission. "Adult Bed-Related Fatalities of Children Under 2 Years of Age." January 1, 1999–December 21, 2001. Accessed at http://www.cpsc.gov/library/02153.pdf.

Chapter 7:

Alberti, Robert E. *Your Perfect Right*. California: Impact Publishers, 1978.

Daley, Martin and Margo Wilson. "Violence against stepchildren." *Current Directions in Psychological Science*, Volume 5, Number 3, 1996: 77–81.

Danielson, Richard, Tom Marshall, John Martin, and Dong-Phuong Nguyen. "Deputies: Four teens raped another in Walker Middle School locker room." *St. Petersburg Times*. In Print: Saturday, May 9, 2009. Accessed in June 2011 at http://www.tampabay.com/news/publicsafety/crime/article999350.ece.

Fensterheim, Herbert and Jean Baer. *Don't Say Yes When You Want To Say No*. New York: Dell, 1975.

Hachman, Mark. *More Kids Using Cell Phones, Study Finds*. The Pew Research Center's Internet & American Life Project, Aug 19, 2009. Accessed on July 10, 2011, at http://www.pewinternet.org/Media-Mentions/2009/More-Kids-Using-Cell-Phones-Study-Finds.aspx.

National Resource Center for Health and Safety in Child Care. "A parent's guide to choosing safe and healthy child care." Undated. Accessed on June 15, 2011, at http://nrckids.org/RESOURCES/ParentsGuide.pdf.

Smith, Keith. *The Men in My Town*. Charleston, SC: BookSurge Publishing, 2009.

The United States Centers for Disease Control. "Injury Center Fact Sheet." Accessed in June 2011, at http://www.nsvrc.org/sites/default/files/IPV%20TDV%20SV%20Fact%20Sheet.pdf .

Chapter 8:

Albert, Bill. *With One Voice 2010: Americans Adults and Teens Sound off About Teen Pregnancy.* Washington, D.C.: The National Campaign to Prevent Teen and Unplanned Pregnancy, 2010.

American Academy of Pediatrics. "Policy Statement on Children, Adolescents and Advertising." *Pediatrics,* Volume 118, Number 6, 2006.

American Psychological Association. *Television Advertising Leads to Unhealthy Habits in Children.* Washington, D.C.: The American Psychological Association, 2004. Accessed at http://www.apa.org/news/press/releases/2004/02/children-ads.aspx.

Athar, Shahid. *Sex Education: An Islamic Perspective.* Accessed at http://www.islamfortoday.com/athar19.htm.

Bersamin, Melina, Michael Todd, Deborah Fisher, Douglas L. Hill, Joel W. Grube, and Samantha Walker. "Parenting Practices and Adolescent Sexual Behavior: A Longitudinal Study." *Journal of Marriage and Family*, 70 (1), 2008: 97–112.

Brody, Gene H. "Siblings' Direct and Indirect Contributions to Child Development." *Current Directions in Psychological Science.* 2004: 124–126.

Finkelhor, D. "Sex Among Siblings: A survey on prevalence, variety and effects." *Archives of Sexual Behavior* (9), 1980: 171–194.

Kolburn Kowal, Amanda and Lynn Blinn-Pike. "Sibling Influences on Adolescents' Attitudes Toward Safe Sex Practices." *Family Relations.* Volume 53, Number 4, July 1, 2004: 377–384.

Ladin L'Engle, Kelly and Christine Jackson. "Socialization Influences on Early Adolescents' Cognitive Susceptibility and Transition to Sexual Intercourse." *Journal of Research on Adolescence* 18 (2), 2008: 353–378. Accessed at http://teenmedia.unc.edu/pdf/Socialization%20Influences.pdf.

Menesini, Ersilia, Marina Camodeca, and Annalaura Nocentini. "Bullying among siblings: The role of personality and relational variables." *The British Jounral of Developmental Psychology*, Volume 28, pt. 4: 921–939.

The Presbyterian Church, USA. *Study Paper on Family Violence*. Louisville, KY: The Presbyterian Church USA, Office of the General Assembly, 1991. Accessed on July 13, 2011, at http://oga.pcusa.org/publications/family-violence.pdf.

Singer, Ken. *Evicting the Perpetrstor: A male survivior guide to recovery from child sexual abuse*. Holyoke, MA: NEARI Press, 2010.

Somers, Cheryl L. and Whitney L. Vollmar. "Parent-Adolescent Relationships and Adolescent Sexuality: Closeness, Communication and Comfort Among Diverse U.S. Adolescent Samples." *Social Behanvior and Personality 34 (4)*, 2006: 451–460.

Chapter 9:

Every Person Influences Children (EPIC). Accessed at http://www.epic-forchildren.org/.

Green Dot.etcetra. Accessed at http://www.LiveTheGreenDot.org.

Muir, Mike. *Research Brief*. The Principals Partnership, 2006. Accessed on April 4, 2011, at http://www.principalspartnership.com.

The Search Institute. Accessed at http://www.search-institute.org/developmental-assets.

Tableman, Betty and Adrienne Herron. "School Climate and Learning." *Best Practice Briefs*, Number 31. University-Community Partnerships @ Michigan State University: 2004. Accessed May 10, 2011, at http://outreach.msu.edu/bpbriefs/issues/brief31.pdf.

The United States Centers for Disease Control and Prevention. "Rape Prevention and Education Program." Accessed at http://www.cdc.gov/ViolencePrevention/RPE/.

Chapter 10:

Albert, B. *With One Voice 2010: America's Adults and Teens Sound Off About Teen Pregnancy*. Washington, D.C.: The National Campaign to Prevent Teen and Unplanned Pregnancy, 2010.

Brown, Jane D., Kelly Ladin-L'Engle, Carol J. Pardun, Guang Guo, Kristin Kenneavy, and Christin Jackson. "Sexy Media Matter: Exposure to Sexual

Content in Music, Movies, Television, and Magazines Predicts Black and White Adolescents' Sexual Behavior." *Pediatrics* Vol. 117, No. 4, April 1, 2006: 1,018–1,027.

Common Sense Media. Accessed at http://www.CommonSenseMedia.org.

The Entertainment Software Rating Board. Accessed at http://www.ESRB.org.

Johnson, Steven. *Everything Bad is Good For You*. London: Penguin Books Limited, 2006.

Jones, Steven. "Let the games begin: Gaming technology and college students." *The Pew Internet and American Life Project*. Washington, D.C.: 2003. Accessed at http://www.pewinternet.org/Reports/2003/Let-the-games-begin-Gaming-technology-and-college-students/2-Gaming-Comes-of-Age.aspx.

Lenhart, Amanda. "Is the age at which kids get cell phones getting younger?" December 1, 2010. Accessed at http://www.pewinternet.org/Commentary/2010/December/Is-the-age-at-which-kids-get-cell-phones-getting-younger.aspx.

Lenhart, Amanda, Rich Ling, Scott Purcell, and Kristen Campbell. "Teens and Mobile Phones." *The Pew Internet and American Life Project*. Washington, D.C.: 2010. Accessed at http://pewinternet.org/Reports/2010/Teens-and-Mobile-Phones.aspx.

Lenhart, Amanda, Joseph Kahne, Ellen Middaugh, Alexandra Rankin Macgill, Chris Evans, and Jessica Vitak. "Teens, Video Games, and Civics." *The Pew Internet and American Life Project*. Washington, D.C., 2008. Accessed at http://www.pewinternet.org/~/media//Files/Reports/2008/PIP_Teens_Games_and_Civics_Report_FINAL.pdf.pdf.

The Motion Picture Association of America. Accessed at http://www.mpaa.org/ratings.

The Recording Industry Association of America. Accessed at http://www.riaa.com/.

Rideout, Victoria J., Ulla G. Foehr, and Donald F. Roberts. "Generation M^2: Media in the Lives of 8- to 18-Year-Olds." The Kaiser Family Foundation, 2010. Accessed at http://www.kff.org.

The United States Federal Trade Commission. *FTC Undercover Shopper Survey on Enforcement of Entertainment Ratings Finds Compliance Worst for Retailers of Music CDs and the Highest Among Video Game Sellers.* 2011. Accessed on August 31, 2011, at http://www.ftc.gov/opa/2011/04/violentkidsent.shtm.

The United States Federal Trade Commission. *Rules for The Childrens Online Privacy Protection Act.* 2000. Accessed at http://business.ftc.gov/privacy-and-security/children%E2%80%99s-online-privacy.

Walsh, David. *Why Do They Act That Way? A Survival Guide to the Adolescent Brain for You and Your Teen.* New York: Free Press, 2004.

Wolok, Janis and David Finkelhor. *Sexting: A Typology.* University of New Hampshire Crimes Against Children Research Center Bulletin, March 2011. Accessed on August 7, 2011, at http://www.unh.edu/ccrc/pdf/CV231_Sexting%20Typology%20Bulletin_4-6-11_revised.pdf.

Wright, Paul J. "Sexual Socialization Messages in Mainstream Entertainment Mass Media: A Review and Synthesis." *Sexuality and Culture.* 2009: 181–200.

Chapter 11:

The American Academy of Pediatrics. *HPV (Gardasil): What You Need to Know.* 2011. Last updated May 31, 2011. Accessed on June 15, 2011, at http://www.healthychildren.org/English/safety-prevention/immunizations/Pages/Human-Papilomavirus-HPV-Vaccine-What-You-Need-to-Know.aspx.

Choi, James, Kimberly L. Cooper, Terry W. Hensle, and Harry Fisch. "Incidence and Surgical Repair Rates of Hyposoadiasis in New York State." *Pediatric Urology*, 2001: 151–153.

Everaerd, Walter, Stephanie Both, and Ellen Laan. "The Experience of Sexual Emotions." *Annual Review of Sex Research*, Vol. 17, 2006: 183–199.

The Guttmacher Institute. "Facts on American Teens' Sexual and Reproductive Health." 2001. Accessed at http://www.guttmacher.org/pubs/FB-ATSRH.html.

National Public Radio. Youth Radio, June 3, 2011. Accessed at http://www.npr.org/2011/06/03/136930347/young-people-talk-about-aids.

Shakeshaft, Charol. *Educator Sexual Misconduct: A Synthesis of Existing Literature.* Washington, D,C.: U.S. Department of Education, Office of the Undersecrectary, 2004. Accessed at http://www2.ed.gov/rschstat/research/pubs/misconductreview/report.pdf.

Singer, Ken. *Evicting the Perpetrator: A Males Survival Guide to Recovery from Childhood Sexual Abuse.* Holyoke, MA: NEARI Press, 2010.

The United States Centers for Disease Control and Prevention. "HPV Vaccine—Questions & Answers." Last updated April 6, 2011. Accessed at June 13, 2011, at http://www.cdc.gov/vaccines/vpd-vac/hpv/vac-faqs.htm.

Chapter 12:

American Academy of Pediatrics. "Gender Identity and Gender Confusion in Children." *Caring for Your School-Age Child: Ages 5 to 12.* 2004. Last updated May 11, 2011. Accessed at http://www.healthychildren.org/English/ages-stages/gradeschool/Pages/Gender-Identity-and-Gender-Confusion-In-Children.aspx.

Euginides, Jeffrey. *Middlesex.* New York: Picador, 2002.

Goldberg, Alan B. and Joneil Adriano. "'I'm a Girl'—Understanding Transgender Children." *ABC News 20/20.* Online, April 27, 2007. Accessed on August 30, 2011, at http://abcnews.go.com/2020/story?id=3088298&page=1.

Grov, Christian, David S. Bimbi, Jose E. Nanin, and Jeffrey T. Parsons. "Race, Ethnicity, Gender, and Generational Factors Associated With the Coming-Out Process Among Gay, Lesbian, and Bisexual Individuals." *The Journal of Sex Research,* Volume 43, Number 2, May 2006: 115–121/

Koch PhD, Patricia Barthalow, Professor of Biobehavioral Health at the Pennsylvania State University, College of Health and Human Development. Personal communication on September 6, 2011.

Maher F. and M. Tetreault. *The Feminist Classroom.* New York: Harper Collins, 1994.

Merriam Webster Inc. "Homophobia." *The Merriam Webster Dictionary*. Accessed on August 30, 2011, at http://www.merriam-webster.com/dictionary/homophobia.

Schlatter, Evelyn. "18 Anti-Gay Groups and Their Propaganda." *The Southern Poverty Law Center Intelligence Report*. Winter 2010, Issue Number: 140. Accessed on August 30, 2011, at http://www.splcenter.org/get-informed/intelligence-report/browse-all-issues/2010/winter/the-hard-liners.

The United States Centers for Disease Control and Prevention. "Lesbian, Gay, Bisexual and Transgender Health." Last updated May 19, 2011. Accessed on July 30, 2011, at http://www.cdc.gov/lgbthealth/youth.htm.

The United States National Library of Medicine, National Institutes of Health. *Intersex*. Last updated August 2, 2009. Accessed on July 2, 2011, at http://www.nlm.nih.gov/medlineplus/ency/article/001669.htm.

Wilcox, Sarah. Interview with Beth Rankin. "Transsexual vs. Transgender: Explaining the Intricacies." *Fusion Magazine*, Spring 2004. Accessed on August 31, 2011, at http://fusion.kent.edu/archives/spring04/trans/transprint.html.

Chapter 13:

American Academy of Child and Adolescent Psychiatry. *Facts for Families # 9*. May 2008. Accessed on March 11, 2011, at

http://www.aacap.org/galleries/FactsForFamilies/09_child_sexual_abuse.pdf.

Annon, Jack S. "Recommended Guidelines for Interviewing Children in Cases of Alleged Sexual Abuse." Institute for Psychological Therapies, 2004. Last updated August 2011. Accessed in September 2011, at http://www.ipt-forensics.com/journal/volume6/j6_3_2.htm.

Douglas, Emily M. and David Finkelhor. "Childhood Sexual Abuse Fact Sheet." Crimes Against Children Research Center, University of New Hampshire, 2005. Accessed in April 2011, at http://www.unh.edu/ccrc/factsheet/pdf/childhoodSexualAbuseFactSheet.pdf.

Faller, Kathleen Coulborn. *Interviewing Children About Child Sexual Abuse: Controversies and Best Practice*. New York: Oxford University Press, 2007.

Finkel, Martin and Angelo Giardino. *Medical Evaluation of Child Sexual Abuse: A Practical Guide*. American Academy of Pediatrics, 2009.

Sedlak, A. J., Jane Mettenburg, Monica Basena, Ian Petta, Karla McPherson, Angela Greene, and Spencer Li. *Fourth National Incidence Study of Child Abuse and Neglect (NIS–4): Report to Congress*. Washington, D.C.: U.S. Department of Health and Human Services, Administration for Children and Families, 2010. Accessed on April 4, 2011, at http://www.acf.hhs.gov/programs/opre/abuse_neglect/natl_incid/index.html.

State of Michigan Governors Task Force on Child Abuse and Neglect and Department of Human Services. *Forensic Interviewing Protocol Third Edition*. 2011. Accessed in April 2011 at http://www.michigan.gov/documents/dhs/DHS-PUB-0779_211637_7.pdf.

U.S. Department of Health and Human Services, Administration for Children and Families, Administration on Children, Youth and Families, Children's Bureau. *Child Maltreatment*. Table 13-3, 2009. Accessed on April 14, 2011, at http://www.acf.hhs.gov/programs/cb/stats_research/index.htm#can.

U.S. Department of Health and Human Services, Administration for Children and Families, Administration on Children, Youth and Families, Children's Bureau. *Child Sexual Abuse: Intervention and Treatment Issues*. Accessed on April 14, 2011, at http://www.childwelfare.gov/pubs/usermanuals/sexabuse/index.cfm.

U.S. Department of Health and Human Services, Administration for Children and Families, Administration on Children, Youth, and Families, Office of Planning, Research, and Evaluation, Children's Bureau. Fourth National Incidence Study of Child Abuse and Neglect (NIS-4) Report to Congress Executive Summary accessed on September 22, 2011, at http://www.acf.hhs.gov/programs/opre/abuse_neglect/natl_incid/reports/nis_execsumm/nis4_report_exec_summ_pdf_jan2010.pdf.

Walker, Anne Graffam. *Handbook on Questioning Children*. Washington, D.C.: American Bar Association Center on Children and the Law, 1999.

Index